HERMENEUTICS AND THE SOCIOLOGY OF KNOWLEDGE

Hermeneutics and the Sociology of Knowledge

Susan J. Hekman

University of Notre Dame Press
Notre Dame, Indiana

US edition
First published in 1986 by University of Notre Dame Press,
Notre Dame, Indiana 46556.

ISBN 0-268-01083-8
LC: 85-5231 1

Typeset by Oxford Publishing Services, Oxford
Printed in Great Britain by Billing and Sons Ltd, Worcester

Contents

1 Social Science and the Sociology of Knowledge 1

- I INTRODUCTION 1
- II THE ENLIGHTENMENT AND THE ORIGINS OF THE SOCIAL SCIENCES 4
- III TOWARD A REDEFINITION OF THE SOCIOLOGY OF KNOWLEDGE 7

2 A Brief History of the Sociology of Knowledge 13

- I INTRODUCTION 13
- II MARX AND THE EARLY HISTORY OF THE SOCIOLOGY OF KNOWLEDGE 16
- III THE *METHODENSTREIT* AND GERMAN SOCIOLOGY OF KNOWLEDGE 22
- IV THE SOCIOLOGY OF KNOWLEDGE IN THE MID-TWENTIETH CENTURY 26
- V THE REALISTS 39
- VI CONCLUSION 47

3 Mannheim's Hermeneutic Sociology of Knowledge 50

- I INTRODUCTION 50
- II MANNHEIM'S SOCIOLOGY OF KNOWLEDGE: THE BASIC STRUCTURE 52
- III MANNHEIM'S CONCEPTION OF KNOWLEDGE 67
- IV MANNHEIM AND ANTI-FOUNDATIONAL THOUGHT 78

4 Gadamer's Hermeneutics and the Methodology of the Social Sciences 91

I *TRUTH AND METHOD* 91

Gadamer's problematic

Art, play and the nature of the human sciences

The nature of the hermeneutic experience

The ontological connection: language, truth and reality

II GADAMER AND WITTGENSTEINIAN SOCIAL SCIENCE 117

Language and the social sciences

Gadamerian hermeneutics and wittgensteinian social science: a comparison

III THE GADAMER–HABERMAS DEBATE 129

IV GADAMER AND THE METHODOLOGY OF THE SOCIAL SCIENCES 139

Action as a text

Hermeneutics and the sociology of knowledge

5 Beyond Objectivism and Nihilism 160

I INTRODUCTION 160

II BEYOND HUMANISM: THE 'DEATH OF MAN' 167

III FOUCAULT: MORAL NIHILISM 171

IV DECONSTRUCTION: CONCEPTUAL NIHILISM 187

Notes 197

References 205

Index 220

Acknowledgements

The idea for this book was conceived during a 1981 NEH Summer Seminar in Berkely, California, on 'The Interpretative Study of Human Beings' led by Hubert Dreyfus. Along the way many colleagues and friends have helped in the development of the thesis. Special thanks are due to Ira Cohen, Michael Shaprio, A. P. Simonds, Richard Ashcraft and Mark Strasser for reading and commenting on an earlier draft of the manuscript. Although I have not always followed their advice, their criticisms have helped me to clarify the thesis presented here.

Parts of Chapter 4 have appeared in different forms in the following journals:

From Epistemology to Ontology. *Human Studies*, Vol. 6, no. 3 (1983), 205–24.

Action as a Text. *Journal for the Theory of Social Behaviour*, Vol. 14, no. 3 (1984), 333–53.

To Evan

1

Social Science and the Sociology of Knowledge

I INTRODUCTION

So much has been written about the 'crisis' in contemporary social science that reference to this state of affairs has become the necessary starting point for all works on contemporary social and political theory. This book, like so many other recent publications in the field, begins with the assumption that the social sciences are, in fact, in a state of crisis. But, unlike many of these works, it also begins with the assumption that it is by no means self-evident what that crisis is, or how it should be characterized. Although attacks on positivist social science and proposals for alternative conceptions have become commonplace in the literature of social and political theory, no resolution of the debate has been forthcoming. Rather, the 'methodological pestilence', as Weber put it, has continued unabated for at least several decades.

Weber justified contributing to the methodological discussions of his day by pointing out that methodological work is necessary when confusions over methodology stand in the way of empirical work. This is certainly true of contemporary social science, just as it was true in Weber's day. The positivist research program in the social sciences that has been seriously discredited in recent decades still serves as the basis for most social scientific research. It has not been replaced by any of the alternative programs that have been proposed, first, because no unanimity exists as to which of these alternatives should be adopted and, secondly, because none of these alternatives offers what appears to social scientists to be a viable methodology for social scientific research. As a result, as many have argued, the social sciences are cast adrift without a theoretical anchor.

Weber's observation thus serves to justify yet another discussion of the contemporary crisis in the social sciences. I will attempt to offer some insights into the nature of this crisis by examining the social sciences from the perspective of what has come to be classified as a rather insignificant subfield of these disciplines: the sociology of knowledge. The sociology of knowledge has been regarded as a legitimate aspect of the social sciences since these disciplines were divided into specific fields in the nineteenth century. The works of Scheler and, later, Mannheim, are generally recognized as marking the beginning of a definite category labelled the sociology of knowledge. They served to define the specific field of the sociology of knowledge and its relationship to the discipline of the social sciences. Since their publication the field has been recognized by most social scientists to be, if not one of the central concerns of the social sciences, at least a part of what is normally considered to fall under the purview of these disciplines.

Using a somewhat broader definition, however, the roots of the sociology of knowledge can be traced beyond Scheler and Mannheim. Much of the work of Marx is generally classified as a version of the sociology of knowledge. The publications of the 'founder' of modern social science, Auguste Comte, have also been identified as falling under the rubric of the sociology of knowledge. Although Comte did not employ the term 'sociology of knowledge', his attempt to construct a science of society rested on a distinction between true knowledge and socially conditioned belief that is definitive of the sociology of knowledge. Further, various other luminaries in the history of social science, most notably Durkheim and Weber, are also credited with formulating a sociology of knowledge. This seems to suggest that the sociology of knowledge is not merely one of many subfields of the social sciences but has actually played a central, perhaps even unique, role in the history and definition of the social sciences.

The nature of this unique role can be illustrated by looking at two contemporary commentators on the sociology of knowledge who have attempted to define its place in the development of the social sciences. In his discussion of the foundations of modern social science, Jeff Bergner remarks that the sociology of knowledge is a peculiar social scientific creation. Unlike epistemology in philosophical studies, the sociology of knowledge 'brackets' the possibility of knowing, that is, it does not engage in epistemological speculations. It thus effectually denies the ideal of essential knowledge, an ideal that is, he argues, precluded by the very structure of modern social science (1981:130–7). For Bergner the sociology of knowledge illustrates the principal failure of contemporary social science, the failure to attain scientific truth. In a very different context, another commentator, A. P. Simonds, also remarks on the special character of the sociology of knowledge *vis-à-vis* the social sciences. In a discussion of the importance of hermeneutics for the sociology of knowledge, he states:

> The sociology of knowledge must be considered not as a special field or sub-discipline, but as a claim respecting the nature of social science itself. (1975:99)

For Simonds, in contrast to Bergner, the sociology of knowledge plays a positive role in the social sciences in that it defines the essentially hermeneutical task of these disciplines.

These two commentators share an important insight while at the same time differing profoundly on the nature of the sociology of knowledge and its relationship to the social sciences. Both argue that the sociology of knowledge is somehow tied to the essence of the social sciences, that is, that it is definitive of the very enterprise of the social sciences. They disagree, however, on what that essence is. For Bergner the sociology of knowledge is a symptom of what he defines as the malaise of modern social science: its abandonment of the ideal of essential knowledge and, thus, its failure to produce what he calls an 'archetectonic' social science. For Simonds, the sociology of knowledge is central to the social sciences for a very different reason. Since he defines the sociology of knowledge as a hermeneutic method, it represents a recognition that the social sciences are engaged in the interpretation of social meaning, not the search for scientific truth.

This book will explore in detail this relationship between the sociology of knowledge and what is essential to the social sciences. This relationship is, as these commentators indicate, a unique one. The sociology of knowledge is not just another subfield of the social sciences but is definitive of these disciplines as a whole. But it is also the case that the definition of the relationship between the social sciences and the sociology of knowledge that has been accepted by most practitioners of the field has been fundamentally misconceived and that what is needed is a redefinition of this relationship as well as a redefinition of the sociology of knowledge itself. Bergner is wrong in his assertion that the sociology of knowledge precludes the possibility of essential knowledge. On the contrary, the sociology of knowledge as it has been traditionally defined necessarily presupposes the existence of 'true knowledge'. On the other hand, Simonds is correct in his assertion that the sociology of knowledge defines the essentially hermeneutic task of the social sciences. But Simonds does not take this argument far enough. Declaring that the sociology of knowledge is an 'interpretive' rather than a 'scientific' enterprise does not go to the root of the problem. Rather, a radical redefinition of both the sociology of knowledge and the social sciences is called for. In order to formulate this definition, however, it is first necessary to understand the original conception of the relationship between the social sciences and the sociology of knowledge that was established at the time of the Enlightenment.

II THE ENLIGHTENMENT AND THE ORIGINS OF THE SOCIAL SCIENCES

Probably the earliest statement of what would come to be labelled the sociology of knowledge can be found in the work of Francis Bacon. Bacon defined the goal of his intellectual work as purging human thought of what he identified as the 'idols' that beset the human mind. In one of the clearest statements of the Enlightenment's attitude toward human reason, he states:

> The formation of notions and axioms on the foundation of true induction is the only fitting remedy by which we can ward off and expel these idols. (1970:89)

It follows that

> Truth is not to be sought in the good fortune of any particular conjuncture of time, which is uncertain, but in the light of nature and experience, which is eternal. (1970:93)

Bacon's statements indicate not only the direction of Enlightenment thought but also the subsequent attitude toward the social sciences that it fostered. The Enlightenment's ambitious program was, as Kant put it, to effect the emergence of human beings from their self-imposed tutelage to unreason. The 'idols' that had beset humans' minds since the dawn of human history were to be stripped away and replaced with the pure light of reason. For Kant this meant a revolt against superstition, prejudice and illusion. It meant freeing the human mind from all that is tied to a particular time and place because these particulars are, as Bacon asserts, uncertain. What is certain and true is that which is eternal, that is, that which is beyond history and culture (Gay, 1966:3–21).

The effects of these Enlightenment attitudes for both philosophy and the natural sciences are well known and need no reiteration here. The implications of Enlightenment thought for the social sciences have also been well documented. Two of these implications are of importance in the present context. First, the Enlightenment's desire to find truth by purging human thought of the uncertainty of particular historical and cultural elements was expressed in the social sciences in the attempt to find a common human nature. 'Truth' in the social sciences would be found not by examining human beings as historical, cultural beings, but by formulating an a-historical conception of human nature free from the distortions or prejudices of particular times and places. Secondly, Enlightenment thought had a profound effect on the conception of social scientific methodology that developed. The Enlightenment witnessed a period of spectacular triumphs in the natural sciences. Beginning with Newton and Galileo, the natural sciences began a conquest of the natural world which was a staggering success. This success did not go unnoticed in the social sciences. Rather, as many commentators have noted, the social sciences were born in the shadow of these triumphs. Furthermore, the methodological lesson that the natural sciences were teaching seemed to be very clear: if the methods of the natural sciences are strictly adhered to then the spectacular success of these sciences could be matched in the social sciences. The social sciences had only to await the arrival of their Newton.

For the social sciences, then, Enlightenment thought dictated a very straightforward program: develop a social scientific methodology based on the eternal truths of human nature, purged of historical and cultural prejudices, and follow the nomological-deductive method of the natural sciences in order to formulate scientific laws about human beings. Even this brief characterization of Enlightenment thought reveals why the sociology of knowledge is central to this conception of the social sciences and why a sociology of knowledge so quickly developed out of Enlightenment thought in the social sciences. If the purpose of research in the social sciences is to separate eternal truth from historical prejudices, and, thus, pure knowledge from the historical prejudices that produce impure knowledge, then it is essential to formulate an understanding of the nature and functioning of historical prejudice. In other words, we cannot separate pure from impure knowledge unless we can recognize and define impure knowledge. And it is the business of the sociology of knowledge as it was conceived in the Enlightenment to do precisely this. The task of the sociology of knowledge was to explore the way in which historical and cultural factors shaped and, by implication, warped, the thought of human beings. The Enlightenment thinkers believed that unless this process were thoroughly understood it would be impossible to formulate the pure knowledge that was defined as the goal of research in both the social and natural sciences.

The Enlightenment definition of the social sciences, is thus unavoidably tied to a sociology of knowledge which sees its task as the definition of the 'idols' that beset the human mind. It should therefore come as no surprise that, beginning with Vico and Montesquieu, the sociology of knowledge has become an integral part of Western social theory (Hamilton, 1974:1–3). From the outset the sociology of knowledge was necessarily linked to what was defined as the principal goal of the social sciences: the pusuit of scientific truth. The two enterprises are interdependent and inseparable; one is not conceivable without the other.

The next chapter's overview of the history of the sociology of knowledge establishes two theses with regard to this relationship between social science and the sociology of knowledge. First, it establishes that, with the partial exception of Karl Mannheim, practitioners of the sociology of knowledge subscribed to the Enlightenment's definition of the social sciences. They thus saw their purpose as formulating the distinction between pure and impure (or objective and subjective) knowledge. Secondly, it establishes that this tradition of the sociology of knowledge, despite its lack of status in positivist circles, embodies the essence of what has come to be modern positivist social science because positivist social science logically depends on establishing the distinction between socially determined and objective knowledge. Further, it shows that neither positivist nor humanist sociologists of knowledge questioned what was the central theme of Enlightenment thought: the exclusive identification of truth with 'scientific method' defined as the exclusion of historical and cultural distortions.[1]

III TOWARD A REDEFINITION OF THE SOCIOLOGY OF KNOWLEDGE

The preceding argument concerning the status of the sociology of knowledge in the tradition of the social sciences raises a particular question with regard to an issue that has dominated the social sciences in recent decades: the critique of positivism. If, as was argued above, the sociology of knowledge occupies a pivotal place in the post-Enlightenment conception of social science, then it would seem to follow that the critics of positivist social science would eschew this approach. But this has not been the case. On the contrary, the sociology of knowledge has experienced a revival of sorts on the part of anti-positivist critics, most notably phenomenologists and critical theorists. Why this is the case, however, is not immediately apparent. The critiques of positivist social science that have occupied the attention of social theorists for nearly the last century have covered a range that defies summary. These critiques have questioned the methods, presuppositions and practices of the positivist program for the social sciences. They have argued, although in very diverse ways, that the social sciences demand a methodology distinct from the natural sciences because their subject matter is radically different. Many of these critics have argued that, if 'science' is defined as the accumulation of 'objective data' on the model of the natural sciences, then the social sciences are not and cannot be scientific.

The reason these anti-positivist critics should espouse the sociology of knowledge can be traced to their adherence to the Enlightenment conception of knowledge. If it is assumed, as the Enlightenment thinkers asserted, that objective, scientific knowledge is that which excludes all historical and cultural distortions, then it follows that, for the anti-positivist, this kind of knowledge is not appropriate to the social sciences. Without questioning that truth is the exclusive product of the scientific method or that the natural sciences have an exclusive claim on this truth, the anti-positivist argues that the social sciences are simply excluded from this realm. But when anti-positivists attempt to identify the kind of knowledge that *is* appropriate to the social sciences they define it as 'subjective' knowledge, that is, knowledge that is culturally and socially determined. This definition coincides precisely with the 'impure' knowledge explored by the sociology of knowledge. The sociology of knowledge, stripped of its 'objective' half – pure knowledge – becomes the perfect tool of an anti-positivist methodology. It allows the anti-positivists to explore the social basis of knowledge and to argue that this exploration does not result in the accumulation of the 'objective knowledge' characteristic of the natural sciences. But it does not entail that they question the basic tenet of the sociology of knowledge: the existence of such objective knowledge. It merely limits this kind of knowledge to the natural sciences, in effect excluding the social sciences from the realm of 'truth'.[2]

In recent years, however, a radically different kind of critique has begun to make an impact on the social sciences. Although this critique is new to the social sciences, it is certainly not new to philosophical discussions. It has its roots in a philosophical tradition going back at least as far as nineteenth century pragmatism. Contemporary discussions, however, usually take their direction from the more recent discussions of Heidegger and Wittgenstein. What sets this group of critics apart from the critics of positivism referred to above is what Richard Rorty has labelled their rejection of 'foundational' thought (1979). These philosophers argue that what both positivists and anti-positivists (that is, humanists or interpretive social scientists) have in common is the Enlightenment conception of 'truth', 'objectivity' and, hence, 'science'. For the Enlightenment, the search for truth meant the search for foundations, that is, an indubitable element of human existence that can 'ground' human knowledge. Although the anti-positivists reject this goal for the social sciences, they do not question its legitimacy as a definition of truth and, in some cases, attempt to formulate an indubitable ground for the social sciences that is suited to these disciplines. The opponents of foundational thought point out, however, that the fact that both camps accept the Enlightenment conception of truth dooms their debate to endless and, ultimately, futile arguments. There can be no resolution because the two sides of the debate are logically dependent on each other.

What these philosophers (who will be labelled 'anti-foundational') suggest, instead, is a re-examination and ultimate rejection of the Enlightenment conception of truth. Jonathan Culler summarizes this anti-foundational attitude very succinctly:

> If 'sawing off the branch on which one is sitting' seems foolhardy to men of common sense, it is not so for Nietzsche, Freud, Heidegger, and Derrida; for they suspect that if they fall there is no 'ground' to hit and that the most clear-sighted act may be a certain reckless sawing, a calculated dismemberment or deconstruction of the great cathedral-like trees in which Man has taken shelter for millenia. (1982:149)

What the anti-foundational philosophers suggest is not a search for 'truth' conceived apart from history and culture, but, rather, an examination of the relationship between human thought and human existence. They argue that the philosopher's task is to explore the way in which background assumptions preform and structure both thought and existence. Further, they argue that the attempt to formulate an a-historical, a-cultural 'truth' involves a radical misunderstanding of both the nature of truth and human existence itself.

That the work of these anti-foundational philosophers has much relevance for the social sciences is becoming increasingly evident to social theorists. It is also evident that their thought is specifically relevant to the tradition of the sociology of knowledge. The anti-foundational philosophers' concern is to explore the relationship between human thought and human existence, an endeavor that falls under the rubric of the sociology of knowledge. But it is a sociology of knowledge divorced from the Enlightenment assumption of the distinction between objective and subjective knowledge. It is a sociology of knowledge that examines human thought and existence without presupposing, as the Enlightenment did, that this examination is subordinate to the really important task of searching for objective knowledge.

The thesis of the following discussion is that this anti-foundational approach to the social sciences provides a much-needed redefinition of the sociology of knowledge, and, more importantly, supplies an understanding of the project of the social sciences that transcends the sterile dogmatism of the positivist-humanist debate. It also transcends the individualist paradigm that has dominated the social sciences in the twentieth century. The kind of 'sociology of knowledge' that can be found in the works of Wittgenstein, Heidegger and Gadamer offers an understanding of what the social sciences are about that definitively rejects the Enlightenment conception of knowledge. What these philosophers reveal is that the sociology of knowledge *is* central to the social sciences. It defines, in fact, the very essence of social science: the examination of the relationship between human thought and human social life. But this sociology of knowledge is not central in the way the positivists thought. It is not logically necessary to the social sciences because it provides a means of distinguishing between objective and subjective knowledge. Rather, it defines the task of the social sciences because it provides a way of analyzing the process by which human beings understand and, hence, structure, the world in which they live. It follows that the sociology of knowledge on this redefinition is not a subset of the larger discipline but defines social science itself.

This analysis raises yet another question concerning contemporary social theory. If, as I am arguing, what these anti-foundational theorists are engaged in is a kind of sociology of knowledge, why have they not espoused the tradition of the sociology of knowledge that has existed in the social sciences? That this has not been the case is quite evident. The first reason for this state of affairs is that the vast majority of what passes for the sociology of knowledge in the social sciences is firmly rooted in positivist assumptions. It is clear that the sociologist of knowledge who defines 'subjective' (socially determined) belief as inferior to objective knowledge is going to have little in common with the anti-foundational theorist who rejects this distinction and the epistemology on which it rests. But there is a less obvious and, ultimately, very important reason: the two sociologies of knowledge operate on different levels of analysis. While the anti-foundational philosopher examines the background assumptions structuring human thought and existence, the traditional sociologist of knowledge examines the relationship between explicit belief systems and particular social groups. Thus the contrast between, for example, Mannheim's analysis of conservatives in nineteenth century Germany and Gadamer's exploration of 'prejudice' lies in the fact that the analyses operate on two very different levels. This difference in levels is definitive of the contrast between the two traditions.

Despite the fact that these two traditions of thought have had little in common, however, it does not necessarily follow that they are antithetical. Rather, a synthesis of the two traditions can be effected that would offer the social sciences both a solid philosophical foundation and a viable research program. On one hand, anti-foundational thought can supply the social sciences with a self-definition that has not been produced in the endless debate over positivism and humanism. On the other hand, the tradition of the sociology of knowledge, purged of its positivist underpinnings, can supply what has been lacking in the anti-positivist critiques in the social sciences – a specific research program for the social sciences. The advantage of this tradition is that it provides a means of examining the relationship between human thought and human existence by analyzing explicit belief systems and their relationship to particular social conditions. In short, these two levels of analysis can be seen as complementary rather than contradictory.[3]

It is, obviously, beyond the scope of a single work fully to substantiate all the claims made above. In the following chapters, therefore, I will attempt a more circumscribed task. Following a brief overview of the history of the sociology of knowledge, I will examine the work of a prominent figure in this tradition, Karl Mannheim. Although Mannheim's work is not free of inconsistencies and positivist assumptions, it comes closer than any other theorist in this tradition to formulating a sociology of knowledge that examines human thought and existence in hermeneutical terms. His work also exhibits a strong affinity to that of Hans-Georg Gadamer, the subject of the second part of the book. The examination of Gadamer's work illustrates the possibility of a connection between these two traditions. Gadamer's work, perhaps more than that of any of the contemporary anti-foundational thinkers, reveals the implications of anti-foundational thought for the social sciences and provides an approach to social scientific methodology free of Enlightenment conceptions about truth. His examination of the role of prejudice in human understanding is the key to the redefinition of the sociology of knowledge that will be attempted. The final chapter outlines the synthesis between these two traditions of the sociology of knowledge on the strictly theoretical level. Although it is certainly an important task to specify the practical methodological implication of the thesis it is not one that will be attempted here. Rather, the aim of the analysis is, first, to establish that anti-foundational thought, and particularly the work of Gadamer, provides an accurate understanding of the task of the social sciences and, secondly, that this understanding is compatible with a specific redefinition of an existing research program in the social sciences, the sociology of knowledge.

2

A Brief History of the Sociology of Knowledge

I INTRODUCTION

The purpose of the following overview of the history of the sociology of knowledge within the social sciences is to sketch the outlines of the major trends in the field, revealing their presuppositions and epistemological assumptions. This overview is not a comprehensive one for a very simple reason: a comprehensive history of the sociology of knowledge would entail no less than a history of social science itself because, as will be argued below, the work of the principal figures in the social sciences, among them Comte, Marx, Weber and Durkheim, was centrally concerned with the sociology of knowledge. Thus to present a complete history of the sociology of knowledge would involve an in-depth examination of the works of these figures, a task far beyond the capabilities of a single study.

The English term 'sociology of knowledge' is a translation of the German *Wissenssoziologie*, a term that is by no means easy to define. Although '*Wissen*' is best translated as 'knowledge', exactly what kind of knowledge it is meant to include has been the subject of much debate from the outset. '*Wissen*' as employed by certain German philosophers and social theorists in the nineteenth century was meant to include knowledge other than strictly scientific knowledge and involved a polemic on the part of those who employed it in this way. Writers such as Weber, Dilthey and Simmel who used the term *Wissenschaften* to describe the products of the social sciences did so to argue that although knowledge in the social sciences is qualitatively different from knowledge in the natural sciences it is nevertheless just as valid. This was denied by their positivist opponents in the then current debate over the nature of the social sciences, the *Methodenstreit*. Thus there is an ambiguity inherent in the name of the field itself. Whether 'knowledge' should include the products of the social sciences, whether this 'knowledge' is distinct from knowledge in the natural sciences, and, later, whether the common-sense knowledge of social actors is also 'knowledge' has been at issue since the nineteenth century. A further complication is introduced by the fact that *Soziologie* is closer to 'social philosophy' than 'sociology' because of the empirical connotations of this term in English (K. Wolff, 1959:560–72). The associations of both these terms in themselves provide an indication of the history of the sociology of knowledge. Practitioners in the field have, from the beginning, been concerned to explore the meaning and extension of 'knowledge' in social life and to do so in a way closer to philosophy than empirical social science.

One of the main difficulties involved in discussing the history of the sociology of knowledge from an anti-foundational perspective is how to deal with the distinction between objective and subjective knowledge. In the previous chapter it was argued that this distinction lies at the heart of both the sociology of knowledge and the social sciences themselves. Yet, from the anti-foundational perspective that will be employed here the distinction itself is a meaningless one because it rests on erroneous epistemological assumptions. Gadamer's position is a good example of the antifoundational position on this issue. He does not argue, as do several nineteenth-century social theorists, that all knowledge in the social sciences is subjective. This assertion, he argues, presupposes the existence of objective knowledge and the legitimacy of the Enlightenment's distinction between the two kinds of knowledge. He claims, rather, that understanding in all of its guises is historically conditioned and, thus, that the distinction itself is wrong-headed. From an anti-foundational position, it is thus difficult to discuss the history of the sociology of knowledge because it is defined by the effort to distinguish between objective and subjective knowledge.

The second problem with this distinction is semantic. The distinction between objective and subjective knowledge and that between objectivity and subjectivity is characterized by confusions, ambiguities and historical changes in definition. The

Enlightenment thinkers cast this distinction in terms of pure and impure knowledge and directed their attention to purging knowledge of its social determinants. It was only in the nineteenth century that the distinction came to be cast in terms of the contrast between the objective and the subjective. The debate among Weber, Dilthey, Rickert and other participants in the *Methodenstreit* revolved around the question of whether and to what extent the social sciences could be 'objective', when 'objective' was defined in terms of the pure, universal and absolute knowledge of the natural sciences. Although this debate became immensely confused and, as a result, the definitions of objectivity and subjectivity took on new meanings, it nevertheless set the stage for the discussions of the nature of the social sciences in the twentieth century. It also provides the starting-point for Gadamer and other contemporary anti-foundational thinkers. Despite the confusions inherent in this distinction, then, these terms will be employed below. The original definition that equates objective with pure and subjective with impure knowledge will be maintained throughout.

The distinction between pure and impure, objective and subjective knowledge dictated not only the original definition of the task of the sociology of knowledge that emerged from Enlightenment thought but also the principle of investigation adhered to in the field. The purpose of the social sciences in general and the sociology of knowledge in particular was defined as the attempt to separate these two kinds of knowledge, to expose the errors of subjective knowledge, and to enthrone objective knowledge in its proper place, that is, definitive of the realm of 'truth'. This distinction and this principle have informed the sociology of knowledge since its inception. Early practitioners of the field, from Vico, Pareto and Montesquieu to Scheler and Marx, defined their task in these terms. There was no question for any of these writers that objective knowledge existed and that its acquisition was the major task of the social sciences. The sociology of knowledge was thus seen as a kind of subsidiary, but vitally necessary, aspect of the real task of the social sciences. The task of the sociologist of knowledge was to define the nature and functioning of the subjective beliefs of social life so as to facilitate the acquisition of objective knowledge in the social sciences.

As the field developed, however, sociologists of knowledge began to alter their opinions concerning the relative scope of subjective knowledge *vis-à-vis* objective, scientific truth. If one theme can be said to dominate the history of the sociology of knowledge it is the progressive expansion of the concept of subjective knowledge at the expense of that of objective knowledge. While the early writers optimistically defined objective knowledge as having a broad scope and relegated subjective knowledge to a minor role, later writers began to reverse this equation. The sociology of knowledge in the nineteenth and twentieth centuries is characterized by practitioners who define a larger and larger role for subjective knowledge. This is particularly evident in the work of Mannheim and the phenomenological school. Although neither Mannheim nor the phenomenologists question the existence of objective knowledge, they do question its relevance for the social sciences. What they claim, in effect, is that the boundaries of subjective knowledge coincide with the boundaries of the social sciences and, thus, that the exploration of subjective knowledge is not merely a subsidiary aspect of the social sciences but is constitutive of its task as a discipline.

In chapter 4 I will argue for a new definition of the sociology of knowledge that can be found in the work of Gadamer and other contemporary anti-foundational philosophers who discard the distinction between objective and subjective knowledge in both the natural and social sciences and, by extension, the underlaborer conception of the sociology of knowledge that has characterized the field from its inception. For these thinkers it is meaningless to posit a realm of objective knowledge to which subjective knowledge can be contrasted. The history of the tradition of the sociology of knowledge within the social sciences reveals, however, that even in its most 'subjectivist' phases its adherents have not moved to this position. They have not, in short, transcended the Enlightenment conception that informs the tradition.

II MARX AND THE EARLY HISTORY OF THE SOCIOLOGY OF KNOWLEDGE

If the distinction between pure and impure knowledge is definitive of the practice of the sociology of knowledge, then the roots of the discipline extend to the roots of social science itself.

Bacon's reference to 'the idols of the mind' as well as Vico's *Scienze Nuova* and Montesquieu's *Spirit of the Laws* contain a nascent sociology of knowledge. But if the explicit exploration of the social determination of beliefs is used as a starting point for the sociology of knowledge, then it must be argued that this tradition arose out of a particular school of thought in the nineteenth century: the critique of ideology. Largely due to the work of the French philosophes, and, specifically Destutt de Tracy's *Elements d'Ideologie*, the social sciences' task of separating illusion from reality came to be defined in terms of the distinction between science and ideology (Giddens, 1979:165). This is, of course, not at all surprising given the pattern of development in the social sciences. Bacon's 'idols of the mind', those things which divert us from the path of true reason, must be exposed and eliminated if the light of reason is to free us from the bondage of unreason. And in the nineteenth century these idols came to be discussed under the general heading of 'ideology'.

De Tracy's work aims to produce a science of ideas, a scientific description of the human mind. It was through him that Bacon's 'idols' were transformed into 'prejudice' in the French Enlightenment. Bacon's theory of 'idols' was meant to apply primarily to the natural sciences; he saw it as a way to safeguard the understanding of nature. But de Tracy and the philosophes transferred his conception to the social sciences where, it seemed, these idols were more prevalent. Although these thinkers did not, unlike Napoleon soon afterwards, attach negative connotations to the concept of 'ideology', they were nevertheless concerned to separate pure science from ideological conceptions. It is out of this tradition, and particularly the related work of Helvetius, that Marx's thought arises (Lichtheim, 1967:7–9; Barth, 1976:1–29).

Any examination of Marx as a sociologist of knowledge, or, for that matter, any examination of Marx from a particular perspective, confronts a number of important problems. First, there is the problem of comprehensiveness. Marx's work cannot be neatly divided into digestible sections that are complete in themselves. Each aspect of Marx's work can only be properly understood as part of the whole. Secondly, there is the problem of interpretation. Should we interpret Marx as a humanist or as a scientific socialist, that is, should we follow Lukacs or Althusser?

I do not pretend to have solved either of these problems, although I have attempted to come to terms with each. With regard to the first problem, I take the position that Marx's most explicit discussion of ideology in *The German Ideology* is relatively self-contained and reveals the essential points of Marx's position. Secondly, I assume that although the major interpretations of Marx differ in important ways, it is nevertheless the case that in both interpretations Marx claims some form of objectivity for his method and his results. This is the key issue on which Marx's sociology of knowledge must be evaluated.

A cursory examination of Marx's attitude toward ideology seems to lead to the conclusion that it is very close to that of Bacon. His goal, like that of Bacon, seems to be to expose the idols of the mind that cloud the light of reason. Marx's exposure of false consciousness thus seems to be merely an extension of the Enlightenment's rejection of prejudice and cultural-historical distortions. But Marx's approach to ideology and, hence, the sociology of knowledge, is marked by a significant departure from this Enlightenment tradition. This is most evident in his discussion (with Engels) in *The German Ideology*. At the beginning of this work he notes:

> Hitherto men have constantly made for themselves false conceptions about themselves, about what they are and what they ought to be. . . . The phantoms of their brains have gained the mastery over them. . . . Let us liberate them from the chimeras, the ideas, dogmas, imaginary beings under the yoke of which they are pining away. . . . Let us teach men, says one, to exchange these imaginations for thoughts which correspond to the essence of man. (1947:1)

This passage could have been written by an Enlightenment philosopher in the eighteenth century. It expresses the basic principle of the Enlightenment: the triumph of reason over unreason. But what is important about this passage is that Marx's intention in writing it is to expose the follies of the Young Hegelians, not to advance his own position. Far from expressing Marx's own thoughts, the passage is intended to mock the program of the Young Hegelians, not to advance his own position. Later in the book Marx attacks the German socialists on similar grounds, criticizing their attempt to replace false conceptions with true ones.

Precisely what is wrong with these conceptions emerges in the subsequent discussion. In all ideological thought, Marx asserts, men and their circumstances appear upside down. (It is in this context that he makes his famous reference to the *camera obscura*.) Instead of interpreting thought as a product of material life processes, ideology depicts material life as a product of thought. This is where the Young Hegelians are in error. They think that by replacing false ideas with true ones, unreason with reason, truth will emerge. But Marx points out that this contains an important mistake because

> The phantoms formed in the human brain are also, necessarily, sublimates of their material life processes, which is empirically verifiable and bound to material premises. (1947:14)

For Marx all concepts are a product of material existence. This informs his famous statement that 'Life is not determined by consciousness, but consciousness by life' (1947:15). Although ideological concepts are no exception to this rule they are unique because ideologists claim *truth* for their concepts, truth that is presumed to supercede real (material) conditions. This position emerges clearly in Marx's discussion of why the concept of 'true property' is ideological: it defines real private property as a semblance whereas it views the concept abstracted from this real property as the truth or reality of the semblance (1947:98).

It follows that, for Marx, the solution to the problem of ideology lies not in formulating different concepts that are, like ideological concepts, abstracted from real conditions. Such concepts can never be 'true' in the sense that their proponents claim. This is the error of the German socialists who, Marx claims, abandon the realm of real history for the realm of ideology and, since they are ignorant of the real connection, merely fabricate 'some fantastic relationship' (1947:80). What is required, rather, is an understanding of the fact that the class which has control of material production engages in another form of production as well: the mental production of ideological concepts. Thus

> The ruling ideas are nothing more than the ideal expression of the dominant material relationships, the dominant material relationship grasped as ideas; hence of the relationship which makes the one class the ruling one, therefore the ideas of its dominance. (1947:39)

Although in *The German Ideology* Marx does not propose a specific alternative to the position of the Young Hegelians and the German socialists, the tenor of his subsequent work makes his position quite clear. In *Capital* the *camera obscura* model that he uses in *The German Ideology* is replaced with a distinction between phenomenon and essence, but the central principle on which both ideas rest remains the same. In both conceptions Marx reveals his conviction that there must be a criterion by which knowledge and ideology can be distinguished (Barth, 1976:48). Marx is, like the Enlightenment thinkers, opposing ideology to truth or reality, but for Marx reality is defined as the material conditions of human beings, conditions that are historically and socially determined, not the 'reality' of true concepts. Thus Marx proposes an analysis of the human condition in terms of the real, material conditions of human beings, not in terms of concepts abstracted from those material conditions. Marx's sociology of knowledge, therefore, can be seen as both an extension of and a departure from Enlightenment thought. Marx does not depart from the basic premise of the Enlightenment: the distinction between objective and subjective knowledge. Like the Enlightenment thinkers, Marx wants to expose the distortions of ideology, but he does so by appealing to the reality of material conditions rather than the truth that is the product of pure reason. Furthermore, like the Enlightenment thinkers, Marx claims to have found pure knowledge which exposes the falsity of ideology. For the Enlightenment the distinction between objective and subjective knowledge rested on the science–ideology distinction. For Marx it rests on the distinction between concepts abstracted from real conditions (ideological concepts) and concepts rooted in the material conditions of social life.

Furthermore, for Marx the false consciousness of ideological thought (subjective knowledge) would be replaced by true consciousness (objective knowledge) with the rise of communism:

> This whole semblance, that the rule of a certain class is only the rule of certain ideas, comes to a natural end, of course, as soon as society ceases at last to be organized in the form of class rule, that is to say as soon as it is no longer necessary to represent a

particular interest as general or 'the general interest' as ruling. (1947:41)

One commentator has labelled this position the Doctrine of Proletarian Truth (Abercrombie, 1980:27). In a society without classes there will be no class interest and hence no distortion of belief. In a communist state there is no reason why phenomenal forms would conceal their true substance (Sayer, 1979:11). Thus the revolution of the proletariat will ensure the production of non-ideological social knowledge (Hamilton, 1974:31). In other words, it will produce objective knowledge, knowledge that eludes those who seek it in the conceptual realm.

It is not necessary to reiterate at length the problems with Marx's concept of ideology as presented in *The German Ideology*. Marx's materialist sociology of knowledge has been frequently attacked in the voluminous literature on Marxist method. Two of these commonly cited criticisms of Marx's position are particularly relevant in the present context. First, Marx's espousal of the Doctrine of Proletarian Truth directly parallels the Enlightenment's concept of the light of pure reason. Both claim to correct the falseness of ideological concepts and thus both fall prey to all the problems inherent in the distinction between subjective and objective knowledge. Secondly, Marx's discussion of ideology rests on the distinction between ideological concepts, which are, by definition, partial, and universal history. In making this distinction Marx incurs the problem of assuming an Archimedean point from which all of history can be assessed. Many commentators have attacked him for this assumption and, furthermore, pointed out the contradiction in the assertion that all positions are historically conditioned except his own (Giddens, 1979:173).

But despite these problems with Marx's account his thought also represents a significant breakthrough for the sociology of knowledge. Most importantly, Marx succeeds in revealing the error of the Enlightenment thinkers' conception of reason. He replaced their assumption that 'truth' resides in abstract concepts divorced from the social and historical realm with the assertion that truth is grounded in social-historical reality and must be apprehended through empirical investigation. He rejects the notion that there are trans-historical covering laws from which essential relations can be inferred and asserts instead that all economic categories are historical and transitory products (Sayer, 1979:114–44). In terms of the sociology of knowledge this is a sea change in the evolution of the discipline. More than any other post-Enlightenment thinker Marx established the basic principle of the sociology of knowledge: all thought is socially and historically determined. Where Marx goes astray, however, is in his assertion that although all consciousness is conditioned by existence it can also rise above existence (Lichtheim, 1967:21). The fact that this implies a contradiction is less important than the fact that it entails the existence of an Archimedean point somewhere beyond social reality.

III THE *METHODENSTREIT* AND GERMAN SOCIOLOGY OF KNOWLEDGE

In the late nineteenth and early twentieth centuries a series of discussions among German economists, historians and sociologists produced a climate of opinion that was to have a profound effect on both the social sciences and the sociology of knowledge. This debate, known as the *Methodenstreit* pitted the defenders of a positivist social science against those who argued for a more interpretive approach to the *Geisteswissenschaften*. The positivists argued that the social sciences should adopt the methodology of the natural sciences because there is no essential difference between the two branches of science. The humanists, on the other hand, argued that the social sciences are qualitatively different from the natural sciences and thus require a different methodology. While it is impossible to discuss the details of this debate here, it is nevertheless important to note a number of points that are of relevance to the present argument.[1] First, neither side in the dispute questioned the basic principle of Enlightenment thought: the exclusive identification of truth with scientific method. Rather, the dispute was conducted over whether the scientific method is appropriate to the social sciences and, if so, what form it should take. Secondly, neither side in the dispute questioned the place of the sociology of knowledge in the social sciences. Both assumed that uncovering the social bases of some forms of knowledge and distinguishing these from 'pure' knowledge is essential to the practice of the social sciences. They differed only as to the extent of socially determined knowledge in the social sciences.

The issues of the *Methodenstreit* played an important part in the formulation of the approaches to the sociology of knowledge that were influential in the early twentieth century. In this period three variants of the sociology of knowledge developed: the German sociological-philosophical school, the French Durkheimian school, and the 'Chicago school' (Curtis and Petras, 1970:3). In terms of the evolution of the discipline the German school is the most significant because it deals with issues that are central to the fundamental bases of the sociology of knowledge and presages the concerns that will later be taken up by the anti-foundationalists. The discussions of the sociology of knowledge produced by both the Durkheimian and Chicago schools, on the other hand, although valuable in some ways, side-step the problems that are crucial to a proper understanding of the sociology of knowledge. Durkheim's fundamental claim with regard to the social sciences, that society produces human consciousness, would seem to be a blanket endorsement of the sociology of knowledge. But Durkheim, without offering specific arguments in defense of his position, assumes that social scientists' observations are based on the scientific method and thus that they occupy a privileged position in society that amounts to an Archimedean point. The question of whether this is possible and, if so, how it is, is precisely the question that the sociology of knowledge must address. By avoiding it, Durkheim's approach fails to provide an adequate basis for the approach. The Chicago school commits a different but equally important error. The adherents of this school adopt an individualist and distinctly psychological attitude toward the sociology of knowledge that ultimately makes the *social* construction of knowledge problematic. The difficulties with this approach, difficulties shared by some offshoots of the German school which will be discussed in the next section, revolve around the problem of moving from individual consciousness to social reality.

In contrast to both these schools a number of theorists in the German school, and particularly those actively engaged in the *Methodenstreit*, make valuable contributions to an understanding of the complexities of investigations in the sociology of knowledge. Weber's extensive studies of the interdependence of economics, religion and society provide a basis for the sociology of knowledge even though he does not explicitly examine the epistemological questions of the field.[2] On a more philosophical plane, Dilthey's theory of interpretation provides a kind of cultural hermeneutics that interprets the 'objective' elements of social life as products of cultural processes. Simmel extends Dilthey's cultural hermeneutics into a developed theory of interpretation that in many ways anticipates the conceptual approach of Gadamer's hermeneutics (Simmel, 1980). But the theorist of this school who made the most lasting contribution to the sociology of knowledge (apart from Karl Mannheim himself) is Max Scheler. Scheler's sociology of knowledge can be defined as the first sustained attempt to define the parameters of the field.[3] Although it is clear that Marx engaged in a sociology of knowledge, Scheler is the first to make a self-conscious attempt to formulate an approach to the discipline.

It may seem curious, but Scheler's sociology of knowledge and Marx's theory exhibit a basic commonality. Like Marx, Scheler bases his discussion on the distinction between ideology and real (material) factors. But in Scheler there is an unresolved tension between the real and ideal factors that provides a contrast to the clear hierarchy between the two found in Marx. For Marx real factors determine ideology, but for Scheler the two exist in an interdependent relationship; he specifies no hierarchical relationship between them. In this respect and in a number of other areas, Scheler's sociology of knowledge is confusing and somewhat contradictory. This confusion can be traced to his effort to integrate a number of incompatible elements in an attempt to solve some of the methodological problems that were central to the *Methodenstreit*.

Foremost among these problems is Scheler's approach to what he sees to be the problem of relativism. Scheler attacks the issue by arguing, on one hand, that the *form* of all knowledge is socially conditioned. But he also claims that all of these forms arise out of one 'ontic ordered realm of ideas' through which the contingent real world passes (1980:41). Although this may sound like a form of idealism, Scheler hastens to add that ideas can only become weapons in history if they align themselves with material conditions. Thus although he asserts that the absolute realm of ideas and values is lifted above factual historical systems, these ideas and values can only be realized through the material (real) conditions of historical societies. As a further defense against idealism he states that a theory of instinct drives is a necessary prerequisite of a sociology of real factors (1980:35). Thus one possible reading of Scheler's thought is that he is advocating not a sociological determination of ideas, but rather a psychobiological determination of human life (Child, 1942:155).

As Scheler sees it, this metaphysics entails that the sociology of knowledge must be concerned with the 'group soul' and the 'group mind'. Since the fixed law that orders the origin of our knowledge of reality is always manifest in particular historical circumstances, the sociologist of knowledge must be concerned about the way in which the customs and manners of particular societies shape social knowledge (1980:69–70). The sociology of knowledge that Scheler advocates is thus opposed to both positivist sociology of knowledge and Marxist sociology. Unlike the positivist, Scheler argues that the scientific world view is not the only true and absolute representation of 'absolute things' (1980:122). Rather, it is only one of a number of different types of knowledge. The relativistic overtones of this position, however, are dispelled by Scheler's argument against the Marxists. Unlike Marx, Scheler argues that a sphere of absolute reality exists based on ideas rather than material factors. Scheler's sociology of knowledge introduces what he labels the 'relative natural view of world'. He posits that the world view of a group subject belongs to whatever is generally given to the group without question, and, further, that the composition of the world view differs from group to group.

Scheler's sociology of knowledge goes into great detail on the parameters of this 'relative natural view of world' but the problems with his conception are clear from even this brief summary of his approach. Scheler offers little defense of his 'ontic realm of ideas' nor does he specify its relationship to material factors. His wedding of Marx and a kind of Catholic absolutism of values needs much more defense than he provides for it. His attempt to solve the problem of relativism by introducing certain absolutist elements while at the same time maintaining that all knowledge is socially conditioned is also problematic. If all knowledge is socially conditioned, what is the status of the ontic realm of absolute ideas that he posits? Sixty years after Scheler wrote his treatises on the sociology of knowledge these problems can hardly be overlooked and it seems fair to conclude that Scheler's approach is seriously flawed. From the perspective of contemporary concerns Scheler's greatest contribution is his challenge to the hegemony of scientific rationality, an advantage shared by the other participants in the humanist side of the *Methodenstreit*. Unlike the Durkheimian school he sees through the façade of the scientists' claim to absolute truth. And, unlike the Chicago school, he emphasizes the social rather than the individual psychological construction of reality. But despite these advantages, Scheler cannot surmount the problems posed by his advocacy of an absolute realm of values, a position that has little to recommend it in contemporary discussions.

IV THE SOCIOLOGY OF KNOWLEDGE IN THE MID-TWENTIETH CENTURY

Although I have been arguing that the roots of the sociology of knowledge lie in the beginnings of social science itself, the advent of the sociology of knowledge as a distinct subfield of the social sciences is usually associated with the works of Mannheim and Scheler. Both theorists specifically defined the field and offered comprehensive approaches that identified the range of topics falling under the rubric of the sociology of knowledge. Their work includes analysis of the empirical relation between knowledge systems and social factors, the role of intellectuals, and the construction of the everyday understandings of social actors. In the decades that followed the publication of their seminal works, however, the field split into various branches that focused on one or another of the different aspects of the field as they had defined it. Two of these branches are of particular importance in the development of the field. One group of theorists concentrated on the analysis of the social origins of everyday knowledge (common-sense reality); a second examined the empirical relationship between knowledge and social factors.

The branch of the sociology of knowledge that defines its subject matter as the analysis of the common-sense reality of the social actor has its roots in the phenomenological tradition. Both Scheler and Mannheim were deeply influenced by the phenomenological writings of the early twentieth century and this influence is reflected in their work on the sociology of knowledge. Thus it is not surprising that a distinctly phenomenological school of the sociology of knowledge should arise. Neither Scheler nor Mannheim explored the full potential of the phenomenological tradition for the sociology of knowledge. This task fell to one man who almost single-handedly established this tradition: Alfred Schutz. Unlike Scheler and Mannheim, Schutz did not identify his approach to the social sciences primarily in terms of the sociology of knowledge. Rather, he defined his task in the broadest possible terms: establishing a foundation for the methodology of the social sciences. The goal of Schutz's social phenomenology is to explain the constitution of meaning in the social world and, derivatively, the construction of the common-sense reality in which the social actor moves. In order to achieve this goal, Schutz relies on the impressive arsenal of concepts in Husserl's phenomenology: bracketing, the epoche, internal time consciousness, intentionality, and intersubjectivity. But he also goes beyond Husserl to employ a number of concepts that are peculiar to a social phenomenology. Schutz discusses the construction of common-sense social reality in terms of levels of anonymnity, we-and-they relationships, face-to-face relationships, finite provinces of reality and systems of relevences. Armed with these concepts, Schutz creates a comprehensive method by which social reality can be analyzed and understood.[4]

But although Schutz prefers to define his social phenomenology in these broad terms, it is not difficult to argue that his approach is just as much a sociology of knowledge as the work of Mannheim and Scheler. Schutz's goal is to examine the creation of 'knowledge' in the social world. He defines knowledge in the broadest possible way: everything that members of a particular social group claim to 'know'. Further, he makes it explicit that his aim is to examine the specifically social basis of this knowledge. In fact his principal thesis is that all knowledge is, by definition, social, or, as he puts it, intersubjective. Thus it is plausible that the entire corpus of Schutz's work has been defined as a sociology of knowledge; it has come to be a commonplace among his commentators. The best illustration of this is Berger and Luckmann's *The Social Construction of Reality* (1966) in which a specifically Schutzian social phenomenology is developed into what the authors define as a 'treatise on the sociology of knowledge'.

The work of Schutz thus served the important function of providing the sociology of knowledge with a fully developed phenomenological basis. But it served another function: it shaped American social scientists' perception of the sociology of knowledge and provided a link between the phenomenological school and a distinctly American branch of the sociology of knowledge associated primarily with the work of George Herbert Mead. When Schutz immigrated to America in the 1930s and was exposed to American social science, he began to see links between his work and various American theorists, most notably Mead and William James. In the articles he published while living in America the influence of these American thinkers began to be evident in his work and he adopted a number of concepts and theories utilized by the Americans. It followed that Schutz's discussion of a phenomenological sociology of knowledge was couched in language already familiar to American readers. This removed some of the stigma that the sociology of knowledge had previously held for American social scientists. As one commentator put it, before Schutz's American writings appeared the sociology of knowledge was regarded as 'an unassimilated European import of interest to only a few colleagues with a slightly eccentric penchant for the history of ideas' (Berger, 1970:373).

Both Schutz's social phenomenology and, to a lesser extent, Mead's social psychology represent important contributions to the sociology of knowledge in a specific sense. By focusing on the analysis of the construction of common-sense reality in social life, Schutz is calling attention to a hitherto neglected aspect of the sociology of knowledge. As such he makes a valuable contribution to the understanding of the nature of social reality. But from the perspective being developed here, Schutz's approach is seriously flawed on two counts. First, and most importantly, Schutz is trapped by his acceptance of a conception definitive of the Enlightenment conception of knowledge: the individualist paradigm and the subject-object dichotomy on which it rests. Schutz's adherence to the individualist paradigm stems from his reliance on the basic postulate of Husserlian phenomenology: all meaning is constructed through intentional acts of the individual ego. Although Schutz is very careful to specify that meaning in the social world is intersubjective, that is, constituted by the interaction of social actors in the social world, he nevertheless bases his social theory in Husserlian phenomenology and, thus, ultimately defines meaning in terms of individual intentionality. Reliance on individual intentionality as the basis of meaning, however, makes the distinctly social character of knowledge problematic. In taking this position he makes the error, revealed by both Gadamer and Wittgenstein, that it is not precisely correct to say than an 'I' speaks. Rather, both argue that, using the social medium of language, social actors participate in the meanings supplied by language. Thus to speak of individual constitution of meaning is to misunderstand how language operates in the constitution of meaning. It follows that Schutz, by failing to transcend the Husserlian concept of the individual constitution of meaning also fails to comprehend how knowledge is produced in the social world.[5] This shortcoming is a consequence of his adherence to the objective-subjective dichotomy that is central to the Enlightenment concept of knowledge. Although Schutz redefines subjectivity and objectivity to suit his own purposes, he does not altogether discard these concepts and hence remains within the conceptual net of Enlightenment thought.

The second related problem with social phenomenology and the Meadian social psychology with which it has come to be associated is that it lends itself to a form of psychological explanation. Instead of providing the sociology of knowledge with a philosophical basis, social phenomenologists have tended to emphasize individual psychological explanations. This criticism applies more to Schutz's followers and to Mead than to his own work, but it is nevertheless significant. It is one thing, for example, to explain how the concept of a generalized other arises for the child in human society, and quite another to explain the phenomenon of human understanding as Gadamer and Heidegger have done. The sociology of knowledge requires a philosophical basis that avoids the pitfalls of psychological reduction and, on the whole, social phenomenology has failed to provide this. Although Schutz and Mead provide valuable insights into the construction of social reality, their followers have compromised these insights by a retreat into psychological explanation.

Of even more importance, what an analysis of these thinkers

reveals is that unless the Enlightenment conception of knowledge is definitively rejected investigations into the nature of knowledge in the social world inevitably fall into error and confusion. Schutz's approach illustrates this very aptly. Although he makes a serious effort to define the *social* basis of knowledge through his examination of the intersubjective constitution of meaning, his effort ultimately falls into confusion because he does not reject Husserlian intentionality. He cannot have it both ways – social (intersubjective) meaning constitution and individual intentionality. What is needed at this point is a complete transcendence of the old epistemology. Such a transcendence is found in Gadamer's insight that language is not a game that we, as social actors, play but, rather, it plays us.

The second branch of the sociology of knowledge that developed in the wake of the work of Mannheim and Scheler is concerned not with the constitution of common-sense social reality but with the empirical relationship between a particular body of knowledge and the social factors that determine it. This branch can be said to represent the more 'classical' tradition in the sociology of knowledge. Unlike the phenomenologists, this branch is primarily concerned with the distinction central to the Enlightenment tradition, that between socially determined and 'objective' knowledge. In the twentieth century this aspect of the sociology of knowledge is further divided into the positivist and materialist camps. The positivists' attitude toward the sociology of knowledge is characterized by the goal of separating 'scientific' or 'objective' knowledge from socially determined belief. The goal of materialist (usually Marxist) sociology of knowledge, on the other hand, is to reveal the social determination of ideological beliefs and to contrast these beliefs to 'material reality'. Although the Marxists are less explicit than the positivists in separating ideological from 'true' knowledge in this sense, making this distinction is also at the root of their analyses. The split between the positivist and materialist approaches to the sociology of knowledge, furthermore, has largely coincided with the split between the American and European camps (K. Wolff, 1959). In general the Americans have adopted the positivist approach which stresses individual factors and an a-historical methodology, while the Europeans have assumed the materialist approach which stresses social factors and emphasizes historical determinants.

Like many other aspects of European social science, the sociology of knowledge was 'discovered' in America in the first half of the twentieth century. This discovery prompted a spate of American publications on the sociology of knowledge: a series of articles on epistemology and philosophy by Child (1941a; 1941b), Sorokin's massive work on culture (1947), and works specifically devoted to the sociology of knowledge by Maquet (1951), DeGre (1955) and Stark (1958). These works can be classified as positivist because, despite the professed 'hermeneutic' bent of several of them, all adhere to the basic principles characteristic of positivist sociology of knowledge: the distinction between pure and impure knowledge that rests on the Enlightenment conception of knowledge and the exclusive identification of 'truth' with the scientific method. Thus, even more than the phenomenological school, positivist sociologists of knowledge fail to transcend the Enlightenment conception of knowledge that has defined the tradition of the sociology of knowledge since its inception. Their more explicit espousal of the crucial distinction between pure and impure knowledge leads them, moreover, to a position that involves a blatant misunderstanding of the constitution of social knowledge, a position that has by and large been abandoned today. It is worth exploring, however, because it continues to influence many social scientists' perceptions of the sociology of knowledge.

Positivist sociology of knowledge developed a distinctive principle that has come to characterize this particular branch of the sociology of knowledge. All these authors, with the notable exception of Child, make a distinction between the origin of thought and its validity and assert that the sociology of knowledge is to be concerned only with origins, not with the epistemological issues raised by questions of thought's validity. This question, they claim, is the province of philosophy and should not be explored by the sociologist of knowledge (Dixon, 1980:2). Child's epistemological investigations, although an exception to this rule, did not alter the positivists' conviction that epistemological issues are not their concern. In a series of articles published in the early 1940s, Child analyzed some of the basic philosophical and epistemological problems of the sociology of knowledge and, specifically, the problem of imputation. He came to the conclusion that the tradition was seriously deficient in these respects; he found Mannheim's work to be inconsistent and inadequate and the sociology of knowledge lacking because it failed to produce a 'coercive ground for the objectivity of social determination' (1941b:413). His conclusion, however, seemed only to reinforce the positivists' conviction that investigations should avoid philosophical and epistemological issues in favor of 'empirical' problems in the sociology of knowledge. The conclusion reached by one commentator characterizes this attitude very aptly: the claim that the sociology of knowledge has epistemological relevance is based on a confusion (Hinshaw, 1943:59).

Exactly what this group of writers had in mind when they claimed that the sociology of knowledge must be empircial is most clearly displayed in Sorokin's work. Sorokin attempts an impressive quantitative study of what he identifies as epistemological systems. He asserts that the world has witnessed three major systems of truth, cognition, or knowledge: the ideational system, the sensate system, and the idealistic system (1947:610). Although he claims that each system determines the content of mental productions created while that system is dominant, this influence is not total, but exists, rather, only at the level of broad trends of philosophical thought. Sorokin's basic approach is followed by Maquet in his ambitious work on the sociology of knowledge. Although Maquet finds Sorokin's use of quantification 'curious and somewhat sacrilegious', he nevertheless follows Sorokin in defining the sociology of knowledge as the study of mental productions empirically related to social or cultural factors (1951:5). Further, he adheres to the positivist dictum that a distinction must be made between the sociology of knowledge and the philosophy of knowledge. While the sociology of knowledge is concerned to clarify the manner in which social factors influence mental productions and provides scientific theories to explain them, the philosophy of knowledge explores the 'profound nature' of knowledge (1951:97). He admits a contact between the two, but concludes that they 'have different objectives, different methods, and move on different planes of reality' (1951:247).

These themes are reiterated in the works of DeGre and Stark. Adhering to the distinction between origin and validity, DeGre claims that the validity of a proposition is found in syntactical rules, not its social origin. Thus it is our knowledge that is determined by existential factors, not what our knowledge is about; the real world is independent of our knowledge about it. In a particularly clear statement of the positivist misunderstanding of the sociology of knowledge he asserts:

> True knowledge is that knowledge which the knower would have if the proposition which he formulates about the objective reality were exactly isomorphic to the reality. (1955:165)

Stark echoes these themes in his claim that the validity of thought is the province of the philosopher, its origin that of the historian (1958:152–60). And, like DeGre, Stark identifies a constant 'real world', the sphere of nature, that is the same for all societies (1958:165).

But Stark, unlike his predecessors, is sensitive to what he identifies as the 'hermeneutic' element in the sociology of knowledge, and in this he moves away from a strictly positivist position. Defining the sociology of knowledge as 'an essentially hermeneutic or explanatory method' (1958:142), he follows Weber in claiming that values lie at the basis of all perception and that these 'objective values' are a product of the society in which we live.

> So deep then is this axiological determination of historical thought, even in its most 'objective' scholarly or 'scientific' form, that it extends not only to concretely determined facts but even to abstract modes of determining facts. (1958:139)

But Stark ultimately shies away from what he sees to be the relativistic implications of this statement. He claims that the 'solution' to the 'problem' of relativity lies in the development of a comprehensive doctrine of man, that is, a philosophical anthropology that can provide an Archimedean point, even though such a position cannot be identified as entirely beyond history (1958:196–210).

In retrospect it seems clear that positivist sociologists of knowledge, and Sorokin in particular, were attempting to make their discipline conform to the empirical standards of behavioral social science. It is also clear that as far as behavioral social science was concerned the sociology of knowledge failed to achieve this goal. In 1959 Thomas Merton wrote:

> After enjoying more than two generations of scholarly interest, the sociology of knowledge remains largely a subject of meditation

> rather than a field of sustained methodological investigation. (1970:507)

By the standards of behavioral empiricism, the problems of the sociology of knowledge seemed vague and elusive (Holzner, 1972:17). The nature of these deficiencies are evident in Ernst Nagel's classic work, *The Structure of Science* (1961). Nagel states that there is no evidence for Mannheim's thesis that the principles employed in social inquiry for assessing intellectual products are necessarily determined by the social perspective of the inquirer. Noting that Mannheim exempts analysis in the natural sciences from social determination, Nagel asks why the social sciences cannot be exempted as well. He argues, in short, that the thesis of the sociology of knowledge that all analysis in the social sciences is socially determined, has not been established and thus that social scientists need not take it all too seriously (1961:498–502).

Nagel's remarks indicate that at mid-century the positivist social scientist adopted one of two related attitudes toward the sociology of knowledge, attitudes that still characterize their assessment of the field and are shared by those few positivists who still engage in research in it. Some argue with Nagel that the sociology of knowledge has no empirical validity and thus no place in a scientific social science. Others argue that a scientific sociology of knowledge can be formulated but only if it is divorced from both philosophical and epistemological questions (Stehr, 1981:227). There is some disagreement as to exactly what such a scientific sociology of knowledge would entail, however. One group maintains that the investigator would distinguish socially conditioned from objective knowledge within the social sciences. As Horowitz puts it:

> If the possibility of objectively measuring truth and error in sociology is not assured, the enterprise of the sociology of knowledge is reduced to a naive philosophical relativism. (1961:97–98)

Others take the more radical view that all knowledge in the social sciences is socially conditioned and that objective knowledge is the exclusive province of the natural sciences (K. Wolff, 1959). But it is important to note that, in both these cases, the positivist position on the sociology of knowledge has not departed significantly from the Enlightenment conception of knowledge from which it springs. Along with the Enlightenment thinkers, the positivist social scientist claims that the distinction between socially conditioned and scientific knowledge is necessary and, further, that only scientific knowledge can be labelled 'objective'. What has changed in the two centuries since Bacon declared war on the 'idols of the mind' is the conception of the scope of objective knowledge. The Enlightenment thinker confidently assumed that objective knowledge could be defined in both the natural and the social sciences and, further, that as science progressed investigations in both branches of science would result in the steady accumulation of objective knowledge. Modern positivists, however, are less optimistic. Many are even ready to concede that objective knowledge as the Enlightenment defined it is not possible in the social sciences. But what ties them to the Enlightenment and makes them true heirs of this tradition is their conviction that objective knowledge does exist and is the unquestioned goal of science, both natural and social.

The claim that recent Marxist and neo-Marxist sociology of knowledge is also heir to the Enlightenment tradition of 'objective knowledge' is more difficult to establish than to argue the same thesis for the positivists. Although the positivists are generally quite clear in their assertion of the distinction between distorted (or ideological) and scientific knowledge, the Marxists make this distinction with more awareness of the social construction of knowledge and hence avoid some of the more obvious traps involved in the positivists' assertion of objectivity. This awareness is particularly evident in the work of critical theorists who make extensive use of 'interpretive' approaches such as phenomenology and ordinary language analysis. The strictly materialist sociology of knowledge found in Marx's work is significantly altered in the work of these contemporary writers. But despite these concessions to interpretive thought, contemporary Marxist and neo-Marxist sociology of knowledge still clings to the distinction between pure and impure knowledge that informed the work of both Marx and the Enlightenment thinkers.

Any discussion of contemporary sociology of knowledge that is heir to the Marxist tradition must confront the impressive work of one man: Jurgen Habermas. In fact, given the prominence of

Habermas's work, other Marxist sociology of knowledge is relatively insignificant.[6] Habermas, like other contemporary neo-Marxists is very sensitive to the advantages that phenomenology, ordinary language analysis and hermeneutics offer to the study of the social sciences. The context in which Habermas sets forth his most explicit sociology of knowledge is his discussion in *Knowledge and Human Interests* (1971). His argument centers on the assertion that the points of view from which reality is apprehended have their roots in the 'natural history of the human species'. He identifies three such points of view or 'cognitive interests': the technical, the practical and the emancipatory. Habermas attempts to establish that these interests are common to all human social life and can be identified with particular aspects of our natural history. His more immediate concern, however, is that each corresponds to a particular form of knowledge in modern social analysis. Technical interest generates the knowledge produced by the empirical-analytic sciences, practical interest produces the knowledge characteristic of the historical-hermeneutic sciences, and emancipatory interest produces 'critical' knowledge. It is this third form of knowledge that is the focus of Habermas's attention. He argues that it was the interest in emancipation that informed the Greeks' attempt to separate appearance from reality and thus liberate individuals from the false appearances of the social world. This interest has, he claims, been abandoned by modern social theorists due to the influence of positivism and only the renewal of emancipatory interest can restore theoretical inquiries to their proper role (1971:308 ff.).

Precisely what Habermas intends as a model for analysis in the social sciences, however, is most clearly revealed in his *Zur Logik der Sozialwissenschaften* (1970). In the critique of interpretive social science found in this work Habermas makes a point particularly relevant to an analysis of his view of the sociology of knowledge: he rejects the relativism implicit in these approaches. Arguing against the notion that social actors' concepts are constitutive of social reality, Habermas asserts instead that social action is constituted in an 'objective framework':

> But the objective framework of social action is not exhausted by the dimension of intersubjectivity intended and symbolically transmitted meaning. . . . *Social actions can only be comprehended*

> *in an objective framework that is constituted conjointly by language, labor and domination.* (1970:289)[7]

It is his assertion of an objective framework of social action that commits Habermas to an approach to the social sciences that, although clearly not positivist, is yet consistent with the Enlightenment distinction between pure and impure knowledge. To put it most simply, for Habermas there is a position outside socially constructed reality by which that reality can be assessed. At various points in his work this position has been expressed in different ways. In *Knowledge and Human Interests* it is defined in terms of an analogy to Freud's psychoanalysis. Later, after his 'linguistic turn', this Archimedean point is defined in terms of the ideal speech situation (1979). Finally, in his most recent work he is moving toward a kind of philosophical anthropology as the basis for his critique of social reality. But, in theoretical terms, these approaches all come to much the same thing. In each, Habermas is positing a realm of objectivity from which what he sees to be the subjective, ideological conceptions of social reality can be assessed and criticized (Giddens, 1979:177).[8]

Attempting to establish that Habermas is positing an Archimedean point of objectivity for the social sciences is difficult, however, because he carefully avoids any explicit discussion of the precise nature of this objectivity. Although it is clear from his work that he sees the form of objectivity suitable to the social sciences as distinct from that of the natural sciences, he does not explain the character of this difference. In her commentary on Habermas's work, Hesse claims that Habermas is moving toward an 'objective hermeneutic method appropriate to the human sciences' (1980:185) and, significantly, compares Habermas's program with that of Francis Bacon. She states:

> Like Bacon, Habermas gives concrete content to the character of the idols or ideologies, but unlike Bacon he is not so specific about the methods then to be pursued in valid argumentation. (1980:215)

This seems to be the most accurate assessment of Habermas's position on objectivity that is possible. Hesse, along with many other commentators on Habermas's thought, sees his social theory as a continuation of the Enlightenment's quest for pure knowledge.[9] Although he clearly rejects both the relativism of the humanists and the scientism of the positvists, he claims the right to identify and criticize what Bacon labelled the idols of the mind.

It should be noted, however, that Habermas, unlike the positivists, is well aware of the role of historical and cultural forces in shaping social reality. He is very careful to define the 'objective framework' of social action as constituted at least partially by history and culture. In his most recent work, *The Theory of Communicative Action* (1984), Habermas strongly emphasizes the determining role of history and culture. Even in this work, however, he intends to offer a theory that can in some sense step outside the social reality created by these historical and cultural influences. Providing an adequate response to what he sees to be the 'problem' of relativism is one of the central themes of the work. It is in another context, however, that Habermas's position on this issue is most clearly stated: his on-going debate with Gadamer on the nature of the social sciences.[10] Gadamer objects to Habermas's theory on the grounds that it posits 'real factors' outside the scope of language and that this position is 'absolutely absurd' (1976b:31). Habermas replies to this that implicit in the activity of social scientific analysis is the intention to inquire behind the apparent meaning of everyday language (1970:236–44). And, most significantly, he argues against Gadamer that the Enlightenment embodied a 'tradition' that he adheres to: the separation of illusion from reality.

Habermas's debate with Gadamer and the thrust of his theoretical work both point to the same conclusion. Despite his significant differences from the positivists, Habermas is, like them, positing a form of objectivity for the social sciences and, like the Enlightenment thinkers, relying on the distinction between pure and impure knowledge. Although all Marxist sociology of knowledge cannot be indicted on the basis of Habermas's work, it nevertheless seems fair to conclude that, given the clearly objectivist and materialist basis of Marx's work, it is improbable that a Marxist theorist would significantly depart from some variant of this position. It follows that, from the perspective offered by the anti-foundational position, Habermas and his fellow Marxist and neo-Marxists can be identified as heirs to the Enlightenment tradition of knowledge that gave rise to the sociology of knowledge.

V THE REALISTS

Interest in the sociology of knowledge as a specific field of investigation has not been a pronounced trend of twentieth-century social theory. Positivist research in the sociology of knowledge has all but disappeared and the materialist approach has been absorbed into the broader concerns of the critical theorists' position. The only exception to this characterization is a group of British social theorists who have produced a body of work dealing specifically with the sociology of knowledge. These theorists, who can be placed under the general label of 'realists', are of particular interest in the present context because their approach seems to be very similar to that of the anti-foundationalists. The realists' program involves an attack on the sacredness of science and its exemption from social determination, a theme that is also central to the anti-foundational position. The realists criticize Mannheim's sociology of knowledge, for example, because Mannheim fails to extend his critique of scientific method to include the natural sciences and mathematics. The realists' 'strong program' in the sociology of knowledge has stimulated more interest in the field than any approach since the work of Mannheim. In this they have made a valuable contribution to the field. But a careful examination of the realists' position will show that it has little affinity to the anti-foundational position. Although the realists claim to be debunking the sacredness of science they are, in essence, redefining the scientific method and using the new definition to claim more territory for the domain of science.

The realist label attached to these theorists originates in current debates in the philosophy of science. It is frequently noted that contemporary philosophy of science is divided into two camps: the realists and the instrumentalists (or relativists). Although it is difficult to characterize either side in this debate in general terms because of the diversity of positions on both sides, the following summaries can, broadly, be said to apply. The instrumentalists (Kuhn, Feyerabend, etc.) take the position that no transcendental or trans-theoretical criteria of rationality or method exist in science or any other activity. Rather they argue that each theoretical system creates not only its own data but its own criteria of truth, validity and rationality. The realists counter that the real world in a broad sense constrains our knowledge of it. Although contemporary realists do not espouse a naive correspondence theory of truth, they argue against the instrumentalists that not just *any* theory will do. Instead they assert that theories either work or do not work because of their empirical relationship to the world. As one commentator has noted, realism necessarily contains an ontological ingredient because, for the realists, ' the sentences of scientific theories are true or false as the case may be in virtue of how the world is independent of ourselves' (Newton-Smith, 1981:43).

The debate between the realists and the instrumentalists in the philosophy of science has spilled over into discussions in the philosophy of the social sciences. The realist position in the social sciences and, particularly, the sociology of knowledge, has been espoused primarily by three theorists: Barry Barnes, David Bloor and Roy Bhaskar.[11] Barnes' *Scientific Knowledge and Sociological Theory* (1974) and Bloor's *Knowledge and Social Imagery* (1976) contain the initial statements of the position that Bloor labels the 'strong program' in the sociology of knowledge. Bloor's definition of the strong program is the clearest summary of the position:

> All knowledge, whether it be in the empirical sciences or even in mathematics, should be treated, through and through, as material for investigation. Such limitations as do exist for the sociologist consist in handing material over to allied sciences like psychology or in depending on the researches of specialists in other disciplines. There are no limitations which lie in the absolute or transcendent character of scientific knowledge itself, or in the special nature of rationality, validity, truth or objectivity. (1976:1)

The position that science, like other forms of knowledge, should be subjected to the scrutiny of the sociology of knowledge provides the organizing principle of the major works of this approach.

The first extended treatise on the strong program, Barnes's *Scientific Knowledge and Sociology Theory* (1974), begins with the assertion that the 'marked neglect' of the sociology of knowledge that characterized social theory has come to an end. Barnes asserts that the revival of interest in the sociology of knowledge is motivated by the concern to extend its domain to include the study of natural science and mathematics (1974:4). In the course of his various works (1974, 1976, 1981) Barnes developes this thesis in terms of a specific attack on Mannheim. Mannheim clearly states that mathematics and natural science are excluded from his thesis on the sociology of knowledge. This view is erroneous, Barnes claims, because science is theoretical knowledge and, as such, must be subject to sociological causation like any other form of knowledge (1974:12). He states:

> Science enjoys no advantage because its beliefs are in unique correspondence with reality or uniquely rational, hence its processes of cultural transmission will be in no important respect different than those employed by other knowledge sources. (1974:64)

Mannheim's failure to subject science to the scrutiny of the sociology of knowledge rested, Barnes claims, on his adherence to an erroneous conception of knowledge. Against Mannheim, Barnes argues that knowledge can be interpreted in one of only two ways: either as a product of contemplation, that is, disinterested individuals passively perceiving some aspect of reality, or as socially produced by interacting groups in a specific context. He further argues that those, like Mannheim, who exempt science and mathematics from the sociology of knowledge, implicitly accept the contemplative account rather than the social account (1976:1–3). Barnes asserts, rather, that all knowledge is produced by individuals with particular technical interests in particular contexts (1976:19).

What Barnes appears to be advocating in these works is a conception of knowledge that is 'relativistic' in the traditional sense, that is, one that asserts that all knowledge is socially produced and, hence, that there is no universal or absolute standard for knowledge. But a closer reading reveals that this is not Barnes' thesis. There is another aspect to his work, and that of the strong program in general, that belies the relativist approach. The first indication of this can be found in the introduction to *Scientific Knowledge and Sociological Theory*. In an attack on phenomenologists and ethnomethodologists in the sociology of knowledge, Barnes argues that they ignore the question of whether the world in any way constrains our knowledge (1974:viii). Later, he asserts that although 'truth' and 'rationality' do not supply an 'unproblematic baseline' by which beliefs may be judged, 'normality' *does* provide such a baseline (1974:42). In the context of a discussion of Habermas, Barnes asserts that it is his intent to advocate not relativism, but 'naturalism' which 'implies the most intensely serious concern with what is real' (1976:25). Furthermore, following the classical tradition in the sociology of knowledge he defines ideologically determined knowledge as that which is created, accepted, or sustained by concealed, unacknowledged, or illegitimate interests. Although he claims that at present there is no explicit, objective set of rules by which these concealed interests can be identified he argues that all knowledge is not ideologically determined and that 'an institution wherein knowledge is generated and sustained under the impetus of legitimate instrumental interests would seem a realistic and empirically realizable ideal' (1976:43).

The 'institution' that Barnes refers to in this passage is that of science itself. Barnes, along with the other realists, espouses a 'post-empiricist' conception of science based on the assertion that all scientific inquiry, even studies in the natural sciences, involves interpretation and, thus, is 'hermeneutic'. He uses this new definition of scientific inquiry to refute those who claim that the social sciences in general and the sociology of knowledge in particular are not 'scientific':

> But the sociology of knowledge is emphatically not, as its critics often mistakenly believe, itself a denigration of science, on the contrary, it is in many ways modelled upon scientific investigation, and any claims to credulity it comes to have must be closely related to those of science itself. The sociology of knowledge is a matter-of-fact empirical field of study which happens to include, among its subject matter, the knowledge and culture of science. (1982:xi)

A concern with extending the sociology of knowledge to science and an anti-relativist theme also characterize Bloor's *Knowledge and Social Imagery*. Bloor begins by asking why scientists have resisted the attempt to use scientific method to analyze the character of scientific knowledge (1976:ix). Like Barnes, he attacks what he calls Mannheim's 'failure of nerve', that is, his reluctance to subject scientific knowledge to critical scrutiny (1976:8). He is even clearer than Barnes in arguing that what is needed is not merely an examination of scientific knowledge in social terms, but a scrutiny of scientific knowledge using the tenets of the post-empiricist scientific method. What Bloor is advocating, in a sense, is turning the scientific method on itself, that is, using the scientific method to examine the causes of scientific knowledge, not just the causes of erroneous beliefs (1976:4–6). This is necessary, he claims, because unless we adopt a scientific approach to the nature of all knowledge, the sociology of knowledge will be confined to the sociology of error and will be 'no more than a projection of our ideological concerns' (1976:70). In a significant passage, he states that the fear of violating the sacredness of knowledge can only be overcome by those whose faith in it is nearly total (1976:71). What is needed, he concludes, is that the social sciences should follow as closely as possible the methods of other empirical sciences. For Bloor, then, as for Barnes, the problem with the social sciences is not, as many have argued, that they are trying to be too scientific but rather that the scientific method has not been applied as rigorously as it should be in these disciplines (1976:41).

Perhaps the most ambitious attempt to specify the parameters of a realist social science is that of Bhaskar in *The Possibility of Naturalism* (1979). Bhaskar defines the transcendental realist view as the assertion that the essence of science is the movement from knowledge of manifest phenomena to knowledge of the structures that generate them (1979:1). Applying his realist definition of science to the social sciences it emerges that the 'manifest phenomena' of the social sciences are the elements of social life as conceptualized in the experience of the social agents, and the structures that generate them are the structures and practices of society that are the necessary conditions for the agents' activity (1979:32–45). Through an elaborate analysis Bhaskar shows how the transcendental realist view of science does indeed fit the social sciences and how other views, notably both positivist and what he labels 'hermeneutic' social science fail. In conclusion he asserts that the social sciences can be sciences in exactly the same *sense* but not in the same *way* as natural science (1979:203).

There is much to Bhaskar's comprehensive system that, although impressive, is of little relevance here. His comments on the issue of relativism, however, have important implications for the realist position in the social sciences and the sociology of knowledge. Bhaskar's position can be summarized in his assertion that epistemological but not ontological relativism is entailed by his position (1979:69–83). He claims that although all beliefs are societally determined (epistemological relativism) this does not also entail a relativism of being (ontological relativism). Exactly what he means by a denial of ontological relativism, however, is by no means clear. The realist view implies, he states, that people do not create society but, rather, it predates them and is a necessary condition for their activity (1979:45). The failure to see this is the principal error of hermeneutic social science. The hermeneuticist overlooks the fact that the conditions for the phenomena exist independently of their appropriate conceptualization (1979:66). To claim, as they do, that the generative role of actors' beliefs is incorrigible is to fall into 'interpretive fundamentalism' (1979:293). Thus, in Bhaskar's terminology, the hermeneutic social scientist embraces both ontological and epistemological relativism. For the realist, on the contrary, 'science does not produce its intransitive [real] objects of investigation; it produces the conditions for their identification'(1979:53). In the natural sciences the realist presupposes a 'real world' that limits and constrains the theories proposed about it. In the social sciences the same is true but the 'real world' that is presupposed is that of society. It thus follows that social actors' concepts do not produce society, but, rather, it exists independently of their conceptualizations. And, although all beliefs are socially determined and thus epistemological relativism is correct, ontological relativism does not follow because society predates socially determined beliefs.

Bhaskar's position, along with the realist approaches of Barnes and Bloor, raises a number of issues important to the formulation of an anti-foundational sociology of knowledge. For a clarification of the philosophical implications of the realist position it is useful to turn to a philosopher whom all three theorists refer to extensively: Mary Hesse. In *Revolutions and Reconstructions in the Philosophy of Science* (1980) Hesse emphasizes that the locus of the debate in both the philosophy of science and the philosophy of the social sciences has shifted in recent years. At the turn of the century the debate in the social sciences revolved around whether positivism, the accepted approach to the natural sciences, was an appropriate method for the social sciences as well. Since that time, however, the positivist approach to the natural sciences has been seriously discredited. As Hesse points out, the three premises of the empiricist (positivist) conception of knowledge, naive realism, universal scientific language and the correspondence theory of truth, have all been undermined (1980:vii). Further, she notes that almost every point made by the humanists about the social sciences to establish the argument that positivism is not an appropriate method for the social sciences has now been made about the natural sciences as well. Thus, for example, most philosophers of science now assert that the claims that data are not detachable from theory and that meaning is determined by theory are just as true for the natural sciences as they are of the social sciences (1980:172–3). The real debate today, she argues, is between the rationalists-evolutionists who see our language and science as the high point of the evolution of ideas and the relativists who eschew any notion of absolute or universal criteria of truth and rationality.

Hesse also argues that if the realists are correct, then the old issue of the distinction between the natural and the social sciences is moribund. If neither the natural nor the social sciences conform to the positivist ideal of knowledge then the argument for the distinction between them based on the failure of the social sciences to match this ideal is meaningless (1980:xxi). It follows that continuity, rather than dichotomy more aptly describes the relationship between the two branches of science. Finally, Hesse asserts that although the strong program advocated by the realists does not necessarily entail relativism, neither does it, as she puts it, exclude necessary truth (1980:45). Rather she argues that the relativity of conceptual frameworks can be contrasted with the real attainment of approximate truth (1980:xxv). It should be evident that this definition of relativism is a departure from the positivist-Enlightenment conception. But it should also be evident that for Hesse as well as for the theorists discussed above, relativism is not an acceptable position; it is still a 'problem' to be 'solved'.

From an anti-foundational perspective the realists' strong program in the sociology of knowledge has both advantages and disadvantages. Positively, they have shown the error of Mannheim's exclusion of science and mathematics from the sociology of knowledge and decisively extended the sociology of knowledge into these fields. They have also shown that the positivist distinction between natural and social sciences based on the distinction between pure and impure knowledge is untenable. Relying on recent discussions in the philosophy of science they show that the ideal of objective knowledge, that is, knowledge defined as free from interpretation and social conditioning, is a false ideal that neither the social nor the natural sciences can or should aspire to. It follows that because both branches of science involve interpretation, natural as well as social science must be classified as 'hermeneutic'. Both of these positions are consistent with the anti-foundational approach. Although Gadamer does not specifically criticize Mannheim, one of the principal arguments of *Truth and Method* is the attack on the ideal of 'pure' knowledge in the natural sciences and its exclusive identification with 'truth'. The assertion of the hermeneutic character of the natural sciences is also compatible with Gadamer's account. His thesis of the universality of hermeneutics necessarily entails that both the natural and the social sciences are hermeneutic. The realists' argument on this point both complements and completes Gadamer's position (Toulmin, 1982:93 ff.).

But despite these undeniable advantages the realist position in the social sciences has a number of serious liabilities.[12] First, and most importantly, although the realists redefine 'scientific method' they nevertheless reify that method. It is clear from the work of both Bloor and Barnes that they see the natural sciences as definitive of the realm of science and attempt to make the social sciences more 'scientific' in this sense. And although they acknowledge the hermeneutic character of the natural sciences what they advocate is not the extension of the hermeneutic thinking of the social sciences into the natural sciences, but, rather, the extension of the scientific method into the social sciences. They thus see their redefined conception of the scientific method as the basis for understanding in both the natural and the social sciences. In sum, instead of stressing, as does Gadamer, the hermeneutical character of all understanding, they stress instead the scientific character of all true knowledge.

Secondly, the realists in the social sciences, like their natural scientific counterparts, presuppose a 'real world' that limits and constrains their conceptions. This is the basis of what might be labelled the 'ontological absolutism' of Bhaskar. This position, and the related 'naturalism' of Bloor and Barnes is seriously confused. Bhaskar makes the point that society predates social actors; it is the 'real world' that must be presupposed. But this assertion of a 'real world' in both the natural and the social sciences reveals the realists' failure to transcend the Enlightenment conception of knowledge. Despite their redefinition of the scientific method, it is evident that the realists continue to seek a *foundation* for their conception of knowledge provided by the 'real world'. Their uneasiness with the concept of relativism is a further indication of this failure. As a result the 'ontological absolutism' proposed by Bhaskar is a far cry from Gadamer's ontological position. While the realists posit a 'real world' that grounds our knowledge of it, Gadamer rejects the notion of grounding altogether. His position is rooted in an existential ontology that reveals the error of the belief in a 'real world' independent of our conceptions.

Finally, the realist position lacks an awareness of what Gadamer defines as the 'fusing of horizons'. Although the realists' position in the sociology of knowledge acknowledges that all knowledge is socially conditioned and, thus, that even scientific knowledge must be examined in terms of this social conditioning, they nevertheless fail to see that this applies to the sociologist of knowledge as well as the object of investigation. They overlook the fact that the investigator's position as well as the position of the investigated is socially determined and that the interpretation that emerges is a product of the fusing of these two positions. Although they do not explicitly claim an Archimedean point for the observer, it is implicit in their approach. Like the historicists whom Gadamer attacks, they fail to extend their thesis of the social determination of knowledge to themselves.

VI CONCLUSION

The purpose of the foregoing has been to sketch the major schools of the sociology of knowledge in order to reveal the basic epistemological assumptions underlying those schools and, thus, the fundamental deficiency of the approaches. The analysis has established three major points. First, the sociology of knowledge, despite its focus on the social determination of thought, is rooted in the Enlightenment conception of the distinction between objective and subjective knowledge, the belief that the acquisition of objective knowledge is the goal of science, and the position that only scientific knowledge is 'true'. The field was thus central to the emerging social sciences because it enabled these disciplines to make the distinction between pure and impure knowledge that is the basis of the Enlightenment conception. Further, the sociology of knowledge has played a significant and necessary role in the development of those sciences throughout their history and up to the present time.

Secondly, practitioners of the sociology of knowledge have, throughout its history, turned increasingly to an analysis of subjective (socially determined) knowledge. The immediate sucessors of the Enlightenment assumed that the realm of objective knowledge would be progressively expanded and predicted that the subjective sphere would be proportionally reduced as the light of reason penetrated its errors. As the field developed, however, it became evident that this was not to be the case. Beginning with Marx and continuing with Mannheim, Scheler and the twentieth-century phenomenological school, sociologists of knowledge defined a progressively larger sphere for knowledge that is socially determined. Furthermore, as the field developed there was a marked tendency among its practitioners to avoid epistemological issues that would force them to confront the contradictions inherent in this division between objective and subjective knowledge. Some theorists even went so far as to exclude objective knowledge from the social sciences altogether. But, significantly, none questioned the distinction itself nor the existence of objective knowledge. Even the realists-naturalists, although they redefine objective knowledge, still make a clear distinction between scientific knowledge and social belief.

Thirdly, the branch of the sociology of knowledge that offers the most hope of transcending this Enlightenment conception and providing the field with a new foundation – the strong program in the sociology of knowledge – fails in a number of important ways. Although the realists reject the Enlightenment's distinction between objective and subjective knowledge they replace it with a conception that is equally problematic. Their 'ontological absolutism' and their unquestioning reification of scientific method prevent them from grasping the essential problem of the sociology of knowledge: the examination of the relationship between human thought and human existence. Thus even though they take important steps toward a new foundation for the sociology of knowledge, they fail to transcend the glorification of science and scientific method that is definitive of Enlightenment thought.

To argue that the sociology of knowledge as it has been generally interpreted and expressed by social scientists is an integral part of the tradition of social science that began with the Enlightenment, and that it is central to the variant of that tradition that is dominant today, positivist social science, is not, however, the end of the discussion. A radically redefined sociology of knowledge can and should serve as the basis for a post-Enlightenment and post-positivist social science. A sociology of knowledge conceived as the study of the relationship between human thought and human existence and purged of the Enlightenment distinction between objective and subjective knowledge can provide a new foundation for the social sciences that is not susceptible to the errors attendant on the association of truth with scientific method. An examination of the theorist who comes closest to providing such a basis, Karl Mannheim, facilitates a description of the parameters of such a sociology of knowledge. Mannheim's work, primarily because of its affinity to the anti-foundational thought of Gadamer, is suggestive of what a truly hermeneutical sociology of knowledge would entail. An examination of his approach thus indicates how a rejection of the Enlightenment conception of knowledge affects the sociology of knowledge, and, by extension, social science itself.

3

Mannheim's Hermeneutic Sociology of Knowledge

I INTRODUCTION

If there is any approach to the sociology of knowledge that is familiar to the contemporary Anglo-American intellectual community it is that of Karl Mannheim. This is most likely due to the fact that Mannheim spent the last half of his academic career in England and thus, unlike the other early proponents of the sociology of knowledge, his writings were immediately accessible to an English-speaking audience. But this availability is not the only reason for the popularity of Manhnhiem's work among contemporaries. It is also due to the fact that many of the issues he examines are relevant to current intellectual discussions. Mannheim's work, like that of Weber, is a product of the *Methodenstreit* and, as many scholars have noted, the issues in that debate are very similar to issues debated in contemporary discussions. Mannheim's theory, because it is sensitive to the intellectual currents of his day and makes a serious attempt to respond to the problems posed in these discussions, has caught the attention of contemporary writers because they are grappling with similar problems.

The contemporary relevance of Mannheim's position is the first reason for the close examination of his work that follows. Mannheim's sociology of knowledge has a striking affinity to the anti-foundational approach of Gadamer. Like Gadamer, Mannheim attacks the Enlightenment conception of truth and espouses an approach that, although he does not label it 'hermeneutic', is a theory of interpretation that has much in common with contemporary hermeneutics. Mannheim's approach is not, however, equivalent to Gadamer's on the philosophical level. It is much less philosophically sophisticated, partly because Mannheim eschews philosophical and epistemological issues. It also contains elements of naive historicism and a sympathy for positivism that are antithetical to anti-foundational thought. Nevertheless, Mannheim presents a theory that has important similarities to the basic program of Gadamer's hermeneutics. His explicit attack on the concept of truth utilized in the natural sciences and his espousal of a theory of interpretation that, like Gadamer's, acknowledges the inescapability of 'prejudices' on the part of both interpreter and interpreted provide a ground of commonality between the two approaches.

These links to Gadamer also provide a second reason for focusing on Mannheim. It was stated at the outset that the attempt to formulate an anti-foundational sociology of knowledge encounters a significant problem: the philosophers who argue for an anti-foundational position fail to provide even an indication of the kind of social scientific methodology that is consistent with their approach, but the sociologists of knowledge who might be expected to supply such a methodology cannot be relied on because they cling to some form of a foundation metaphor. Mannheim's work is significant because he lays the groundwork for solving this problem. Unlike the philosophers, he is very much interested in method and, unlike other sociologists of knowledge he comes very close to rejecting an appeal to foundations and grounding altogether. His approach thus offers an indication of the structure an anti-foundational sociology of knowledge would take.

The third reason why Mannheim's sociology of knowledge is useful in the present context is also methodological. The anti-foundational sociology of knowledge for which I am arguing must be able to establish a continuity between two kinds of investigation that have been separated in most twentieth-century thought: the philosopher's investigation of the underlying preunderstandings that constitute human social life (for example, Heidegger's *das Man* and Gadamer's 'prejudices') and the examination of explicit belief systems and their relationship to specific social groups. The sharp break between these two kinds of investigation that has characterized twentieth-century thought stands in the way of a proper understanding of the relationship between thought and existence. Mannheim's work, unlike that of both philosophers and most sociologists of knowledge, establishes that there is a continuum between these two kinds of investigation. He states explicitly that he sees his task as a sociologist of knowledge as picking up where the philosopher leaves off. More importantly, he defines the two kinds of investigation as connected, arguing that the philosopher's concern with what Heidegger calls '*das Man*' marks the beginning of the sociologist's task (1952:197–8). Mannheim's work can thus be used to establish the argument that a continuum exists between these two kinds of investigation and that the sociology of knowledge, correctly understood, encompasses them both.

II MANNHEIM'S SOCIOLOGY OF KNOWLEDGE: THE BASIC STRUCTURE

Mannheim was concerned with the sociology of knowledge and related epistemological and methodological issues in the early part of his academic career. After emigrating from Germany in 1933 Mannheim turned his attention to other issues (his last reference to the sociology of knowledge occurs in 1931), particularly social planning. But in his early work, roughly from 1921 to 1931, he examines the various facets of the sociology of knowledge in a comprehensive fashion. Mannheim formulates his approach to his subject matter in terms of his objections to a number of philosophical and sociological positions prominent in his time. An examination of these objections is thus the best place to start in an analysis of these writings. The intellectual world that Mannheim addressed at this time was, in his view, dominated by four schools: positivism, formal apriorism, phenomenology and historicism (1952:150 ff.). Mannheim has serious objections to each of these schools even though he identifies his position as a form of historicism.

In an early article based on his doctoral dissertation, 'Structural Analysis of Epistemology' (1953:15–73), Mannheim attacks the problem of how meanings are constituted from a neo-Kantian position and, under the influence of Lukacs's *History and Class Consciousness* and Heidegger's *Being and Time* moves toward his mature position in *Ideology and Utopia* (Congdon, 1977:13). But despite his rejection of neo-Kantianism in later writings, a residue of it remains in his works published between 1923 and

1925. In these works Mannheim makes it quite clear that he sees all meaning to be historically determined. But he is still uncomfortable with the concept of relativism and attempts to find an alternative to the 'historicist relative theory of truth' (1953:39). Mannheim approaches his problem by advancing, first, a critique of the four schools mentioned above and, secondly, an outline of his conception of the sociology of knowledge. What is important about his presentation in these articles is that they reveal a serious rethinking of the relationship between reason and relativism that constitutes a departure from the position taken in his dissertation, And, significantly, Mannheim articulates his position by launching a comprehensive attack on the Enlightenment conception of reason in a manner that presages Gadamer's work.

Mannheim's attack on the Enlightenment revolves around revealing its basic presuppositions and showing them to be historically specific. He points out that the Enlightenment conception of reason and, derivatively, that of relativism, is flawed because 'the ideal of an eternally identical reason is nothing other than the leading principle of an epistemological system constructed *post factum*' (1952:92). He states:

> Finally, what if it can be shown that the accusation of relativism derives from a philosophy which professes an inadequate conception of 'absolute' and relative; a philosophy which confronts 'truth' and 'falsehood' in a way which makes sense in the sphere of so-called exact science, but not in history, since in the latter there are aspects of the same subject-matter which can be regarded, not as true or false, but as essentially dependent on a given perspective or standpoint which can co-exist with others? (1952:93)

Mannheim's answer to this question is that this *can* be shown and, further, that his analysis has shown it. It follows that the charge of relativism leveled by the followers of the Enlightenment need not be taken seriously. Rather, the charge can be turned back on the accusers:

> There is no more relativistic solution than that of a static philosophy of Reason which acknowledges a transcendence of values 'in themselves', and sees this transcendence guaranteed in the *form* of every concrete judgment, but regulates the material content of the judgment into the sphere of utter relativity –

> refusing to recognize in the actual historical cosmos of the realizations of value any principle of approximation of the transcendent values as such. (1952:128)

Mannheim argues that the error of the Enlightenment approach stems from the tendency of its followers to look for one correct solution to a problem and then to identify their own position, a position peculiar to their own time, as that solution (1952:30). In this early series of articles Mannheim lays the groundwork for this position but does not state it explicitly. By the time he published *Ideology and Utopia* in 1929, however, Mannheim's position on this issue is considerably clearer. In this work he confidently rejects the whole problem of relativism as the product of an 'older' system of thought that denies the legitimacy of 'subjective' knowledge (1936:79). This is a significant step. It means, first, that Mannheim repudiates the Enlightenment's appeal to 'timeless Reason', an appeal that characterizes his own earlier work and, secondly, that he is holding up what he calls 'subjective knowledge' as a legitimate form of knowledge, refusing to exclude it because the Enlightenment identifies it as relativistic.

But although this is an important step, Mannheim's position leaves some important problems unanswered: Is 'subjective knowledge' equivalent to the 'objective knowledge' touted by the Enlightenment? Is it inferior, or, as Gadamer suggests, in reality the grounding for what the Enlightenment labelled 'objective knowledge'? Mannheim offers a number of contradictory answers to these questions in the course of his work. At this point he argues that in the objective knowledge that characterizes investigations in the natural sciences meanings do not change over time as they do in the subjective knowledge of the cultural sciences. It follows that in the natural sciences we can identify progress toward a 'correct' knowledge (1952:170). This position implies, as so many critics have argued, a position of inferiority for the cultural sciences. It also clashes with Mannheim's rejection of relativism as a pseudo-problem and his attack on the 'timeless Reason' of the Enlightenment. The only possible explanation for these ambiguities is that although the logic of Mannheim's account leads him to a rejection of the concept of objective knowledge in all spheres, he is not willing to take this radical step.

Mannheim's critique of the Enlightenment forms the basis for his approach to the four contemporary schools of thought that have developed what he sees to be flawed approaches to the sociology of knowledge. Three of these schools – positivism, formal apriorism and phenomenology – Mannheim identifies as falling prey to the Enlightenment conception of 'timeless Reason'. He dismisses positivism as a 'deluded school' that hypostasizes a particular conception of empiricism and asserts that human knowledge can be complete without metaphysics and ontology. Formal apriorism, likewise, is rejected because it rests on an unwavering (and unfounded) faith in 'Reason' (1952:150–3). Establishing that this is true of phenomenology as well, however, is more involved. Mannheim claims that phenomenology (and here he is thinking primarily of the work of Scheler), like the other two schools, appeals to a realm of 'supra-temporally valid truths'. Although the phenomenologist claims access to this realm through 'essential intuition', Mannheim sees an affinity between this claim and the positivists' appeal to objective knowledge (1952:154–5). Both deny that knowledge is always acquired from a particular perspective. Both also claim that we stand in a 'supra-temporal vacuum of disembodied truth' (1952:148).

It is important to note, however, that Mannheim does not totally reject the perspectives of either positivism or phenomenology. At various points in his work he utilizes the insights of both approaches and, interestingly, has been labelled by some critics as a phenomenologist, by others as a positivist. But although he sees merit in both approaches he makes it clear that his basic objection to each of them stems from their adherence to the Enlightenment conception of 'timeless Reason'. It is in the context of his analysis of historicism, however, that he offers his most complete critique of Enlightenment thought.

Although it is evident that Mannheim identifies his position most closely with that of historicism, the position that he advocates is one that is distinctly different from what is commonly taken to be the historicist view. Mannheim begins his critique by asserting that the conflict between historicism and the Enlightenment revolves around the question of whether reason is static or historically dynamic. He traces the concept of static Reason to Kant for whom the knowing subject is completely free of all historically determined conditions (1952:101). This statement and other comments throughout his article on historicism lead to the conclusion that Mannheim is attacking the validity of the concept of objective knowledge *per se*. At another point he states that the 'ultimate task' of the sociology of knowledge is to

> reinterpret the phenomenon of static thought – as exemplified by natural science and by other manifestations in the civilizational sphere in general – from a dynamic point of view, and to ascertain specifically to what extent logic belongs to this sphere. (1952:132)

He also asks:

> Is it not more advisable first to see whether our conception of science is not false, or at least one-sided, because it is exclusively based on the natural sciences, before we reject a factually existing vital area of research, merely because it does not correspond to our conception of science? (1952:126)

In these passages Mannheim seems to be asserting that all knowledge is dynamic, that is, historically conditioned, even the so-called objective knowledge of the natural sciences. Yet other passages suggest that he sees knowledge in the historical sphere as dynamic while that of the natural sciences, logic and mathematics is defined as absolute and unchanging. He asserts that the perspective character of historical knowledge must be recognized as essential to the structure of 'these types of knowledge' (1952: 120). Once again it seems plausible to conclude that Mannheim is reluctant to accept the radical implications of his argument, that is, that all knowledge is 'dynamic' in his sense. In *Ideology and Utopia* he returns to this issue in the context of his discussion of relational knowledge. In this context, however, he turns to another issue: validity. He tries to establish that dynamic, historical knowledge, even though it does not conform to the Enlightenment conception of knowledge, is nevertheless valid. This comes down to the question of how, in the sphere of historical knowledge, we can judge one interpretation correct, another false. He offers two possible criteria of validity: interpretations must be correct, that is, satisfying available criteria and offering internal consistency; and they must be adequate, that is, penetrating their objects to their total depths (1952:122).

In his discussion of criteria of validity Mannheim's logic takes a curious turn because he is trying to do a number of potentially contradictory things simultaneously. First, he is attempting to establish 'objective validity' in a sphere in which he has denied the relevance of objective knowledge. Secondly, although he rejects the appeal to absolute values found in Scheler's sociology of knowledge, he nevertheless defines Scheler's position as a challenge and relativism as a 'problem' that must be 'overcome'. The solution he offers in this context is an appeal to 'material evidence' rather than absolute values:

> Guarantees of objective truth which really can overcome relativism can only flow from material evidence, and we cannot have the experience that our actual, historic, cognitive acts do point to something real, or that our action does have positive goodness, unless we somehow have the certainty that the standards we apply in judging cognitive truth or moral goodness have a bearing upon concrete reality as given *hic et nunc*. (1952:128)

His answer to Scheler, then, is that historicism is the only solution to the problem of finding '*material* and concretely exemplified standards and norms for a world outlook that has become dynamic' (1952:132).

It was not until he published *Ideology and Utopia*, however, that Mannheim finally clarified his position on these issues. In this context Mannheim redefines his 'dynamic historicist' standpoint into a defense of his well-known concept of 'relational' knowledge. He begins with the point that relational thought assumes that there are spheres of thought in which it is impossible to conceive of absolute truth existing independently of the subject's values and the social context. It follows that 'what is intelligible in history can be formulated only with reference to problems and conceptual constructions which themselves arise in the flux of historical experience' (1936:79). Furthermore, we should not consider it a source of error that all thought is rooted in historical contexts (1936:80). The knowledge that arises out of our 'life situations' is knowledge nonetheless (1936: 86). Relationism does not entail that there are no criteria of rightness and wrongness, but that it is in the nature of certain assertions that they cannot be formulated absolutely, but only in relationship to a particular situation (1936:283). And, further:

> Even a god could not formulate a proposition on historical subjects like 2 × 2 = 4, for what is intelligible in history can be formulated only with reference to problems and conceptual constructions which themselves arise in the flux of historical experience. (1936:79)

What Mannheim is claiming in these statements is that investigations in the historical realm are legitimate even though they do not conform to the standards of 'timeless Reason'. He states this unambiguously when he asserts that our task must be to re-ask Kant's question, 'how is knowledge possible?' for the qualitative as well as quantitative realm (1936:291). One of the best examples of what Mannheim means by this can be found in his discussion of why there is no 'science' of politics (1936:109–91). In this discussion he defends an essentially Weberian view of politics, arguing that it *is* a science, but that the criteria of judgement applicable in this sphere are not that of the 'too-narrow' scientific conception modelled on math and geometry (1936: 165). In social and political knowledge the perspective of the observer, and, thus, an irradicable value element, cannot be removed. In other words, he proposes a science of politics that incorporates the inevitability of ideology (Cox, 1979:212). In the end he claims that this sphere of knowledge operates according to a different logic than that of the natural sciences (1936:117).

The problem with Mannheim's position, however, is that he still vacillates on whether all thought, or just historical knowledge, is relational. Several passages point to the more comprehensive view. He argues that 'All knowledge is oriented toward some object and is influenced in its approach by the nature of the object with which it is preoccupied' (1936:86). Further, he states:

> Just as the fact that every measurement in space hinges upon the nature of light does not mean that our measurements are arbitrary, but merely that they are only valid in relation to the nature of light, so in the same way not relativism in the sense of arbitrariness but *relationism* applies to our discussions. (1936:283)

These passages contradict the assertions made in the sections quoted previously that his analysis of relational knowledge only applies to the sphere of historical knowledge. Yet Mannheim makes no effort to deal with this contradiction.

That Mannheim still avoids the radical implications of his advocacy of relational knowledge is evident in the contradictions between these sets of passages. It is also evident in his discussion of the issue of relativism in *Ideology and Utopia*. Mannheim offers a new argument for how the sociology of knowledge can avoid the relativism that he still sees as a 'problem'. In discussing the current intellectual position he states:

> It is imperative in the present transitional period to make use of the intellectual twilight which dominates our epoch and in which all values and points of view appear in their genuine relativity. We must realize once and for all that the meanings which make up our world are simply an historically determined and continuously developing structure in which man develops, and are in no sense absolute. (1936:85)

Mannheim argues in this and other contexts that the particular historical period in which we live offers us a unique opportunity. Not only can we see all meanings in their 'genuine relativity' but also, because of this perspective, we can effect a synthesis among these different meanings. The possibility of such a synthesis is very important to him because it means that we can transcend the relativity of these diverse viewpoints. In his words, we have a much more comprehensive grasp of history because we can utilize the 'new and ever more comprehensive central ideas' that are available in our era (1952:177).

Mannheim's position on this issue has earned him the criticism of a number of commentators. Dixon argues that, like Marx, Mannheim is guilty of 'dual residualism', the position that the superiority of the investigator's position derives from his particular social location and his position in the historical process (1980:34). Remmling claims that for Mannheim historicism is the approach that will permit modern men to penetrate the innermost structure of the world (1971:539). Both imply that, for Mannheim, if something is to be called 'knowledge' it must have a grounding beyond historical relativity, even if that is only an appeal to our position in the evolution of thought in history and the particular advantage this affords us.

These criticisms are correct in the assertion that in his advocacy of a synthesis Mannheim is looking for a way to transcend relativism, but they nevertheless obscure an important point. In this theory Mannheim is taking a position that most historicists denied: that the investigator's position is just as historically determined as the investigated. Rather than claiming an Archimedean point of objectivity for his analysis, a claim implicit in most historicists' writings, Mannheim claims that his view, and even the comprehensive synthesis that is possible because of this historical position, is determined by particular historical circumstances. His position on the possibilities afforded by our particular historical era, which might be labelled an 'evolutionary' perspective, is particularly evident in his explanation of the development of the sociology of knowledge as a discipline and, hence, its tasks. It is quite clear in this discussion that Mannheim is, in effect, turning his method in on himself, something most historicists failed to do. He is asking how he and other sociologists of knowledge came to embark on the kind of investigations characteristic of their discipline. His answer is that a number of historical trends laid the groundwork for this kind of investigation. The breakdown of what he calls the 'unitary world view' is the first development that leads to the sociology of knowledge. The decisive fact of the modern world is the shattering of the monopoly of ecclesiastical interpretation of the world (1936:11). More specifically, he argues that four factors were instrumental: first, the self-relativization of thought and knowledge; secondly, the rise of the 'unmasking' form of mind; thirdly, the appearance of a system of reference, the social sphere, in which thought could be conceived as relative; and, fourthly, the aspiration to make this relativization total (1952:134–44).

The foregoing analysis of Mannheim's positions on relationism, relativism and the Enlightenment's 'timeless Reason' is a necessary preliminary to an examination of his specific discussion of the discipline of the sociology of knowledge. This discussion is closely connected to Mannheim's understanding of the structure of the discipline and the tasks it must undertake. For example, Mannheim's understanding of the reflexivity of knowledge leads him to assert that it is one of the primary tasks of the sociology of knowledge to examine the conditions of its own emergence, that is, why the 'unmasking form of thought' arose in this particular era. Mannheim identifies the sociology of knowledge as a branch of sociology and divides it into two parts. As a theory, its task is the analysis of the relationship between knowledge and existence and as a method of research its aim is to trace the forms which this relationship has taken in the intellectual development of mankind (1936:264). Within these two divisions Mannheim defines several tasks the sociology of knowledge should embrace:

(1) defining criteria for the discovery of the relationship between thought and action;
(2) developing a theory of the significance of non-theoretical conditioning factors in knowledge (1936:264);
(3) specifying the various intellectual standpoints on which thought is based which are possible in various periods;
(4) uncovering hidden metaphysical premisses;
(5) finding the social strata making up the intellectual strata in question (1952:189).

Mannheim takes pains to distinguish his position on the sociology of knowledge from that of Marx. His assertion that we must examine the 'existentially conditioned genesis' (1952:180) of various standpoints is contrasted to the 'crude materialism' of Marx's task (1952:188). The sociology of knowledge, on Mannheim's account, explores the 'functional dependence of each intellectual standpoint on the differentiated social group reality standing behind it' (1952:190). We cannot, he claims, identify each intellectual standpoint with a particular class as Marx seeks to do. The sociological category of class is a 'narrow framework' that bypasses individual perceptions and reactions (1956:103–9). What we should seek is the rootedness of thought in what he calls the underlying historico-social reality (1952:182). Mannheim sees Marx's view, the motivation by interest, as a partial case of a broader phenomenon: existential determination.

Throughout his discussion of the tasks of the sociology of knowledge Mannheim consciously avoids an issue that is nevertheless central to his concerns: epistemology. The reasons for his position on epistemological issues are complex. First, in his early, neo-Kantian stage Mannheim was centrally concerned with the issue of epistemology. His rejection of this issue in his later work thus represents his rejection of the neo-Kantian position itself. Secondly, Mannheim claims that the sociology of knowledge he is seeking requires an ontology, not an epistemology. The sociology of knowledge's 'relationizing enables philosophical ontology to revise particulars previously posing as absolutes' (1971:270). This struggle for an ontology causes him to turn to Heidegger whose philosophy is concerned with the question of ontology (Congdon, 1977:14). Thirdly, Mannheim makes it clear that he is attacking the traditional epistemology of the Enlightenment, but, as he admits in his later writings, he is not offering a clear alternative to that epistemology. He realizes, like Gadamer, that the Enlightenment epistemology must be rejected, but, unlike Gadamer, does not offer a clear alternative to the epistemology. As a consequence of this complex attitude his position on epistemology results in some seemingly contradictory statements. He asserts both that the sociology of knowledge will not supplant epistemological investigation and that it will not be irrelevent to such investigations (1936:287). Further, he claims on one hand that the sociologist of knowledge need not be concerned with 'ultimate truth' (1936:84) and on the other that epistemology is an integral part of the theory of the sociology of knowledge (1936:267).

Mannheim's rejection of Enlightenment epistemology and the ambitious goals with which it is identified informs his definition of what the sociology of knowledge can hope to accomplish. The most we can anticipate, he asserts, is that the sociology of knowledge can overcome the 'talking past one another' of various groups by revealing the sources of partial disagreement among them (1936:281). The task of the sociologist of knowledge, one that was impossible until the present time, is, first, to examine the social bases of knowledge and, secondly, to juxtapose the many different viewpoints prevalent in the present day. The result is a 'new type of objectivity' attainable through the 'critical awareness and control' of evaluations (1936:5). This juxtaposition of different viewpoints allows for the assimilation and transcendence of particular points of view (1936:106). What this amounts to is a very Weberian viewpoint. Mannheim asserts that by assimilating particular views a comprehensive whole emerges that is built on the particularity of the viewpoints, not the 'objectivity' of any one of them.[1]

A central element in Mannheim's hopes for achieving the tasks of the sociology of knowledge is the 'free-floating intelligentsia' for which he is so well known. His understanding of the possibilities open to this group is closely tied to his thesis of the historical development that has made the sociology of knowledge possible. The historical evolution that created the 'unmasking form of mind' also creates a class that is relatively unattached to the economic process (1936:155). This class embodies the 'detached' perspective that Mannheim claims is demanded by the sociology of knowledge (1936:182). Although he asserts that class and status do not become completely irrelevent for this group the fact that modern intellectuals, unlike their priestly counterparts, are not recruited from a single class with definable interests places them in a unique position (1936:156).

This unique position provides the intellectual with the opportunity to formulate what Mannheim sees to be the goal not only of the sociology of knowledge but of sociology itself: a synthesis of the varying viewpoints represented in the modern world (1936:151). Mannheim's logic in arriving at this conclusion, however, is somewhat curious. On one hand he argues that such a synthesis is the goal that the sociologist should strive for above all else. But, on the other hand, he argues that a group whose class position is not definitely fixed, that is, the intellectuals, has a 'wider area of choice and a corresponding need for total orientation and synthesis' (1936:161). Thus the sociologist of knowledge who is part of this free-floating intelligentsia is both consciously striving for this synthesis and existentially conditioned to look for it. The two factors can be said to merge, however, when intellectuals become aware of their social position and the mission implicit in it (1936:160).

Mannheim has been widely criticized for his position on the free-floating intelligentsia. It is therefore important to be clear about what he is and is not asserting about this group. First, he is arguing that their position offers them the *possibility* of a detached perspective and the formation of a synthesis. It does not guarantee that such a synthesis will be forthcoming nor that it will be valid.[2] Furthermore, he specifically states that it will not be 'objective' in the Enlightenment's sense of this word. Secondly, Mannheim is not claiming that the synthesis for which the intellectual strives is a total or absolute one. On the contrary, he explicitly rejects the possibility of a 'total' view and again takes the Weberian position that reality can best be grasped by studying it from as many different angles as possible (1936:151).

The various aspects of Mannheim's position on the sociology of knowledge culminate in his discussion of the concept for which he is most famous–ideology. One would think, given the title of his famous work, that the concept of 'utopia' would be equally central to his theory. But such is not the case; his discussion of the latter concept is relatively unimportant. He distinguishes the two concepts by arguing that ideologies are situationally transcendent concepts that never succeed in the realization of their goals, but, nevertheless, project realizable aims. Utopias, on the other hand, although they also fail to transform reality according to their goals, present aims that cannot be realized in existing social situations (1936:194–6). As a result utopias, unlike ideologies, have a shattering effect on the social order precisely because they do not conform to it (1936:192). Ideologies, because they are so rooted in the status quo, fail to perform this function. What is important about these definitions is that Mannheim specifies that both concepts contain 'the imperative test with reality' (1936:98). But by 'reality' he does not mean the foundational concept the Enlightenment employed. Rather, he defines reality as 'a concrete historically and socially determined reality which is in a constant process of change' (1936:198).

This concept of reality is crucial to an understanding of Mannheim's important distinction between the two different conceptions of ideology, the particular and total conceptions. It is also central to an understanding of the significance of his departure from the accepted definition of ideology. His distinction between the particular and total conceptions of ideology is Mannheim's most important innovation and lays the groundwork for the redefinition of the sociology of knowledge along anti-foundational lines. Unlike previous investigations of ideology that seek, in one way or another, to unmask conscious or unconscious deceptions, Mannheim presents a sociology of knowledge that examines the relationship between knowledge and social existence. He assumes that the reality to which ideology is compared is a socially and historically conditioned reality and, further, that 'ideology' as he defines it is a general aspect of the human condition.[3]

Mannheim's best description of the distinction between the particular and total conceptions of ideology can be found in the first pages of *Ideology and Utopia*. He defines the particular conception as referring to the conscious disguise of the real nature of a situation. The particular conception always designates only part of an assertion as ideological. Further, it operates on the psychological level and is concerned primarily with the psychology of interests. The total conception, on the other hand, refers to the 'ideology of an age'. It refers to all, not just some assertions and operates on the 'noological' level. Finally, the total conception always refers not to individuals but to groups (1936:55–9).

Mannheim identifies the rise of the total conception of ideology with the same social and historical developments that produced the sociology of knowledge itself. Although Mannheim, like most other commentators on ideology, traces the concept back to Bacon, he sees the rise of the total conception as a distinctly different stage in the development of the concept. What made possible the development of the total conception was the rise of the historical school and their definition of ideology in historical terms. Also important was the emergence of class analysis which moved away from the concept of consciousness as such. The theory of ideology develops into the sociology of knowledge, Mannheim argues, with the realization that both the positions of the observer and that of the observed must be subjected to ideological analysis (1936:65–78).

Mannheim labels the conception of ideology that arose out of this development the 'non-evaluative' conception. Exactly what he means by this, however, is not always clear. First he states that the non-evaluative conception 'unwittingly leads to an evaluative one' (1936:88), then, later, that the evaluative conception takes on a non-evaluative form in order to lead to an evaluative solution (1936:99–100). What this confusion comes to is, first, that Mannheim is denying the positivist position that concepts, to be objective, must be non-evaluative, non-metaphysical and non-ontological. He argues instead that although we are still prey to 'positivistic prejudices' that demand freedom from metaphysics and ontology, all concepts must necessarily have these presuppositions. Secondly, he is asserting that the analysis of total ideology is non-evaluative in the sense that it is not looking to unmask 'deceptions' but, rather, to describe an unavoidable aspect of human social existence common to all historical periods. Finally, he argues that the analysis of total ideology inevitably leads to evaluative procedures and ontological judgements although the values of an era can never be regarded as absolute (1936:94). He summarizes this with the injunction that 'Thought should contain neither less nor more than the reality in whose medium it operates' (1936:98).

Mannheim's conception of ideology forms the basis of his distinctive approach to the sociology of knowledge and his definition of this conception reveals all the ambiguities and confusions as well as the strengths of that approach. On one hand the conception reveals that Mannheim has not entirely freed himself from Enlightenment epistemology. He still appeals to an 'objective' point of view even if he insists it is a kind of objectivity peculiar to to historical studies. Further, his insistence on the possibility of a synthesis that transcends the relativity of particular viewpoints is evidence of his failure to break completely with that epistemology. But, on the other hand, his conception takes giant steps in the direction of an anti-foundational sociology of knowledge in two important respects and thus represents a radical break in the history of the discipline. First, Mannheim asserts that the total conception of ideology is self-reflexive, that is, that observers see their own perspective as an ideology as well as the perspective of those they observe. This view represents an important break with historicism. The historicist assumes that the interpreter occupies an Archimedean point of objectivity while at the same time claiming that that which is interpreted is historically determined. Mannheim's position in effect extends the historicist's maxim that all meaning is historical to both elements of the interpretive situation. Secondly, for Mannheim the sociology of knowledge is not the study of 'more or less conscious deceptions and disguises of human interest groups' but, rather, is concerned 'with the varying ways in which objects present themselves to the subject according to the differences in social settings' (1936:265). In other words, he assumes that objects will always be apprehended from the perspective of a particular social setting, that is, that 'ideology' is part of the human condition. He also assumes that the 'reality' to which we compare ideological thought is itself socially constructed. The result is that, through his total conception of ideology, Mannheim definitively rejects Bacon's definition of ideology as 'idols of the mind' and replaces it with a conception that rejects an absolute grounding in reality *per se*.

III MANNHEIM'S CONCEPTION OF KNOWLEDGE

Implicit in Mannheim's examination of the sociology of knowledge is his understanding of the status of knowledge in both the natural and the social sciences. Since this issue will be the focus of the analysis in subsequent chapters, it is important that his definition of knowledge be carefully examined. At various points in his work, and particularly in his early phenomenological stage, Mannheim attempted to grapple with the broad questions of meaning, understanding and knowledge. These discussions are far from definitive, but they do reveal that Mannheim does not merely follow the strict historicist line on these issues. Rather, he espouses what amounts to a hermeneutical theory of understanding that has a great deal of affinity with Gadamer's critique of historicism.

The basis of Mannheim's exploration of meaning and understanding is his stated goal of finding a methodology for the cultural sciences. The first step in the achievement of his goal, Mannheim insists, is to 'emancipate oneself from the methodological principles of natural science' because its thought patterns are not even 'faintly analogous' (1952:37). In his discussion of how to study *Weltanschauungen*, Mannheim presents a distinction among three different types of meaning that form the basis for his discussion: objective, expressive and documentary meaning. In this early work Mannheim approaches the issue in explicitly phenomenological terms, organizing his discussion around the question of how different cultural objects, among them *Weltanschauungen*, are 'given' to us.

Mannheim's discussion of the three types of meaning appears to be an odd combination of phenomenological, Hegelian and what he labels 'positivistic' elements. Objective meaning, first, is based on the 'objective social configuration' and makes no reference to the subject's intentional act. Expressive meaning, on the other hand, refers to the subject's stream of psychic experience and thus cannot be divorced from the subject. Documentary meaning, however, goes beyond the subject's conscious activity. In Mannheim's words, it is 'profoundly influenced by the location within the historical stream from which the interpreter attempts to reconstruct the spirit of a past epoch' (1952:61).

But Mannheim goes on to make a further distinction among these three concepts. Objective and expressive meaning, he asserts, are 'fixed' in a way that documentary meaning is not. Although he claims that 'historical preparation' is necessary to understand objective and expressive meaning, once this has been accomplished they can be declared unambiguously true or false. Documentary meaning, on the other hand is 'dynamic', that is, it is subject to change over time. Different ages will interpret past epochs differently because, Mannheim claims,

> To understand the 'spirit' of an age, we have to fall back on the 'spirit' of our own – it is only substance which comprehends substance. (1952:61)

This is due to the fact that historical understanding, unlike understanding in the natural sciences and mathematics, is not timeless, but is shaped by the 'historical process of self-reflection' (1952:62).

It is documentary meaning, Mannheim makes clear, that is the subject of his analysis. The central question that he poses with regard to documentary meaning is whether the method of analysis employed in its study can be given the status of a 'science' that rivals the method of the natural sciences. Mannheim's answer to this question is a firm 'yes'. The study of documentary meaning can be declared 'scientific' because documentary interpretation can and must be subjected to standards of validity; every interpretation does not have the same claim to be accepted. If different interpretations are proferred we must ask which one of these interpretations is adequate, that is, has the 'greatest richness' and the 'greatest substantive affinity' with the object (1952:62). Documentary interpretations that meet these criteria can be treated as 'given'. It follows that:

> Once it is shown that in every cultural product a documentary meaning reflecting a global outlook is given, we have the basic guarantee that *Weltanschauungen* and documentary meaning are capable of scientific investigation. (1952:70)

At this point in his argument, Mannheim introduces what can only be labelled his 'phenomenological positivism'. Insisting that, for positivist method, scientific investigation is only possible for what is given beforehand, he argues that for a 'correctly understood' positivism, that is, one that accepts the phenomenological principle that each sphere of reality has its own givenness, positivist methods, with which he claims to agree, can be used to analyze documentary meaning and, hence, *Weltanschauungen*. What he is arguing is that in both the natural scientific and the social sphere objects can be said to be 'given' to investigators and this commonality allows both to be subjected to scientific analysis. But he also argues that the nature of the 'givenness' in each sphere is distinct. In the cultural sphere objects are given to us differently, in the natural sciences they are apprehended uniformly. Further, in the cultural sciences when the observer takes a new attitude toward the observed it does not involve a mere theoretical shift as it does in the natural sciences, but, rather, it involves a change in the attitude of the 'total phenomenological subject toward its object' (1971:118). This discussion culminates in Mannheim's attempt to catalogue all the possible spheres of 'givenness' and their appropriate methods of interpretation, extending from the most subjectively oriented to the most abstract positivistic methods (1971:126–30).

Mannheim's discussion in this context is seriously confused and, furthermore, appears to contradict directly the effort to portray his position as hermeneutical. But, despite the obvious problems of this account, Mannheim's theory of documentary meaning has its merits as well as its demerits. The principal error of Mannheim's account stems from his use of the labels 'positivist' and 'phenomenological' when his theory is, in actuality, neither. What Mannheim calls 'positivist' method, the scientific analysis of different spheres of reality that are 'given', is nothing any positivist would recognize. Not only do positivists *not* recognize different spheres of reality as equally valid, but they also reject the phenomenological notion of 'givenness'. What Mannheim is presenting is not positivism, but, in actuality, a hermeneutical method for the analysis of *Weltanschauungen*. This is clear from his assertion that:

> We derive the 'spirit of the epoch' from its individual documentary manifestations – and we interpret the individual documentary manifestations on the basis of what we know about the spirit of the epoch. (1952:74)

What he is asserting here is that historical phenomena are to be analyzed using a method that interprets these phenomena in terms of the understandings and presuppositions of the age in which they are manifest, in other words, a hermeneutic method. He argues that this method is appropriate to analyses in the historical sphere while the logic of the positivist method utilized in the natural sciences is not. His claim that a 'correctly understood positivism' would condone the use of a different method for a different sphere of reality, is however, very dubious.

Mannheim's claim that his approach can be labelled phenomenology is also tenuous. His discussion includes talk about 'givenness' and 'intentionality', concepts that are central to the phenomenological enterprise. But his use of these concepts is highly idiosyncratic. First, he fails to answer the question of how something (in this case, documentary meaning) can be 'given' in many different ways. He argues that criteria – adequacy and substantive affinity – separate correct from incorrect interpretations. But this usage hardly accords with Husserl's concept of 'givenness'. For the phenomenologist, that something is given means that it is unquestioned, not that it is subject to tests of validity. Secondly, Mannheim's use of 'intentionality' can also be questioned on the grounds that it departs from normal phenomenological usage. It is an open question whether, even in his discussion of expressive meaning, Mannheim means to refer to 'inner psychic life'.[4] Further, in his discussion of documentary meaning Mannheim incorporates intentionality into a broader framework of meaning and it is this framework, one that does not refer to subjective meaning, that is the focus of his analysis.[5]

Once these misapplied labels are discarded several elements of Mannheim's theory of meaning emerge as significant contributions. First, his approach is based on a clear rejection of the use of the methods of the natural sciences in the social sciences and an explicit avowal of hermeneutic method. Secondly, Mannheim stresses the self-reflective character of hermeneutic knowledge. He states unambiguously that the 'spirit' of a work is something that can be grasped only if subjects utilize their own 'historic substance'. As a result, the history of documentary interpretation of past ages is, in essence, a history of the interpreting subjects themselves (1952:63). This is crucial because it means that Mannheim does not commit the error of assuming an Archimedean point of objectivity, an error common to historicists as well as positivists and phenomenologists.[6] Furthermore, this self-reflective character of Mannheim's hermeneutic approach has striking similarities to Gadamer's conception of effective historical consciousness.

A third advantage of Mannheim's position is his attitude toward causal interpretation. Obviously, causality (and determinism) is an issue of some importance for the sociology of knowledge. Many sociologists of knowledge have run into serious difficulties over the whole set of problems associated with attempting to establish a direct causal relationship between social existence and patterns of thought. Mannheim's approach to causality, however, neatly avoids these problems. He defines the relationship between social existence and human thought in hermeneutical terms, and thus for him it is a problem of meaning and understanding, not one of causal imputation. This is not due to the fact that he rejects the validity of causal analysis, but, rather, because he sees it as occupying a sphere separate from meaning analysis. He argues that there is no rivalry between causal and interpretive explanation because they describe different things, and thus there can be no causal, genetic explanation of meanings (1952:81).

In summary, although it is not accurate to argue that Mannheim's theory of interpretation is without flaws, his position has much to recommend it despite its confusions. The key to Mannheim's theory is his clear distinction between the scientific sphere exemplified by the natural sciences and the cultural sphere. He not only claims legitimacy and validity for the cultural sphere, but also argues that the natural scientific conception of reason is in itself erroneous. Furthermore, like Gadamer, Mannheim sees the social rootedness of thought as a positive possibility of knowledge rather than a liability. The fact that knowledge in the social and cultural sciences is 'existentially determined' is not the end, but the beginning of inquiry for Mannheim. Finally, Mannheim, once more anticipating Gadamer, implies that the kind of knowledge offered by the natural sciences is a special case of knowledge, not the absolute model for all knowledge.[7]

These conclusions throw new light on the controversy that has arisen over Mannheim's rejection of relativism and his advocacy of 'relational' knowledge. Many commentators reject this distinction as a sleight of hand on Mannheim's part designed to dispel the threat of relativism while, in essence, embracing it (Shils, 1974:83). The preceding analysis reveals, however, that Mannheim's distinction between relativism and relationism is a significant aspect of his approach. Mannheim rejects relativism because it derives from a conception of knowledge, that of static reason, that he finds to be in error. His advocacy of relationism is not merely relativism in another guise, but, derives from a set of radically different epistemological assumptions. At the very least Mannheim insists that knowledge in the cultural sciences is always from a particular perspective, thus denying the universality of the Enlightenment model of knowledge. He states:

> A positivist, a follower of the historical school, a Hegelian, a Marxist will in each case base their accounts on different principles of selection and different patterns of synthesis, or categories, depending on their varying historico-philosophical positions. (1952:102)

But, as was noted above, Mannheim at times extends his concept of relational knowledge to all spheres of knowledge. In a discussion of Heisenberg's uncertainty principle he asserts:

> Because, as long as we see only relational determinabilities in the whole realm of empirical knowledge, the formulation of an 'as such' sphere has no consequences whatsoever for the process of knowing. (1936:306)

Mannheim seems to be implying here that empirical knowledge in both the natural and social sciences is relational in his sense. He sometimes refers to this as 'perspective knowledge' and stresses that this knowledge contains an 'activist' element;[8] in another context he uses the term 'conjunctive knowledge' (1982:191 ff.). In all these contexts he is attempting to make the same point, that knowledge in the cultural sciences always reveals the perspective of its author and the group from which the author comes. This is an aspect of thinking that is more than a mere 'formal determination of thinking', but refers to a qualitative element in the structure of thought overlooked by formal logic (1936:272). In his discussion Mannheim once again emphasizes the positive possibility of knowledge that is relational, perspectivistic and activistic, not the deficiencies of this means of knowing.

These observations lead to the conclusion that Mannheim's theory of relational knowledge takes important steps in the direction of an anti-foundational approach to the social sciences. It would be convenient if Mannheim had articulated his position more clearly and, particularly, if he had defined his views on a number of issues central to social scientific methodology. Unfortunately he does not do so. But it is nevertheless possible to reconstruct his position on some of these issues from his scattered remarks. The first of these is his attitude toward the natural sciences. As has frequently been noted above, Mannheim's attitude toward the relationship between the natural and social sciences is confused. At times he seems completely to reject the natural sciences' claim to absolute knowledge by rejecting the legitimacy of such knowledge, while at other times he only seems to be asserting that this ideal is inapplicable to the cultural sciences. Although it is impossible to gloss over this confusion, the reason for Mannheim's ambiguity on this issue can be identified. At various points in his work Mannheim refers to the dominance of the methodological ideal of the natural sciences and the resulting dualism between the natural and social sciences. In a footnote to his article on historicism he asserts that he recognizes that his own position is 'positionally determined' by this dualism between the natural and cultural sciences (1952:130). In another context he argues that in each particular time period epistemological primacy is accorded to one mode of thought and, in our time, this mode is that of the exact natural sciences (1952:206). This point is more clearly stated in his summary of the tenets of the sociology of knowledge:

> The particularity of the theory of knowledge holding sway today is clearly demonstrable by the fact that the natural sciences have been selected as the ideal to which all knowledge should aspire. (1936:290)

These statements offer further support for the interpretation of Mannheim that has been advanced above. Although the logic of Mannheim's account leads him to a Gadamerian position of the rejection of the ideal of absolute knowledge, he cannot definitively assert this position because he is bound by the epistemological assumptions of his day. In these passages Mannheim all but admits this to be the case. The purpose of his discussion of the natural sciences is, in all instances, to reject the legitimacy of the model of knowledge for the cultural sciences, and, in doing so, to question the legitimacy of the model *per se*. He asserts that the methods of the natural sciences will not allow the social sciences to ask the kind of questions that must be asked (1936:51). His discussion of the differences between the methods of the two kinds of sciences is extensive and always aimed at reinforcing this point (1971:117–19). Insisting that our 'intellectualism' will stimulate us to seek a point of objectivity, he concludes that 'this objective cannot be attained without doing violence to the subject matter' of the cultural sciences (1936:171). Finally, he argues that the attitude that the social sciences are waiting for their Galileo has fostered the 'vain effort to graft the methods of the natural sciences on to the cultural sciences', an effort that has resulted in 'positivist blindness' (1982:76).

Mannheim's position on a second issue that is central to social scientific methodology can also be reconstructed. On the subject of 'truth' and what it means for the social sciences Mannheim makes one thing very clear: he rejects the notion of a realm of truth 'as such'. He states unambiguously that 'We must reject the notion that there is a "sphere of truth in itself" as a disruptive and unjustifiable hypothesis' (1936:305). He argues that it is 'extremely questionable' whether it is worthwhile to seek 'fixed and immutable ideas', even claiming that those who look for absolutes are 'unable to look life in the face' (1936:87). Further, he argues that the absolutist definition of truth is, like all conceptions of truth, a product of the epistemological assumptions of the particular mode of thought from which it arises (1952:227; 1936:292). What is called for instead, Mannheim argues, is a new conception of truth that rejects the search for absolutes. Rather than looking for absolute truth we should recognize that all 'truths' are products of modes of thought:

> As long as we do not believe in some kind of supra-historical standpoint that suddenly descends upon us, and instead keep firmly in mind that we are trying to understand the historical from a standpoint which is itself historical we shall not only be incapable of overcoming our point of departure: we shall not want to overcome it. (1982:274)

Determining what is true and false in relational knowledge, on

Mannheim's account, involves the juxtaposition and comparison of all existing modes of thought (1936:294). Mannheim realizes, furthermore, that this position has epistemological implications. He claims that the sociology of knowledge demands a new epistemology because the findings of their investigations are relevant to the establishment of truth (1936:285).

But Mannheim's remarks on truth also lead him to a confusion. His position entails that 'truth' as the Enlightenment defined it is the product of a particular mode of thought. Yet he cannot entirely relinquish the absolutist goal that he claims to be rejecting. He argues that if knowledge is always from a particular perspective, then the juxtaposition or combination of as many different perspectives as possible must offer some 'larger' kind of truth. He rejects the idea that his 'dynamic relationism' is nihilistic precisely because it seeks to overcome the narrowness of particular standpoints (1971:267). Ideas are true, he claims, if they reflect our *actual* situation, a situation determined by the many different perspectives possible in a given historical epoch. This conception, as many commentators have noted, retains some of the idealized vision of truth informing the absolutist view (von Schelting 1936:667; Vallas 1979:469).

If Mannheim's call for a new conception of truth is somewhat confused, his definition of a closely related issue, objectivity, is more precise. He begins his discussion of objectivity with the theme that dominated his examination of truth. The question, he states, is not how to get a non-perspectivistic view or to apologize for the necessity of taking a particular perspective, but rather, it is how 'by juxtaposing the various points of view, each perspective may be recognized as such and thereby a new level of objectivity attained' (1936:196–7). He develops his argument with regard to objectivity along two lines. First, he claims that objectivity is different but not impossible in the cultural sciences. Unlike the natural sciences, objectivity in the cultural sciences is based on the recognition of perspectivistic knowledge. Secondly, he argues that there are different levels of objectivity possible in different spheres of cultural knowledge (1953:57). When a common universe of discourse is shared, observers will arrive at the same result, but when observers have different perspectives, objectivity is obtained by translating one mode of discourse into another (1936:301).

At the heart of Mannheim's definition of objectivity is the distinction between conscious evaluation and the evaluative element present in all thought (1936:100). He claims that the 'objective' is not the non-evaluative, but, rather, the intersubjective. In his essay on political conservatism he argues that the elements of his analysis are 'objective' not in the sense of eternally and universally valid, but in the sense of 'apart from individual experience'. Objectivity for Mannheim is not obtained by methodological fiat, but by scrutinizing the viewpoints of both observer and observed. The 'objective analysis', in other words, is that which gives us greatest comprehensiveness (1936:301).

Mannheim's definition of objectivity has a certain affinity with that of Weber as well as the American pragmatists. It is thus tempting to criticize Mannheim's conception on the same grounds as these conceptions have been criticized, that is, by arguing that the positivist conception of objectivity has been so altered by their redefinition that the term itself ought to be discarded. But although this is a valid criticism, and Mannheim, along with the other anti-positivist critics, should have employed another word to express his meaning, Mannheim's definition of objectivity has an advantage: the emphasis on self-reflexiveness. Built into Mannheim's definition of objectivity is the maxim to examine one's own viewpoint, one's own definition of 'truth', along with that which is being observed. This hermeneutical insight is less explicitly stated in both the Weberian and pragmatist approaches.

These observations on Mannheim's approach to some of the perennial problems of social scientific methodology, the relationship between the natural and social sciences and the status of truth and objectivity, lend support to the argument that he is not only definitively rejecting the methodology of positivist social science but is also moving toward a new epistemological basis for the cultural sciences. This argument can be strengthened further by looking at an issue that was a central question in social scientific methodology in Mannheim's day even though it is rarely discussed today: the 'genetic fallacy'. Mannheim has frequently been criticized for falling prey to the genetic fallacy by positivist critics in the middle of the twentieth-century as well as by his contemporaries. Because condemnation of the genetic fallacy was a nearly universal tenet of logical thought in

Mannheim's day he confronts the issue very directly. He states unequivocally that:

> The historical and social genesis of an idea would only be irrelevant to its ultimate validity if the temporal and social conditions of its emergence had no effect on its content and form. (1936:271)

This statement implies that Mannheim is simply discarding the genetic fallacy as invalid for, as he has often stated, temporal and historical conditions *do* have a profound effect on the content and form of ideas. But a more careful reading of his work reveals a subtler position. Mannheim argues that those who fall prey to the genetic fallacy *are* in error, but not because the genesis of an idea has nothing to do with its validity. Rather, they are in error because they assume an individualistic generation of meaning. What Mannheim calls the 'psychogenetic' approach is wrong because it looks for the genesis of meaning in the individual rather than the collective context (1936:25–7).

In this instance, once again, Mannheim is changing the terms of the argument by attacking the basic assumptions of his opponents. By asserting that meaning is always tied to social and historical conditions he reveals that the issue that the genetic fallacy addresses is spurious. But by denying the validity of individual genesis of meaning he avoids the psychologism of the other theorists of his day who denied the legitimacy of the genetic fallacy. In short, he shows the fallacy to be not false in itself but based on false epistemological presuppositions.

With regard to this issue as well as the other issues of social scientific methodology discussed above Mannheim presents a position that transcends the epistemological assumptions of his opponents. In the case of each of these issues, but particularly that of the genetic fallacy, Mannheim's critics have interpreted his position in radically different ways.[9] This difficulty with the interpretation of his work is, however, an indication of his break with the accepted, that is, positivist methodology of his day. The purpose of this review of Mannheim's views on these issues of social scientific methodology has been to show that the value of his approach lies precisely in this epistemological break.

IV MANNHEIM AND ANTI-FOUNDATIONAL THOUGHT

The preceding overview of Mannheim's work is based solely on work published up to 1931 (with the exception of the addition to *Ideology and Utopia* written in 1936). Mannheim's later work, concerned almost exclusively with social planning, is, from the point of view of social theory, uninteresting.[10] My argument for the significance of Mannheim's work, does not however, rest on the assertion that the whole corpus of his thought places him in the ranks of a Weber or a Durkheim. This is quite obviously not the case. Nor does it rest on the claim that his work is a seamless whole presenting a consistent, unified viewpoint on the methodology of the social sciences. Mannheim himself admits that this is far from being the case. In a letter of 1946 he states that there are inconsistencies in his thought because 'I want to break through the old epistemology radically but have not yet succeeded fully.' He even goes so far as to justify these inconsistencies as a necessary product of the methodological approach he espouses:

> I use this method because I think that in this marginal field of human knowledge we should not conceal inconsistencies, so to speak covering up the wounds, but our duty is to show the sore spots of human thinking at its present stage. In a simple empirical investigation or straightforward logical argument, contradictions are mistakes; but when the task is to show that our whole thought system in its various parts leads to inconsistencies, these inconsistencies are the thorn in the flesh from which we have to start. (quoted in K. Wolff, 1959:571)

Mannheim comes closest to expressing the position that I am advancing with regard to the importance of his work in these quotations. Without denying or excusing the inconsistencies in Mannheim's thought it has been my goal to argue that these inconsistencies are a result of his attempt to make a radical break with Enlightenment and positivist epistemology. He is, as he admits in this statement, not entirely successful in his attempt to make this break. The preceding discussion has revealed that positivist elements remain in his thought. His adherence to the dualism between the natural and social sciences, as he himself admits, is a major stumbling block to transcending Enlightenment thought. One commentator has argued that had Mannheim had access to contemporary research in the philosophy of natural science he could have overcome his faith in the objectivity of natural science (Mulkay, 1979:16). But the fact remains that he did not and consequently could not accommodate the relationism of natural science in his theory. His uncertainty over the definition of 'truth' and his insistence on retaining the search for 'objectivity' are further indications of the 'old epistemology'. But this discussion has also revealed that despite these inconsistencies, Mannheim's theory goes a long way toward creating a truly hermeneutic method for the social sciences. By defining the task of the social sciences as the analysis of the relationship between thought and existence and calling into question the 'absolute Reason' of the Enlightenment, he lays the groundwork for an anti-foundational social science even though it is not entirely realized in his own work. The hermeneutic social science that he envisions, like that of Gadamer, involves 'other ways of experiencing and knowing arising out of an altogether different kind of relationship between subject and object' (1982:155).

In the foregoing I have not attempted to review all the critical commentaries on Mannheim's work, focusing instead on an exposition of the texts. But it should be noted at this point that the interpretation of Mannheim generally advanced by his critics is not in accord with the argument advanced here. Paradoxically, even though Mannheim is generally recognized as the founding father of the sociology of knowledge, he is criticized by both positivist and anti-positivist commentators (House 1977:207). The majority of Mannheim's critics have faulted him for his inconsistencies and argued that his 'relativistic' stance is an inadequate basis for the sociology of knowledge. Even his more recent critics who are sympathetic to his interpretive stance fault him for his 'vicious relativism' or his 'unsatisfactory' relationism (Hollis, 1978; Hamilton, 1974; Simon, 1982). With the notable exception of A. P. Simonds (1975; 1978) none of these commentators sees Mannheim as a forerunner of anti-foundational social science. This judgement is, in many instances, based on a misinterpretation of Mannheim's work. But in those cases where Mannheim's position is correctly understood, he is commonly dismissed for the reason that a 'groundless' philosophy of social science is unthinkable.[11]

Far from being unthinkable, however, the groundless philosophy of social science that Mannheim proposes offers a number of distinct advantages for the social sciences. First, more clearly than any other sociologist of knowledge, Mannheim defines the task of the social sciences as hermeneutic interpretation. Although others of his era (Weber and Simmel, for example) emphasized the interpretive role of the social sciences, Mannheim is more explicit about the hermeneutic procedure involved in investigations in the cultural sciences. He is also very clear about the role of the quantifying methodology of the natural sciences for the interpretive task of the social sciences. He states unequivocally that it is not applicable to the social sciences because it does not answer the kind of questions social scientists ask. The second advantage of Mannheim's theory is closely related to this point: self-reflexivity. Unlike the historicists with whom he identifies his theory Mannheim makes it clear that in social scientific analyses the observer as well as the observed must subject their perspectives to examination. His clearest statement of this point comes from his discussion of the interpretation of *Weltanschauungen*:

> The 'spirit' or global outlook of an epoch is something the interpreting subject cannot grasp without falling back upon his own historic 'substance', which is why the history of documentary interpretations of past ages is at the same time a history of the interpreting subjects themselves. (1952:63)

In another significant passage he states:

> The *concrete values* which serve as a standard have *developed* in their fullness of meaning *organically out of the same historical process* which they have to help interpret. (1952:104)

In these passages Mannheim comes close to taking the position that Gadamer is later to define as 'effective historical consciousness'. Mannheim's discussion of documentary meaning, which he sees to be the primary task of the cultural sciences, reveals his affinity to Gadamer's hermeneutics most distinctly. It also reveals his departure from the historicists' position, the position that Gadamer defines as his principal point of attack. For Mannheim understanding is always from a particular perspective, and he makes it clear that this maxim applies to observer as well as observed. Even though the historicists recognized the interpretive role of the social sciences, they posited an Archimedean point of objectivity for the observer. Mannheim, like Gadamer, offers a corrective to this historicist view.

The third advantage of Mannheim's thought is that, again like Gadamer and unlike interpretive social scientists and historicists, he defines the 'perspective' which structures knowledge in collective rather than individual terms. The focus of his sociology of knowledge, Mannheim claims, is not individual thought, but the social setting. He states this point very forcefully in the introduction to *Ideology and Utopia*:

> Strictly speaking it is incorrect to say that the single individual thinks. Rather it is more correct to insist that he participates in thinking further what other men have thought before him. (1936:3)

Furthermore, Mannheim asserts that the emphasis on the individual has been one of the major defects of modern thought. He states: 'That the individual is the primary seat of reality is of course an assumption that seems inescapable to us' (1956:110). But he also asserts that it is the task of the sociological approach to correct this error. Against the individualistic approach Mannheim argues that individuals do not construct a view of the world from their own experiences but, rather, 'it is much more correct to say that knowledge is from the very beginning a co-operative process of group life' (1936:29).

Several critics have identified Mannheim's de-emphasis on the individual mind as a serious liability of his approach. Shils condemns Mannheim for identifying the individual mind as a 'fiction' (1974:84) and Hartung notes that because he asserts the existence of a thought system which is carried neither by individuals nor by an identifiable group his sociology of knowledge is deficient (1970:696). But from an anti-foundational perspective Mannheim's position on this issue is an asset rather than a liability. For Mannheim the background perspective that structures the thought of both individuals and groups cannot be identified with any particular individual or group because it makes thought itself possible for the entire age in which they live. This position sounds very Heideggerian, and at one point Mannheim specifically identifies his position on this background perspective with Heidegger. He states:

> The philosopher Heidegger calls this collective subject who supplies us with the prevailing public interpretation of reality '*das Mann*' – the 'They'. This is the 'They' that is meant in the French

> expressions – such as *Que dit-on*, or *Que dira-t-on* – but it is not merely the collective subject responsible for gossip and tittle-tattle, but also that profounder Something which always interprets the world somehow, whether in its superficiality or its depths, and which causes us always to meet the world in a preconceived form. (1952:197)

These three aspects of Mannheim's work form the core of his distinctively hermeneutic approach to the sociology of knowledge. They also provide the basic argument for the affinity between his position and that of Gadamer. In his extensive work on Mannheim, A. P. Simonds also argues that Mannheim's theory constitutes a hermeneutic method for the social sciences. In making this argument he takes a position that is similar in several respects to that which was argued above. First, he shows that Mannheim's work has a great deal in common with the 'subjectivist' or interpretive social science that has been popular in recent years, particularly that of Schutz, Winch and Taylor. He also argues that because Mannheim retains the possibility of the 'legitimate scientific ideal of intersubjectivity' he adds an important element to the subjectivist position (1978:156).

Simonds makes another important point when he discusses the role of subjective intentions in Mannheim's work (1978:53). Although he argues that Mannheim appeals to the intention of the author or actor in the process of interpretation, this does not entail recourse to empathy or intuition. Rather, as his references to Heidegger make clear, Mannheim sees meaning as a collective phenomenon. As he sees it we appeal to the shared meanings of the socio-historical context to establish the intention of authors or actors, not the inner workings of their psyches. But although Mannheim comes close to rejecting subjective intentionality altogether, as his assertion that the single individual does not think implies, he does not, as does Gadamer, explore the radical implications of this stance. Mannheim goes beyond Weber and Simmel in his treatment of subjective intentionality in that he stresses the determinate character of shared meanings although he does not take the final, Gadamerian step of denying subjective intentionality completely.

Simond's position on another issue, however, the question of semantic autonomy, represents a serious misinterpretation of Mannheim's thought that calls into question the particular understanding of Mannheim's hermeneutic approach that I am presenting. The issue of semantic autonomy in contemporary discussions is an exceedingly complicated question. In its simplest terms, however, the doctrine entails the claim that the intention of the author of the text does not fix the meaning of the text. In contemporary discussions the doctrine has taken two principal forms. First, positivists have used the doctrine to claim that texts should be interpreted in terms of their relationship to certain 'timeless' or 'eternal' truths. Those who espouse this variant of the doctrine of semantic autonomy are looking for the 'objective meaning' of the text which is removed from reference to the author's subjective intention. Finding the 'objective meaning' of the text in this sense thus coincides with the positivists' desire for a 'scientific' approach to the analysis of texts. Secondly, semantic autonomy can take the form of the more recent claim by the structuralists that the analysis of texts should not entail reference to any historical data. The structuralists argue that texts should be interpreted as autonomous entities, not in terms of the presuppositions of the era in which the author lives nor in terms of the author's subjective intentions. Although both these variants of the doctrine reject the notion that the author's meaning fixes the meaning of the text there are nevertheless important differences between them. In the case of the positivists' doctrine of semantic autonomy it is assumed that only one determinate, 'objective' meaning of the text exists and it can be found through careful analysis. The position of the structuralists, in contrast, entails that multiple readings of the text all constitute legitimate interpretations. Since the structuralists reject appeals to both subjective intentions and historical determinates to establish the meaning of the text, multiple readings are both possible and unavoidable.

Simonds makes it clear at the beginning of his analysis that he rejects the doctrine of semantic autonomy and argues that Mannheim also does (1978:53–4). Appealing to the most forceful argument against semantic autonomy, that of Eric Hirsch (1967), he argues that a case against textual autonomy is implicit in Mannheim's work even though it is not explicitly stated. He also claims, as have other critics, that Gadamer presents a case for the autonomy of the text. To establish his claim he quotes a passage from *Truth and Method* in which Gadamer questions the possibility of the sociology of knowledge (1975:107). Simonds then argues against Gadamer that if communication is to be rendered possible we must be able to identify a common core of meaning for any text under examination. He claims that Gadamer denies this with his assertion that the meaning of the text is determined in part by the interpreter's perspective. Simonds takes the position that although the *interpretation* of the text can change with different interpreters, the *meaning* of the text stays the same (1978:94–5). He claims, moreover, that this constitutes Mannheim's position on the issue of semantic autonomy.[12]

Simonds's interpretation of this issue has serious deficiencies. First, he claims that, in determining the meaning of a text, proponents of semantic autonomy, Gadamer among them, ignore the shared meanings that constitute the social and historical understandings of the author's particular time as well as the subjective intentions of the specific author. This involves a basic misunderstanding of Gadamer. Although Gadamer does reject the appeal to subjective intentions, he does not claim that the meaning of the text is determined by the interpreter alone but, rather, that it rests on a 'fusing of horizons' – that of the interpreter and that of the text. For Gadamer the meaning of each of these horizons is established by appealing not to subjective intentions but to the shared meanings, or, as he puts it, the 'prejudices' of the age. He cannot, therefore, be classified as a proponent of semantic autonomy.

It can also be shown that Simonds' argument entails a misreading of Mannheim. As the above discussion has established, Mannheim, like Gadamer, argues that the interpreter's perspective is a key determinate of the meaning of the text or action under observation. His statement that the history of the documentary interpretation of a past age is the history of the interpreting subjects themselves establishes this very clearly (1952:63). It is this thesis of self-reflexivity that sets Mannheim's theory apart despite the fact that he still retains the presupposition of subjective intentionality. Simonds's claim that Mannheim's position entails that the interpretation, not the meaning, of the text changes with different interpretations cannot be substantiated in Mannheim's work. It can be concluded, rather, that Mannheim and Gadamer stand together on this issue and that both claim that the shared meanings, or prejudices, of both interpreter and interpreted establish the meaning of a text.

Simonds's effort to enlist Mannheim in his argument against both the doctrine of semantic autonomy and Gadamer's position ultimately fails. What is important in this context, however, is not merely the fact that Simonds errs in his interpretation of Mannheim and Gadamer, but that the Hirsch–Simonds position on semantic autonomy is itself in error, a point that will be argued more extensively in subsequent chapters. Both Hirsch and Simonds argue that the intention of the author of a text, understood in terms of the shared meanings of the time, ultimately determines the meaning of the text. What this leaves out is precisely what Gadamer and Mannheim argue so forcefully – that the interpreter participates in establishing the meaning of the text. Both Hirsch and Simonds qualify this thesis, first, by rejecting the appeal to 'getting inside the author's head' and, secondly, by conceding that different interpreters will see this meaning in different ways. But no matter how much the thesis is modified it always entails some appeal both to an Archimedean point of interpretation and to a fixed meaning of the text.

Showing Simonds' interpretation in this regard to be incorrect is central to the thesis that will be advanced in subsequent chapters. Simonds uses his claim that Mannheim appeals to socio-historical conditions to establish meaning to argue that his sociology of knowledge is at the same time a hermeneutic method. In contrast he argues that Gadamer's failure to rely on socio-historical understanding to establish meaning entails that his method precludes the very possibility of a sociology of knowledge (1978:70, 89). A careful reading of Gadamer reveals, however, that far from rejecting the socio-historical context of the text, Gadamer bases his hermeneutic method on an interpretation of this context. His insistence that 'prejudice', the historically grounded presuppositions of the age, predetermine meanings entails that his approach is rooted in historical interpretation. This also entails that his approach is not incompatible with Mannheim's approach and does not preclude a sociology of knowledge defined in anti-foundational terms.

The three elements of Mannheim's theory discussed above, hermeneutic interpretation, self-reflexivity and the collective approach to knowledge, constitute the basis of his hermeneutic approach to the sociology of knowledge. In addition to these central features, however, there are two additional advantages of Mannheim's approach that are particularly relevant in contemporary discussions. The first of these is a point that is crucial to the argument for the viability of his hermeneutic method: the application of hermeneutic method to the analysis of action as well as texts. Although Mannheim does not make an explicit argument for the hermeneutic analysis of action, he quite obviously assumes this to be the case. If it were not, his whole program for the sociology of knowledge would collapse.[13] This aspect of Mannheim's approach is especially germane to a comparison with Gadamer's work. From the perspective of its usefulness for the social sciences one of the greatest deficiencies of Gadamer's approach is his failure to extend his hermeneutic method to the analysis of action as well as texts. Although several recent authors have explicitly argued for this connection between action and texts in hermeneutic method (C. Taylor, 1977; Ricoeur, 1977a), it is nevertheless significant that Gadamer himself fails to make this crucial connection. The fact that Mannheim illustrates how hermeneutic method can be employed in this analysis of action thus constitutes an important argument in favor of his approach.

The final aspect of Mannheim's approach that is relevant to contemporary discussions in the social sciences involves another element of his thought for which he does not offer an explicit argument. In the course of his work Mannheim briefly eludes to his position that there is a continuum between the analysis of what Heidegger calls the background of human existence and the more specific social scientific analysis of individual social groups and their particular belief systems. The closest he comes to making an argument for this continuum can be found in his discussion of Heidegger's concept of the 'They'. In the context of a very concrete discussion of a particular social phenomenon, competition and the cultural influences that give rise to it, he states:

> The philosopher looks at this 'They', this secretive Something, but he is not interested to find out how it arose; and it is just at this point, where the philosopher stops, that the work of the sociologist begins. (1952:198)

This position has special importance for the discussion of an anti-foundational sociology of knowledge. Central to establishing the viability of this position is the argument that the two levels of analysis that Mannheim has identified are intimately connected and that a proper understanding of this connection is central to both enterprises. That a 'background' of taken-for-granted assumptions forms the basis of human thought and existence has been the theme of some of the most notable twentieth century philosophers: Heidegger, Wittgenstein and, at least on some readings of his later writings, Husserl. These philosophers have challenged the dominant assumption that the basis of human thought and existence lies in some indubitable realm, whether of objective scientific facts, eternal ethical truths, or the transcental Ego. Many twentieth century social scientists, on the other hand, have been concerned with showing how the basic structure of thought constituting social life dictates attitudes, beliefs, 'ideology', and every other aspect of human existence. As has been argued above, the sociology of knowledge as a discipline is intimately connected with this trend in twentieth century social thought.

These two trends, however, have by and large occupied separate spheres and their proponents have failed to acknowledge the similarity of their approaches. A number of reasons can be cited for this state of affairs. First, most social scientists retain, if only marginally, an allegiance to the positivist search for objective truth. Most assume that underneath the layer of social conditioning that it is their business to describe is a bedrock of objective facts. In the tradition of the sociology of knowledge in particular, many define the search for links between thought and existence in causal terms, further confusing their analyses. Secondly, both philosophers and social scientists assume that they are engaged in distinctly different kinds of analyses. Both groups presuppose that it is one thing to identify what Wittgenstein calls the 'bedrock' of human thought and quite another to examine specific belief structures belonging to particular social groups.

The assumptions that lead to this separation of the two levels of analysis, should however, be re-examined. Although these two endeavors represent different levels of analysis, their examination is nevertheless inextricably linked. The philosopher's examination of the 'background,' 'bedrock', or 'prejudice' that is an inescapable part of human existence establishes that human thought is defined by human existence. This point, made so brilliantly by Wittgenstein, Heidegger and Gadamer, can be linked to the social scientists' analysis very directly by showing that it forms the basis for the more specific analysis of how a particular aspect of human thought is tied to a particular group of humans existing in a given time and place. If, in general, all human thought is existentially formed, then it follows that particular manifestations are formed by particular circumstances. The relationship between these manifestations and these circumstances is not, however, as the positivists thought, one of causal determination. Rather, as Mannheim has shown, the link between a particular thought system is a problem of interpretation to be analyzed by hermeneutic techniques.

Mannheim's support for this thesis can be enlisted not only on the basis of the quotation noted above but also by citing a concrete example of his analysis of the thought of a particular social group and the links between this group and its social standing. In his examination of nineteenth century German conservative thought Mannheim illustrates how hermeneutic technique is used to analyze the relationship between social groups and social existence. Mannheim makes the basic intent of his analysis clear at the outset. He states that the core of his technique is the analysis of *meaning* (1953:77). This statement expresses a thesis that is more carefully stated in his later writings: the rejection of a simple one-to-one causal connection between social class and styles of thought. In another context Mannheim states that Marx's view is one-sided in its dogmatic assertion of the link between social class and styles of thought. What is needed, Mannheim claims, is a more 'elastic' theory that can accommodate other elements of the social situation (1957:146). Marxist analysis is also hampered by the fact that although socialists and communists conduct their analysis in terms of ideology, their analysis is not self-reflexive, that is, they fail to apply that analysis to themselves (1936:125).

What the analysis of social life calls for, Mannheim claims, is finding the 'basic intention' that lies behind a style of thought (1953:78). The sociology of knowledge seeks to find the connection between styles of thought and social history, a task for which Marx's connection through class is insufficient (1936:307). It is precisely this that Mannheim attempts to do in his analysis of German conservatives in the first half of the nineteenth century. Instead of trying to establish a causal link between the class and style of thought of this particular group he tries instead to define the meaning of their beliefs in terms of their social existence and the general pattern of thought in that time period. The result is a thorough analysis of the nature of the thought of this group, how that thought was linked to their particular social standing, and how, in turn it related to certain fundamental assumptions of the age embodied in Romanticism and the Enlightenment.

Because of his connection between these two levels Mannheim's position presents a useful model for the relationship between social science and philosophical thought on the nature of human existence that I am advocating. His position entails that there are two distinct yet related levels of the sociology of knowledge: the examination of background assumptions and the analysis of specific belief systems. Both, however, rest on the same assumption – the intimate and essential connection between human thought and human social existence. Mannheim's work has the advantage of pointing to the fact that there will inevitably be a link between these two levels. As he shows in his analysis of German conservatives, specific styles of thought are derivative of the general patterns of thought characteristic of the time period under examination and the background assumptions on which they rest. Indeed, it is impossible to imagine that this would not be the case.

In attempting to establish this argument the discussion will next turn to an examination of Gadamer's hermeneutics. Gadamer is particularly useful as a foil for Mannheim because he corrects many of the errors and contradictions in Mannheim's theory. He presents a more comprehensive analysis of the first level of the sociology of knowledge, the ontological examination of the background of human existence. But from the perspective of the methodology of the social sciences Gadamer suffers by comparison with Mannheim for he fails to provide any guidance for the second level of the sociology of knowledge, the examination of specific beliefs of particular groups. Although Gadamer specifically argues that his theory is not intended to establish a concrete method for the social sciences, this qualification is not of much use for the problems under consideration here. Given the advantages and disadvantages of both positions, therefore, what will be attempted is a synthesis between the two approaches on the metatheoretical level. Together, the theories of Gadamer and Mannheim can be fashioned into an approach to the sociology of knowledge that defines the enterprise as the analysis of human thought and existence on the level of ontology as well as that of concrete social existence.

4

Gadamer's Hermeneutics and the Methodology of the Social Sciences

In order to establish the argument that Gadamer's hermeneutics is relevant to the current problems of the social sciences and that it is instrumental to the definition of an anti-foundational social science a number of issues must be clarified. First, it is important to begin with a clear understanding of Gadamer's place in contemporary hermeneutics and the goal of his major work, *Truth and Method*. Secondly, the advantages of a Gadamerian approach to the social sciences must be enumerated with regard to some of the central issues and approaches in contemporary social science. Thirdly, the outlines of a methodology rooted in Gadamer's hermeneutics must be sketched.

I *TRUTH AND METHOD*

Gadamer's problematic

Attempting to define the purpose of *Truth and Method* may seem, on one level, a relatively simple task. Gadamer is very explicit with regard to his goal in the introduction and foreword to his work where a precise and unambiguous statement of purpose can be found. But from the perspective offered by the many commentators on *Truth and Method*, clearly defining Gadamer's problematic is not at all simple because his task has been interpreted in widely different ways. Many of the major critics of *Truth and Method* patently ignore the stated goal of the work and attribute to Gadamer quite different purposes. A further difficulty in specifying Gadamer's purpose lies in the subtlety of the course of his argument in *Truth and Method*, a subtlety that belies the unambiguous statement of purpose found at the beginning of the book. It is possible to interpret Gadamer as almost stumbling onto the conclusion to *Truth and Method* and the answer to the question that he poses at the outset. The nature of this conclusion, furthermore, overshadows the importance of the specific topics he discusses in the book and succeeds in placing the social sciences on a radically new footing.

Gadamer's problematic in *Truth and Method* must be understood, first of all, in terms of the basic split that divides contemporary hermeneutics. His work, particularly as it is defined in *Truth and Method*, in large part defines one side of that controversy. Gadamer defines hermeneutics as the philosophical exploration of the character and fundamental conditions of all understanding and rejects the contention that the task of hermeneutics is methodological investigations into the social sciences or any other discipline. The counter to his approach has been labelled 'objective' hermeneutics and claims that the goal of hermeneutics is to identify general methodological principles of interpretation. Its principal spokesman is Enrico Betti whose *Teoria Generale della Interpretazione* (1955) is the definitive statement of this approach.[1] Although most commentators acknowledge this basic split within hermeneutics, questions concerning the definition of Gadamer's 'philosphical hermeneutics' continue to arise, particularly among social scientists. Thus, to cite a contemporary example, Zygmunt Bauman, in his analysis of the relationship between hermeneutics and the social sciences argues that hermeneutic analysis provides the social sciences with a distinctive method that allows them to achieve the same standard of truth and cogency as the natural sciences, only in a different sphere (1978:14). This statement, although it is compatible with Betti's approach, is completely foreign to Gadamer's approach to hermeneutics. In general, the problem encountered in interpretations of Gadamer's work is that, despite his protestations to the contrary, few commentators take seriously Gadamer's vehement denial that he is offering a methodology for the social sciences. Despite his interest in the social sciences it is not Gadamer's aim to offer methodological guidelines, yet many commentators fault him for failing to do so. In one of the supplements to *Truth and Method* Gadamer accuses Betti himself of making this mistake (1975:466). Given the firmness with which Gadamer denies any methodological intent, these misinterpretations are somewhat hard to explain, but the frequency with which they occur necessitates a clear understanding of Gadamer's position on this fundamental issue.

The best place to begin the attempt to characterize Gadamer's hermeneutics is the introduction and foreword to *Truth and Method* where Gadamer defines the purpose of his work. In the introduction he states:

> The hermeneutics developed here is not, therefore, a methodology of the human sciences, but an attempt to understand what the human sciences truly are, beyond their methodological self-consciousness, and what connects them with the totality of our experience of the world. (1975:xiii)

In his foreword to the second edition he makes this even more explicit:

> Therefore I did not remotely intend to deny the necessity of methodological work within the human sciences (*Geisteswissenschaften*). Nor did I propose to revive the ancient dispute on method between the natural and the human sciences. . . . The question I have asked seeks to discover and bring into consciousness something that methodological dispute serves only to conceal and neglect, something that does not so much confine or limit modern science as precede it and make it possible. (1975:xvii)

These passages offer a clear statement of what Gadamer is and is not trying to do in his book. He claims that it is his aim to discover what the human sciences truly are; by this he means he wants to know 'what kind of insight and what kind of truth' can be found in the human sciences (1975:xi). Here we get the first glimmerings of the conflict between truth and method that is to dominate the book. If the question of the human sciences goes beyond the question of method but encompasses that of truth, then it follows that truth itself must be beyond the question of method.

Two themes are introduced here that are of crucial importance to an understanding of the project of *Truth and Method*. The first is found in the statement that his intent is to search for what the human sciences truly are. This search leads Gadamer to an analysis of the evolution of the human sciences, the influence of the 'spirit of modern science' on their development and the fact that they have retained certain basic elements of the humanistic heritage (1975:xvii). This is the theme that informs the analysis of the first half of the book in which he explores, first, the basic humanistic concepts as they are defined by Vico, Dilthey and other representatives of the humanist tradition and, secondly, an analysis of the experience of art that, he claims, is closer to the experience of truth encountered in the human sciences than that characteristic of the natural sciences.

The second theme introduced here is, however, of greater importance because it reveals the central concern of *Truth and Method*: how is understanding possible (1975:xviii)? Although Gadamer's immediate goal in the book is to discover the nature of the human sciences, in order to do so he must tackle the infinitely more difficult question of how understanding itself is possible. Since it is clear to him that the self-understanding of the human sciences is fundamentally erroneous he is forced to take on the question of what kind of understanding *is* appropriate for the human sciences and, consequently, the universal question of what understanding itself is. His answer to this question is that all understanding is hermeneutical and, thus, that an analysis of the nature of understanding is coincident with an analysis of 'universal hermeneutics'. Initially Gadamer defines hermeneutics as the 'basic being-in motion of There-being which constitutes its finiteness and historicity and hence includes the whole of its experience of the world' (1975:xxii). The study of hermeneutics is thus the study of Being, and, ultimately, the study of language, because 'Being that can be understood is language' (1975:xxii).

The answer to the question that Gadamer poses at the beginning of *Truth and Method*, the nature of the human sciences, is thus that all understanding is linguistic and that understanding in the human sciences is therefore to be examined through the medium of language. It may seem to be belaboring the obvious to state that the linguisticality of understanding is thus the key to Gadamer's approach and must be the focus of an explication of his work. But the centrality of this thesis has not been obvious to many of Gadamer's commentators and it is important to underscore its significance. In setting out to discover the nature of the human sciences in *Truth and Method* Gadamer engages in the discussion of a broad range of issues: the nature of aesthetic experience, the role of play, the history of the human sciences and ontology. It is easy to get caught up in the minutiae of

Gadamer's analysis of these various topics, and many of his critics have done precisely this. There have been lengthy discussions of Gadamer's understanding of these issues and, particularly, of his approach to the difficult question of ontology. These discussions miss the real thrust of Gadamer's work because they lose sight of the importance of his conclusion. Ultimately, the one issue that is important, the one that must be understood because it is the key to understanding all the others, is language. This issue overshadows all the subsidiary issues that Gadamer discusses and provides a perspective by which those other issues must be approached. Thus, for example, instead of trying to discover Gadamer's position on ontology it would be more fruitful to ask how language reveals Being; the question of language supercedes that of ontology and dictates how the question must be approached. There is even a sense in which Gadamer's initial question is transposed by his conclusion. His analysis leads to the discovery that, as he puts it, the theory of the human sciences is really philosophy itself (1979:112).

The thesis of the centrality of the linguisticality of understanding will be the basis of the following analysis of Gadamer's work. Gadamer's approach goes a long way toward establishing a position that is crucial to the thesis of this book – that philosophy and the social sciences are intimately connected and that this connection lies in the nature of linguistic understanding. My position is that although Gadamer is most definitely not offering a methodology for the social sciences in his work, his position has profound implications for the social sciences. The distinction between these two positions is important and involves much more than a mere definitional quibble. To argue that Gadamer offers a method for the social sciences entails that he takes the position that the social sciences need a distinctive 'method' just as the natural sciences need a method if they are to be classified as sciences. This position is the antithesis of Gadamer's approach. But to argue that Gadamer's work has profound methodological implications is to assert that he defines a philosophical perspective that so revolutionizes the way the social sciences are conceived that it calls into question our very notion of method. It follows that his position on language and the human sciences and the anti-foundational thrust of that insight necessarily dictate a methodology that is radically different from that conceived by most social scientists and certainly most sociologists of knowledge. Finally, an analysis of Gadamer's work from this perspective reveals that if, as Gadamer argues, the theory of the human sciences is philosophy itself, then there can be no gap between the problem of understanding in the social sciences and understanding in philosophy.

Art, play and the nature of the human sciences

In the foreword to the second edition of *Truth and Method* Gadamer states:

> My starting point is that the historic human sciences, as they emerged from German romanticism and became imbued with the spirit of modern science, maintained a humanistic heritage which distinguishes them from all other kinds of modern research and brings them close to other, quite different, extrascientific experiences, and especially those proper to art. (1975:xvii)

This statement dictates the subject matter of the first two major parts of his work, the examination of the experience of art and an overview of how the human sciences evolved out of the thought of the nineteenth century. Gadamer begins with a brief discussion of what he identifies as 'leading humanistic concepts', an analysis predicated on the assumption that:

> What makes the human sciences into sciences can be understood more easily from the tradition of the concept of *Bildung* than from the concept of method in modern science. (1975:18)

Throughout this section and the critique of objectivism in the human sciences that succeeds it Gadamer's aim is to show that an understanding of the human sciences lies not in the nineteenth-century's narrow concern with method and the relationship to the natural sciences but in the 'unbroken tradition of rhetorical and humanist culture' (1975:23). But since the human sciences have been cut off from this tradition by the objectifying trends of the nineteenth century they must find a way to reclaim it. They must rediscover that understanding in the social sciences does not involve the discovery of general laws, but entails understanding a phenomenon in its 'unique and historical concreteness' (1975:6). The way to effect this rediscovery, Gadamer claims, is through an analysis of the experience of art. Why art? Because art reveals the limitations of the Enlightenment concept of truth. He asks:

> Is it right to reserve the concept of truth for conceptual knowledge? Must we not also admit that the work of art possesses truth? We shall see that to acknowledge this places not only the phenomenon of art but also that of history in a new light. (1975:39)

This is the case, in Gadamer's view, because aesthetic experience is not just a mode of experience but represents the essence of experience itself (1975:63).[2]

Gadamer's more immediate goal in his analysis of the experience of art, however, is to show that the mode of understanding found in this experience is closer to that of the human sciences than that of the natural sciences, even though, since the nineteenth century, the human sciences have been mimicking the method of the natural sciences. It is this self-understanding of the human sciences that Gadamer wants to call into question. In order to do so he identifies two key elements of the mode of understanding characteristic of the experience of art that are antithetical to the method of the natural sciences: understanding in the aesthetic experience is always self-understanding that takes place in relationship to something else that is understood; and the aesthetic experience always takes those experiencing it out of the context of their own life and relates them back to the whole of their existence (1975:63, 86). Having identified these two characteristics Gadamer next turns from aesthetics proper to an analysis of play, claiming that the aesthetic experience is a kind of play and, furthermore, that play is the clue to ontological explanation (1975:91). His analysis of play reveals three more characteristics of the mode of understanding he is exploring: play is always 'subjectless', that is, 'play has its own essence, independent of the consciousness of those who play' (1975:92); play always involves self-representation (1975:97); and play always includes a participating spectator who is 'involved in the communion of being present' (1975:117).

The significance of this digression into the aesthetic experience and play becomes evident when Gadamer asserts that the essence of the play of art is representation or reproduction and that this is also the essence of any kind of reading. It follows that literature is the point where art and science meet (1975:145). It also follows that not only is the aesthetic experience a branch of hermeneutics, but science must also be classified as hermeneutical because it involves reading and, hence, reproduction. What Gadamer has accomplished in this digression into the nature of the aesthetic experience is thus quite significant. He has identified a number of important attributes of a mode of understanding that is, he claims, characteristic of the human sciences. But, more significantly, he has also discovered that these characteristics are antithetical to analysis in the natural sciences, that the mode of understanding characteristic of the human sciences is hermeneutical and, finally, that science itself is hermeneutical. Although important in this context, these points will assume even greater significance later in his investigations.

In the next section of *Truth and Method* Gadamer embarks on a set of critiques that are of immediate relevance to the present thesis. He examines the work of a number of nineteenth and twentieth century thinkers whose works have been influential in shaping the self-understanding of the human sciences. These critiques are important because in each one Gadamer, although praising the thinker for moving away from the more blatant excesses of positivist objectivism, nevertheless reveals that each has introduced into his own theory an element of objectivism that mimics that of positivism. By criticizing each of these thinkers in turn Gadamer presents an outline of the human sciences that is purged of all objectivism and rejects any appeal to absolute foundations. These critiques thus give the best indication of the kind of social science that Gadamer is advocating, one that is radically anti-foundational.

Only a few of the elements of these critiques must be noted to indicate the thrust of Gadamer's argument in this regard. He begins by claiming that his aim is to free the human sciences from Dilthey's influence and identifies that influence as the attempt to link the certainty of science with the certainty of life philosophy, that is, knowledge (1975:147). Although Dilthey concedes that there is a difference between the historical and scientific modes of knowing, he nevertheless claims the same kind of objectivity for the natural and social sciences.[3] This objectivism in Dilthey's thought, Gadamer claims, is overcome in the phenomenology of

Husserl. Husserl's concept of the life-world is the antithesis of all objectivism because it posits the life-world as the inevitable ground of all knowing. But Husserl's approach is also flawed. Although Husserl makes the important move of grounding the human sciences through his analysis of the life-world and showing that it is prior to objective science, both Husserl and Dilthey fail to bridge the gap between speculative idealism and the experiential standpoint, because, for both, the concept of experience is primarily epistemological (1975:60, 219, 229). Ultimately, Gadamer argues, it is to Heidegger that we must turn in order to complete the move begun by Husserl. Heidegger transcends both Dilthey and Husserl by arguing that:

> Understanding is not a resigned ideal of human experience adopted in the old age of the spirit, as with Dilthey; nor is it, as with Husserl, a last methodological ideal of philosophy over against the naivete of unreflecting life; it is, on the contrary, the original form of the realization of There-being, which is being-in-the-world. (1975:230)

The nature of the hermeneutic experience

With the completion of his critique of objectivism in the human sciences Gadamer arrives at the heart of his investigation and must now reveal the specific nature of the mode of understanding that he has only outlined thus far. Immediately following the passage quoted above he declares that 'The present work is devoted to this new aspect of the hermeneutical problem' (1975:230). In defining this 'new aspect' Gadamer relies heavily on the work of Heidegger, or, more properly, his particular interpretation of Heidegger's work. As Gadamer sees it Heidegger's radical breakthrough was to reveal the ontological significance of understanding, that is, to reveal that the concept of understanding is not a methodological but an ontological problem. Heidegger defines hermeneutics as an ontology of understanding and interpretation, and Gadamer turns to this definition to discover 'if Heidegger's radicalisation can contribute to the construction of an historical hermeneutics' (1975:232–3).

Precisely what Gadamer accomplishes through his excursion into Heidegger's thought is very significant and should be carefully noted. In the previous section he has shown that the emphasis on epistemological problems and, consequently, method has led the social sciences to an impasse. They have been unable to transcend the Enlightenment's conception of truth and method because they are still concerned exclusively with epistemological questions. It is to solve this problem that Gadamer turns to Heidegger's ontology. But he selects only particular aspects of Heidegger's thought to utilize in his argument and, furthermore, transposes those aspects to suit his own purposes. Heidegger's ontology, particularly in his earlier works, has distinct transcendental overtones.[4] He thus incurs the danger of replacing the epistemological absolutism he is criticizing with ontological absolutism. Gadamer avoids this problem by casting his discussion of ontology in terms of, first, the linguisticality of all understanding and, secondly, historicity. As a consequence Gadamer's approach to ontology follows Heidegger's lead in emphasizing that Being is always understood through language and in time but avoids what can be interpreted as the transcendentalism of Heidegger's ontology. Gadamer makes it clear that his interest in Heidegger's thought stems from his success in overcoming the transcendental conception of philosophy propounded by Husserl (1981a:435) and also that it was not until Heidegger's later work (after the '*Kehre*') that Heidegger himself overcame the transcendental conception of self (1981c:195).

Gadamer focuses on three principal elements of Heidegger's approach. First, by using Heidegger's discovery that the horizon of being is time, he avoids the main problem of Husserl's transcendental phenomenology – its ontological groundlessness (1975:227). Husserl's discussion of subject and object takes the subject out of the world as a spectator, one who has no place in the world. Heidegger changes this by freeing understanding from the problem of communication with another person. His fundamental ontology is firmly grounded in the world itself. It pays careful attention to the modes in which human beings exist and the manner in which things are encountered in the world (Ricoeur 1978:152–3). This insight becomes the basis of what Gadamer calls the 'hermeneutics of facticity'. Against Husserl he argues that no freely chosen relationship to one's own being can go beyond the facticity of this being (1975:234). Gadamer later incorporates this element of Heidegger's approach into his own theory under the label of the historicity of understanding. The second element of Heidegger's work that Gadamer utilizes is his concept of the 'fore-structure' of understanding. This element is the basis of Gadamer's concept of 'prejudice', the cornerstone of his particular approach to hermeneutics. Gadamer relies on Heidegger's understanding of 'fore-structure' to advance the claim that the prejudice that is presupposed in all understanding is not arbitrary. As he puts it:

> But understanding achieves its full potentiality only when the fore-meanings that it uses are not arbitrary. Thus it is quite right for the interpreter not to approach the text directly, relying solely on the fore-meaning at once available to him, but rather to examine explicitly the legitimacy, i.e. the origin and validity, of the fore-meanings present within him. (1975:237)

The third element of Heidegger's approach that attracts Gadamer's interest is his conception of the hermeneutic circle. It is significant that, unlike other hermeneutic philosophers, Gadamer does not dwell on the subject of the hermeneutic circle. The reason for this can be found in Heidegger's definition of the concept. Heidegger makes it clear that the hermeneutic circle is not a liability, that is, it is not 'vicious' because it does not describe a methodological problem. Stated in terms of the opposition of subject and object the hermeneutic circle can only appear 'vicious'. Heidegger redescribes the hermeneutic circle, however, as 'an ontological structural element in understanding'. For Heidegger and also for Gadamer the hermeneutic circle is not a 'formal circle', but describes understanding as the interplay of the movement of tradition (Gadamer, 1975:261). Because Gadamer, following Heidegger, defines the hermeneutic circle as a necessary and positive element of the ontology of understanding, not a methodological 'problem' that must be 'solved', there are no extensive discussions of this issue in Gadamer's work. Instead there is an attempt to describe the 'interplay of the movement of tradition' and the consequences that flow from it.

Relying on these elements of Heidegger's approach Gadamer develops his own particular theory of hermeneutical understanding. As was noted above, the cornerstone of that theory is the concept of prejudice, a direct heir to Heidegger's notion of fore-structure. Gadamer identifies prejudice as the concept that 'gives the hermeneutical problem its real thrust' and also that which the tradition of the Enlightenment most seriously misunderstood. He states this departure from Enlightenment thought very explicitly: 'the fundamental prejudice of the enlightenment is the prejudice against prejudice itself which deprives tradition of its power' (1975:239–40). What is needed in the 'new hermeneutics' that Gadamer is proposing is a 'fundamental rehabilitation' of the concept of prejudice and a recognition of the fact that there are legitimate prejudices (1975:246).

Gadamer's theory of prejudice leads him to a discussion of the related concepts of reason and authority. It is his contention that the opposition between reason on the one hand and prejudice and authority on the other, the opposition that is the foundation of Enlightenment thought, is fundamentally wrong. Reason and logic are not, as the Enlightenment thought, 'gifts of God', that is, absolutes that transcend time and space. Reason, rather, 'exists for me only in concrete, historical terms, i.e., it is not its own master but remains constantly dependent on the given circumstances in which it operates' (1975:245). An understanding of the role of prejudice, furthermore, also involves a re-evaluation of the concept of authority. Specifically, it involves the understanding that authority is not based on the surrender of reason but rather on recognition and knowledge. The recognition of authority is always based on the concept that what authority states is not arbitrary but can be shown to be true (1975:249).

Gadamer's connection between the concept of prejudice and the concept of truth is absolutely crucial to an understanding of his definition of hermeneutics but is also one of the most misunderstood aspects of his thought. His basic position is that, far from ruling out the possiblity of truth, the concept of prejudice is the means by which it is established. The connection between prejudice and truth is what Gadamer identifies as the 'positive possibility of prejudice', a connection that he defines in terms of the concept of temporal distance. He first makes the point that there are true and false prejudices, and thus that it is the task of the hermeneutical philosopher not merely passively to accept the role of prejudice in the process of understanding, but actively to examine prejudices. The 'tyranny' of hidden prejudices, he claims, is one of the greatest impediments to understanding (1975:239). The central question of historical hermeneutics is to establish the ground of legitimate prejudices. It is, he states, the 'undeniable task of critical reason' to distinguish legitimate from illegitimate prejudices (1975:246). This task is accomplished through the effect of temporal distance:

> It is only this temporal distance that can solve the really critical question of hermeneutics, namely of distinguishing the true prejudices by which we understand, from the false ones by which we misunderstand. (1975:266)

The claim that Gadamer's position entails relativism, arbitrariness and the abandonment of truth and reason has become one of the stock criticisms of his approach. The problems and ambiguities with Gadamer's position on truth and prejudice will be discussed later. It should be emphasized at this point, however, that these passages establish without question Gadamer's allegiance to the concept of truth and, significantly, even to that of 'critical reason'. For Gadamer the concept of prejudice does not entail a passive surrender to the forces of unreason. Nor does it commit him to a position in which he must accept any passing fancy as legitimate as any other. Central to his position is the assertion that there are true and false prejudices and that it is the task of hermeneutics to make the crucial distinction between them. The assumption that Gadamer must abandon the possibility of truth because he espouses the inevitability of prejudice is based on the acceptance of the Enlightenment dichotomy between prejudice and truth, a dichotomy he has shown to be in error.

Gadamer begins to explain how we fulfil the task of historical hermeneutics by introducing a concept that is closely connected to that of temporal distance: effective historical consciousness (*Wirkungsgeschichtliche Bewusstsein*). When he first discusses this concept it is in the context of his examination of temporal distance and the necessity of historical consciousness in the process of understanding (1975:266). Historical consciousness entails an awareness of the prejudices governing one's own understanding, or, as he puts it, 'Understanding proves to be a kind of effect and knows itself as such' (1975:305). Effective-historical consciousness is the acknowledgement of the fact that the effect of historical events influences our study of them.

Ignoring this necessary element in the act of understanding, a characteristic of scientific method, leads to distortion of knowledge (1975:267–68).

Central to the understanding of effective-historical consciousness is the fact that it has the structure of an experience (1975:310). The attempt to objectify experience, to purge it of all historical elements, is the principal characteristic of scientific method. This objectification, however, misunderstands the fundamental nature of all experience: its inner historicality. In order to establish this point and to reveal the error of the scientific concept of experience, Gadamer suggests that effective-historical consciousness is analogous to the I-Thou relationship that occurs between individuals (1975:323; Palmer, 1969:193). In the I-Thou relationship I open myself to the other; I am dominated by the will to hear rather than to master and I am willing to be modified by the other. Analogously, in historical understanding I open myself to tradition, that is, I let it speak to me, allowing the true meaning hidden in it to become clear. Both the I-Thou situation and effective-historical consciousness involve a dialogic relationship, but while in the I-Thou situation it is a relationship between individuals, in effective-historical consciousness it is a relationship between interpreter and text (cf. Bleicher, 1980:111).

Gadamer identifies the phenomenon that occurs when effective-historical consciousness operates as the 'fusing of horizons'. He defines the concept of horizon, following Nietzsche and Husserl, as the 'range of vision that includes everything that can be seen from a particular vantage point' (1975:269). Gadamer uses this definition to make a strong point against the nineteenth century historicists. These thinkers argued that in order to comprehend past events one must understand them in terms of the historical horizon of those events. What these writers did not understand, however, is that another's historical horizon cannot be understood by abandoning one's own, that is, by adopting an Archimedean point of objectivity. Gadamer argues that not only is such a point of objectivity impossible to achieve but it entails a self-alienation that is the antithesis of understanding. We must already have a horizon in order to understand another's (1975:271). We can only regain the concepts of the historical past by comprehending them through our own concepts (1975:337).

What the historicists misunderstood is that the projecting of an historical horizon is only the first phase in the process of understanding. The second, equally necessary phase is understanding through an appreciation, recognition and examination of one's own historical horizon. The fusing of the two horizons is the successful completion of an act of understanding. Gadamer identifies the conscious act of this fusion as the task of effective-historical consciousness (1975:273–4).

Gadamer's concept of the fusion of horizons is another centerpiece of his theory of hermeneutic understanding. The critics of that theory have pointed to the deficiency of this conception as a principal way of attacking his approach. It is claimed that with this conception he is abandoning the possibility of distinguishing true from false interpretations because neither horizon, neither that of the interpreter nor that of the text, can be clearly specified, and thus 'fusing' them is an incoherent notion. But this criticism misses Gadamer's point in this context. To assert that a horizon is a *range* of meaning entails that it encompasses more than one element, but it also entails that it excludes other elements. In other words horizons are definable. They are not 'incoherent' as Gadamer's critics claim because they have definite boundaries, boundaries set by the prejudices of the time. To say that I understand the horizon of a text from the horizon of my own time does not mean, first, that there is *one* correct interpretation of that text because both horizons constitute a range of meanings, not just one. But, secondly, it does not mean that any interpretation will do. Horizons are *particular* vantage points which, although they encompass a range, are exclusive as well.

Gadamer draws a number of important conclusions from this analysis of the process of understanding. One of the most significant concerns the kind of understanding that occurs in the natural sciences, a position that has radical implications for the role of both the natural and social sciences. One of the principal characteristics of Enlightenment thought, and, in fact, the starting point of the inquiry that Gadamer undertakes in *Truth and Method*, is its glorification of the method of the natural sciences and its exclusive association of truth with that method. Gadamer's exploration of the process of understanding reveals both that glorification and that association to be in error. Far from being the source of all truth and the only method by which it can be obtained, the method of the natural sciences turns out to be a special case, a sort of aberration of the mode of understanding definitive of human life.

Throughout *Truth and Method* Gadamer gives indications of the nature of the peculiarity of the scientific mode of understanding. He claims at the outset that his aim is not to deny the legitimacy of the methods of the natural sciences or to revive the debate between the natural and the social sciences. Yet his remarks on the nature of scientific method call this mode of understanding into question and even cast doubt on the legitimacy of knowledge in the natural sciences (1975:xvii). The main difference between the two kinds of sciences, as Gadamer sees it, concerns the object of their inquiry. In the human sciences the object of inquiry does not exist in itself but is constituted by the motivation of the inquiry (1975:253). It is for this reason that the model of the natural sciences is inapplicable to the social sciences. But in the course of his analysis of the phenomenon of understanding Gadamer discovers that there are several aspects of the universal process of understanding that are missing in the mode of understanding employed in the natural sciences. The first of these is effective-historical consciousness. Declaring first that effective-historical consciousness is a necessary element in all acts of understanding, he claims that 'when a naive faith in scientific method ignores its existence, there can be an actual deformation of knowledge' (1975:268). When Gadamer extends his analysis of effective-historical consciousness to the structure of experience, however, the indictment of scientific knowledge becomes even stronger. Claiming that effective-historical knowledge has the structure of an experience, he argues that the natural sciences' understanding of experience is seriously flawed. In its insistence on the repeatability of experience the natural scientific method removes all historical elements from experience, thus over-simplifying it and missing its 'real character as a process' (1975:316). True experience, he concludes, is experience of one's own historicity, a process which continually shows generalizations to be false (1975:316–21).

These indictments of natural scientific method are not brought into focus very clearly in *Truth and Method*, but in other contexts Gadamer brings his point home forcefully. He claims that he has discovered that, far from offering the model of all truth, the method of the natural sciences has been revealed as a 'special case' of the concept of objectivity (1979:129). Even more conclusively, he states:

> If *Verstehen* is the basic moment of human *In-der-Welt-sein* then the human sciences are nearer to human self-understanding than the natural sciences. The objectivity of the latter is no longer an unequivocal and obligatory ideal of knowledge.
>
> Because the human sciences contribute to human self-understanding even though they do not approach the natural sciences in exactness and objectivity, they do contribute to human self-understanding because they in turn are based in human self-understanding (1979:106).

It is somewhat ironic that what follows from this is that the legitimacy of knowledge in the natural sciences is called into question by the model of understanding characteristic of the human sciences rather than, as the Enlightenment claimed, vice versa. For if, as Gadamer asserts, natural science is rooted in the notion of freedom from bias and prejudice and if prejudice is a necessary component of understanding, then the question of legitimizing knowledge in the natural sciences becomes very problematic (1976a:10).

Gadamer effectively reverses Enlightenment thought on the relationship between the natural and the social sciences with this theory. For the Enlightenment the natural sciences provided a method that alone could lead to truth. For them the social sciences were, by nature, suspect; they could only attain truth by mimicking the scientific method, and whether they were capable of this was regarded as doubtful. Gadamer has now shown that the reverse is true: the model of understanding characteristic of the human sciences is the universal process by which we, as human beings, attain knowledge; that characteristic of the natural sciences, on the other hand, seriously distorts this process, hence calling into question the legitimacy of this mode of understanding.

Gadamer's exploration of the nature of the hermeneutic experience thus leads him to a sweeping reassessment not only of the human sciences but also of the nature of human understanding itself. The importance of that reassessment is expressed in the thesis that has become the guiding principle of Gadamerian hermeneutics: the universality of hermeneutic understanding. For Gadamer, hermeneutics is not just a theory or, worse, a method to be compared with other methods. Rather, it is an examination of the universal process of understanding, and, he claims, a natural human capacity (1981c:114). Gadamer's description of the full implications of the universality of hermeneutics is found in the final part of *Truth and Method* in the context of his discussion of language. The way in which Gadamer moves from the examination of hermeneutics and its history to the discussion of language should, however, be carefully examined because this transition reveals the central thrust of the work and an understanding of why language is so central to his thought.

Toward the end of his discussion of the nature of hermeneutic experience in Part II Gadamer asserts that experience is characterized by what he calls 'openness' and, further, that the highest type of hermeneutical experience is the openness to tradition possessed by effective-historical consciousness (1975:324). From this he concludes that he must now turn to an examination of the logical structure of openness (1975:325). This logical structure, he declares, is to be found in the dialectic of question and answer. The hermeneutic phenomenon contains within itself the original meaning of the structure of question and answer, and thus it follows that the logic of the human sciences whose task it is to examine hermeneutic phenomena is coincident with the logic of the question. For a text to become an object of interpretation it must ask a question of the interpreter. This is not an arbitrary procedure because a question is always related to the answer that is expected in the text. An examination of the dialectic of question and answer reveals, furthermore, that understanding, like conversation, is always a reciprocal relationship (1975:333–40).

This series of arguments culminates in the claim that the further direction of the inquiry must be an analysis of the medium in which conversation takes place, that is, language. The stages of this rapid transition from the hermeneutic experience to the analysis of language are significant. Gadamer's discussion has the following pattern: first, a discussion of the nature of hermeneutic experience; secondly, an examination of the essence of the hermeneutic experience, openness; thirdly, an analysis of the structure of openness, question and answer; and, fourthly, a consideration of the foundation of the relationship of question and answer, conversation. He then concludes that to understand hermeneutical experience we must understand the basis of conversation, language. Each of these topics is complex and could be the subject of a lengthy excursus. Yet Gadamer explores none of them in any depth and, in each case, the importance of the topic is overshadowed by the discovery of the more comprehensive topic that succeeds it. And all of the topics are, in the end, dominated by the overwhelming importance of the subject of language. Gadamer implies that the other examinations are not complete or even possible without an understanding of language.

What emerges from all this is that, to put it most bluntly, nothing really matters except the examination of language and that the assertion of the exclusive and overriding importance of language is the key to a proper interpretation of Gadamer's argument in *Truth and Method*. Although Gadamer discusses a wide range of topics in his book, all of them are ultimately subsumed by the discussion of language. Two conclusions follow from this interpretation: first, to emphasize any of these other topics unduly is to misunderstand Gadamer's thesis of the centrality of language and thus to distort his thought; secondly, in order to assess Gadamer's importance for the human sciences it is necessary to give language the central role in that assessment, for it is in the examination of language that the significance of his approach will be revealed.

The ontological connection: language, truth and reality

Gadamer's discussion of language begins with his remarks about conversation that concluded the analysis of the hermeneutic experience. His first task is to connect the discussion of the linguisticality of understanding and the conversational model with the previous themes of the fusion of horizons and effective-historical consciousness. He asserts that the merging of meaning that goes on in a conversation is an instance of the fusion of horizons and that the linguisticality of understanding is the 'concretation' of effective-historical consciousness (1975:350–1). Gadamer goes on to apply the conversational model to the particular problem of hermeneutics, textual interpretation. Written texts, he claims, present the real hermeneutic task because writing involves self-alienation. Writing is alienated speech that must be transformed back into speech and meaning (1975:354).[5]

It is therefore the analysis of written texts that occupies Gadamer's attention in the subsequent discussion. Understanding a text, he claims, is always an interpretation and all interpretation takes place in the medium of language. Linguistic interpretation, furthermore, is the form of all interpretation, even when what is to be interpreted is not linguistic in nature. Although all forms of interpretation may not be explicitly linguistic, they presuppose language (1975:360). This is due to the fact that tradition itself is linguistic, that is, it exists in the medium of language (1975:351).

This discussion is siginificant because with each step of his argument Gadamer widens the scope of the domain of language. But his next step is the most decisive one: the connection between language and ontology. In what amounts to a paraphrase of Heidegger he states that language has no independent life apart from the world that comes to language within it.[6] Furthermore:

> Not only is the world 'world' only insofar as it comes into language, but language, too, has its real being only in the fact that the world is re-presented within it. Thus the original humanity of language means at the same time the fundamental linguistic quality of man's being-in-the-world. (1975:401)

In another context Gadamer amplifies this by stating that language carries everything with it, not only 'culture' but 'everything (in the world and out of it) is included in the realm of "understanding" and understandability in which we move' (1976a:25). Thus language is not simply a tool that, like many others, human beings put to use. When we take a word in our mouth we are 'fixed in a direction of thought' (1975:496). Words themselves prescribe the only way we can use them; we cannot use them arbitrarily as we might a tool (1976b:96). We become acquainted with the world and even ourselves through language because language is the universal mode of being and knowledge (1975:445; 1976a:62). It follows that animals, who do not have langauge, cannot 'have' a world (1975:411).

If language gives us a world, then the reverse is also true: our world gives us language. Human communities are always linguistic communities. Invented systems of artificial communication are never languages because they have no basis in a community of life (1975:404–5). This communitarian emphasis in Gadamer's understanding of language informs an aspect of his discussion that is of central importance: the contention that language is 'I-less'. Language is always the sharing of a common meaning (1975:260). Whoever speaks a language that no one else understands literally does not speak (1976a:65). This thesis substantiates a point that Gadamer had made earlier in connection with his critique of nineteenth century historicism, his assertion that we need not go back to the subjectivity of an author in order to understand a text (1975:260). Gadamer can now reinforce this point by asserting that it is more correct to say that language speaks us rather than we speak it. It follows that the time at which a text was written can be determined more exactly from its linguistic usage than from the subjective intention of its author (1975:421). Understanding is not a mysterious communion of souls in which the interpreter grasps the subjective intention of the author. Rather, it is a fusion of the author's horizon with that of the interpreter.[7]

Much has been made of this ontological connection in Gadamer's work. In contrast to the epistemological preoccupation of much of contemporary philosophy, Gadamer follows Heidegger in focusing on ontology rather than epistemology, that is, claiming that understanding is a mode of being not a mode of knowledge. For some contemporary thinkers this move renders Gadamer's work, along with Heidegger's, incoherent (Giddens, 1976:62). For others it is the only proper move because epistemology necessarily presupposes ontology (Jung, 1979:59). Gadamer himself justifies the move by pointing out that the epistemological preoccupation of Enlightenment thought led it to misconceive the process of understanding fundamentally. Gadamer's approach to ontology, as was noted above, is firmly rooted in language and, derivatively, history. Following Heidegger he claims that language is the key to ontology, that it is the 'House of Being'. But because he avoids the transcendentalism and, by implication, absolutism, that characterizes Heidegger's early approach to ontology, Gadamer succeeds in avoiding many of the pitfalls attendant on investigations into ontology. Ontological investigations into ontology, like epistemological analysis, can fall into objectivism (Oliver, 1983:543). By approaching ontology through language and history Gadamer carefully avoids an approach to ontology that presupposes an Archimedean point of objectivity. But he also avoids the opposite error of reifying language. He firmly rejects the notion that '"everything" is only language and language event' (1975:xxii). In short, Gadamer's approach has the advantage of Heidegger's ontological perspective in that it overcomes the obsession with epistemology that characterizes much of nineteenth- and twentieth-century approaches, but it also avoids the errors of traditional ontological investigations because of its emphasis on language and history.

Gadamer's thesis of the linguisticality of understanding and the connection between langauage and ontology provides him with a perspective on a number of issues central to an understanding of the human sciences. One of the most significant of these issues is that of objectivity. Gadamer's radical reassessment of the relationship between the natural and the social sciences necessitates an equally radical redefinition of 'objectivity' in both the human sciences and hermeneutic interpretation itself. The question of Gadamer's stance on objectivity has been one of the principal points of criticism of his work. Because of his alleged 'retreat' on the question of objectivity Gadamer has been accused of being a relativist, a historicist and a subjectivist. That he is none of these because he rejects the epistemological presuppositions on which these charges rest can be established by looking carefully at his comments on objectivity in *Truth and Method*. Although Gadamer is sharply critical of the natural science's approach to objectivity he does not reject out of hand the 'objective situation' of the natural sciences, arguing, rather, that it is 'one of the relativities embraced by langauge's relation to the world' (1975:408). His main point is that this 'special case' is not, as the Enlightenment claimed, the only method by which truth can be obtained. Gadamer's attitude toward the definition of objectivity in the human sciences is not as easily discerned, however. When he uses the word 'objectivity' in connection with the human sciences he frequently puts the word in quotes, calling attention to the fact that it is a word that is inapplicable to the subject matter of these sciences. In a significant passage he uses the word in this way to combat the charge of arbitrariness:

> The only 'objectivity' here is the confirmation of a fore-meaning in its being worked out. The only thing that characterises the arbitrariness of inappropriate fore-meanings is that they come to nothing in the working-out. (1975:237)

Gadamer defines the 'central task' of a truly historical hermeneutics as the examination of prejudice and the distinguishing of legitimate from illegitimate prejudices, a task that is accomplished through the use of 'critical reason' (1975:246). Gadamer's reference to reason in this context is easily misunderstood. He is not claiming as the critical rationalists do that reason transcends language, that is, that it constitutes an a-historical standard by which all cultural products can be assessed. He makes this very clear in a preceding passage in which he states that 'Reason exists for us only in concrete, historical terms, i.e., it is not its own master but remains constantly dependent on the given circumstances in which it operates' (1975:245). It does not follow from this, however, that we must abandon reason in our quest for truth. Later he states:

> The work of understanding and interpretation always remains meaningful. This shows the superior universality with which reason rises above the limitations of any given language. The hermeneutical experience is the corrective by means of which the thinking reason escapes the prison of language, and it is itself constituted linguistically. (1975:363)

This passage is also very difficult to interpret. Having rejected the omnipotence of reason in the previous passage, Gadamer now appears to be celebrating its 'superior universality' in a manner reminiscent of the Enlightenment. In other passages he talks in terms of achieving the 'right horizon of meaning' (1975:269) and attaining a 'higher universality' in the process of understanding because we overcome both our own particularity and that of the other (1975:272). The seeming contradiction here can only be explained by remembering that the thrust of Gadamer's reassessment of Enlightenment thought is to challenge the standard epistemological dichotomies on which it is based. In this case this means that he rejects the notion that we must choose reason *or* prejudice. He asserts instead that we need not abandon reason and even its 'superior universality' despite the fact that we claim the universality of prejudice in understanding.

Even on the most charitable reading what Gadamer offers is a very ambiguous definition of 'objectivity' in the human sciences.[8] Pointing to Gadamer's lack of specificity on this issue many of his critics have claimed that his position entails that 'anything goes' – that one interpretation is just as good as any other.[9] Against these critics it can be argued that although Gadamer's position on objectivity is problematic, it is nevertheless defensible. Two difficulties with his approach stand out: first, his use of the word 'objectivity' and, secondly, his lack of specificity on the criteria by which 'true' and 'false' prejudices can be distinguished. Answers to both these issues can, however, be reconstructed from a Gadamerian perspective. With regard to the first issue the best solution is simply to discard the word itself. The term 'objectivity' connotes precisely the subject-object dichotomy that Gadamer wants to reject. His position would be much stronger (and more consistent) if he were straightforwardly to reject this term together with the epistemology from which it derives. What Gadamer means to express through his use of the word 'objectivity', however, is a coherent and defensible position: that hermeneutical investigations in the human sciences are not arbitrary. To claim that something is not arbitrary is, for the Enlightenment, to claim that it is 'objective'. It is understandable then that Gadamer, in his attempt to reject arbitrariness, resorts to the use of the word 'objectivity'. In doing so, however, he thereby falls prey to the very epistemology he has taken such pains to reject. But although this is an important semantic error, it is not an irredeemable one.

If Gadamer's aim is to establish the non-arbitrary nature of hermeneutical investigations then this leads to the second question posed above: if interpretations are not arbitrary then criteria must exist by which true can be distinguished from false, correct from incorrect. In this regard, Gadamer is again not specific. He clearly wants to make these distinctions but he does not indicate precisely how they can be made. An answer to this question, however, is implicit in his approach. True prejudices can be distinguished from false prejudices by appeal to the commonly shared meanings that constitute the human linguistic community. True prejudices are always self-reflexive, that is, they reveal us to ourselves; they are prejudices that constitute our way of life and our self-understanding. False prejudices do not meet these criteria. As Gadamer puts it, 'they come to nothing in the working out.' The statement that the criteria by which we judge true from false are those supplied by the shared understanding of the linguistic community is not, furthermore, one that is unique to Gadamer. Many twentieth century philosophers have argued precisely this point. Indeed, it is difficult to imagine where these criteria would come from if not from this common base. The existence of these criteria entails that interpretations are not arbitrary, but it does not entail that they are 'objective' in the Enlightenment's sense. To call something objective is to presuppose that the observer assumes an Archimedean point apart from those observed. What Gadamer's position requires, is that the interpreter is situated in history and time and that this situatedness is what protects against arbitrariness. Hermeneutic investigations are neither arbitrary nor 'objective' but are constituted by the self-reflexive analysis of prejudice from within a human linguistic community.

Thus, although Gadamer himself does not offer a coherent position on the 'objectivity' of the human sciences, his approach does offer a means by which the charge of arbitrariness can be refuted. This conclusion is not only significant in light of the general criticisms of Gadamer's work noted above, but it can also be used to refute a more specific charge, the claim that, by denying that the meaning of a text is fixed by the author's intention, Gadamer must relinquish the notion of a correct interpretation. With regard to this issue Gadamer's position entails, first, that what determines the meaning of a text is the fusion of the two horizons of meaning – that of the interpreter and that of the text – and that we can determine the horizon of meaning for both participants in the interpretation. Secondly, it entails that we do not determine the correct interpretation by identifying subjective intentions. Rather, the correctness of an interpretation lies in its conformity to the horizon of meaning from which the interpretation is made and the prejudices that constitute that horizon.

Gadamer's position on language and ontology also provides him with a perspective on two issues closely related to that of objectivity: reality and truth. Gadamer does not deny, as some have claimed, that no 'reality' exists outside language.[10] What he does claim is, first, that our encounter with the reality of the world is always through language and that 'every linguistic experience of the world is experience of the the world, not experience of language' (1975:495). This position has important implications for the debate between Gadamer and Habermas as well as for the comparison between Gadamer's approach and Wittgensteinian social science; it will be discussed more fully in those contexts. In this context, however, it should be noted that it is only those who define langauge narrowly who see a gulf between language and reality. Gadamer's analysis reveals that the dichotomy between language and reality, another product of Enlightenment epistemology, stands in the way of understanding and must be discarded.

Gadamer's position on the question of truth also involves discarding a dichotomy and questioning a connection that is central to Enlightenment thought. In opposition to the dichotomy between truth and prejudice Gadamer argues that truth does not involve the rejection of prejudice. But he is even more forceful in his argument that the Enlightenment's connection between truth and scientific method is erroneous. His clearest statement of this comes in the conclusion to *Truth and Method*:

> Thus there is undoubtedly no understanding that is free of all prejudices, however much the will of our knowledge must be directed towards escaping their thrall. It has emerged throughout our investigation that the certainty that is imparted by the use of scientific methods does not suffice to guarantee truth. This is so especially of the human sciences, but this does not mean a diminution of their scientific quality, but, on the contrary, the justification of the claim to special humane significance that they have always made. The fact that in the knowing involved in them the knower's own being is involved marks, certainly, the limitation of 'method'; but not that of science. Rather, what the tool of method does not achieve must – and effectively can – be achieved by a discipline of questioning and research, a discipline that guarantees truth. (1975:446–7)

Gadamer's separation of truth and method has inevitably led to charges of relativism as well as ambiguity and inconsistency.[11] It is argued that unless we have (methodological) criteria of truth we cannot distinguish truth from untruth. Gadamer confronts this argument in two ways. First, he transcends the dichotomy on which it rests, replacing the opposition between truth and prejudice with the assertion that prejudice – our situatedness in history and time – is the precondition of truth, not an obstacle to it. Secondly, he argues that truth is not something achieved by adherence to methodological guidelines. Rather, it is something that happens to us: 'In understanding we are drawn into an event of truth and arrive, as it were, too late, if we want to know what we ought to believe' (1975:446). We are drawn in, furthermore, by tradition and through the medium of language; it is thus through the examination of language that we are able to understand the event of truth in the human sciences. Once more Gadamer's conclusion is that language is the key that unlocks the door to understanding.[12] The criteria by which we distinguish true from false are found not in 'method' but in the common understandings of the linguistic community and in our critical examination of and openness to tradition.

II GADAMER AND WITTGENSTEINIAN SOCIAL SCIENCE

Language and the social sciences

The theses that Gadamer establishes in *Truth and Method* provide an understanding of the social sciences that is directly relevant to what is commonly acknowledged as the current crisis in social theory. The best way to establish this argument is to present a comparison between Gadamer's position and two other approaches that seek to provide the social sciences with a means of transcending their current problems: Wittgensteinian social science and Habermas' critical theory. Although these two approaches are by no means the only contenders in the present struggle for ascendancy in the social sciences, they are the most relevant to the thesis that is being argued here. Furthermore, like Gadamer's approach, they have both been labelled branches of 'hermeneutical' social science (Howard, 1982). A comparison between Gadamer's position and these two approaches reveals, however, that, although for very different reasons, neither of these two approaches provides the social sciences with the self-understanding appropriate to its current problems.

The comparison between Gadamer's approach and that of Wittgensteinian social science is, at least on one level, easy to facilitate. The similarities between Gadamer and Wittgenstein on the role of language in human social life and, hence, in the human sciences, are striking. But the approaches exhibit a number of contrasts as well. Gadamer approaches some of the problems of language and the social sciences in a manner that is subtly yet significantly different from that of Wittgenstein's followers. As a consequence of these differences Gadamer's approach avoids some of the key problems of the Wittgensteinian approach, problems that have stood in the way of its acceptance as a viable social theory.

Both Gadamer and Wittgenstein are caught up in what has been identified as the 'linguistic turn' in twentieth-century philosophy and it is this common concern with language that defines the similarity between them. But the similarity goes deeper than a mere agreement on subject matter. Both Gadamer and Wittgenstein see language as intimately connected to and even constitutive of human social life. This dictates a number of significant parallels between the two approaches. First, language always entails a way of living for Wittgenstein, a 'form of life', a position that is similar to the communitarian emphasis of Gadamer's approach to language that was detailed above. Secondly, Gadamer's point that language is not like a tool that can be set aside after use is one that Wittgenstein echoes in very similar words. Third, Wittgenstein's famous description of language games finds its counterpart in Gadamer's approach. Like Wittgenstein, Gadamer describes language as a 'game' because, like a game, language is something we enter into, an activity that we share (1975:446; 1976b:62–3, 210–11).

But although these similarities between the accounts of language offered by Gadamer and Wittgenstein are significant, the differences between the two accounts are also quite evident. The first difference is one of particular importance to the social sciences: the approach to the possibility of mediation between language games. Because Gadamer's theory of language is rooted in a theory of interpretation, a central aspect of his approach is an analysis of the nature and function of mediation. The interpreter is, of course, unavoidably involved in translation between langauges. Gadamer defines the task of the interpreter, and thus of hermeneutics itself, as the bridging of personal or historical distance between minds (1976b:95). Wittgenstein, in contrast, has very little to say about this issue, a silence that has not gone unnoticed by his critics (Apel, 1981:249).

It is another aspect of Gadamer's theory of language, however, that represents the most significant contrast between his approach and that of Wittgenstein. It has been shown that following Heidegger, Gadamer defines language in ontological terms. He concurs with Heidegger's central thesis that language is the 'House of Being' and that 'being that can be understood is language.' Although Gadamer avoids the transcendentalism implicit in Heidegger's approach the emphasis on ontology is nevertheless a central aspect of his thought. This view of language, however, conflicts with the primary thrust of Wittgenstein's theory. Although both Gadamer and Wittgenstein see language as the central fact of human life, constitutive of the form of life we know as human, and although both characterize language as a game, a shared activity that we enter into and are encompassed by, Gadamer's ontological definition of language nevertheless provides a sharp contrast to Wittgenstein's essentially epistemological approach. Wittgenstein's interest in language is dictated by the thesis that we can know nothing of that which is beyond language because it is a realm about which we cannot speak. This contrast between the two positions is best illustrated by the different ways in which Gadamer and Wittgenstein define the concept 'language game'. Wittgenstein refers to language as a game in order to emphasize that language is constitutive of human activity, that human beings 'do things with words'. Gadamer's position, however, can best be characterized by the statement, 'words do things with us.' He uses the game analogy to point out that it is not the case that *we* play games, but rather, that games play *us*. He argues that the same is true of langauge:

> Strictly speaking, it is not a matter of our making use of words when we speak. Though we 'use' words, it is not in the sense that we put a given tool to use as we please. Words themselves prescribe the only ways in which we can put them to use. One refers to that as proper 'usage' – something which does not depend on use, but rather we on it, since we are not allowed to violate it. (1976a:93)

Wittgenstein, like many of the other nineteenth and twentieth century philosophers that Gadamer criticizes is still caught up in the epistemological concerns that dominated Enlightenment thought. Although he transcends many of the Enlightenment dichotomies, he fails to make the crucial move from epistemology to ontology that Gadamer has effected. Because Wittgenstein and Gadamer differ in this respect their approaches to social scientific methodology diverge in ways that are significant for contemporary social theory.

Gadamerian hermeneutics and Wittgensteinian social science: a comparison[13]

The most striking similarity between the approaches to the social sciences dictated by Gadamer and Wittgenstein is one that has been frequently noted in criticism of both their approaches: the 'failure' to provide the social theorist with an Archimedean point ouside the social actors' linguistically constituted world by which that world can be assessed. It has been argued that by concentrating exclusively on linguistic understandings both Gadamer and Wittgenstein deny the reflective element that is a necessary component of social science. Albrecht Wellmer has summarized this point very succinctly in his commentary on the two approaches:

> Hermeneutic and linguistic philosophers have denied the (epistemological) possibility of developing a theory which would allow us to reconstruct historical developments and social changes by systematically transcending the self–interpretation of a society and its individuals. They have denied, i.e., the possibility of reconstructing historical processes taking place 'in back' of individual agents who systematically deceive themselves about their mutual social relations and about the meaning of their own action. (1976:253)

In his reply to this criticism, Gadamer, like the Wittgensteinians, freely admits his 'failure' in this respect. His rebuttal, furthermore, has much in common with the replies of the Wittgensteinians to similar attacks. Like Wittgenstein, Gadamer claims that the limits of language are the limits of our world. In his debate with Habermas, Gadamer argues that the claim that the social actors' 'linguistically articulated consciousness' must be supplemented with an analysis of the realities of work and domination is meaningless. Gadamer's principal argument against Habermas, as was noted above, is simply to ask for the justification of this claim to 'reality' transcending the actors' concepts (1975:495; 1971b:68–70; 1971a:242).

This fundamental agreement between Gadamer and the Wittgensteinians that we live in a linguistically constituted world has a number of important implications for the methodological position entailed by each approach. Since both Gadamer and the Wittgensteinians insist on the linguisticality of the social world, it follows that both define analysis in the human sciences as exclusively linguistic analysis. The insistence that, as Winch puts it, language and social relations are two sides of the same coin, has elicited strong objections in the social scientific community. A Gadamerian approach, however, would logically adopt the same position. Both Gadamer and the Wittgensteinians explicitly reject the quest for the natural scientist's definition of 'objective knowledge' in the social sciences and deny that the model offered by the natural sciences is appropriate to inquiry in the social sciences. The arguments that Gadamer offers in support of his position, furthermore, are remarkably similar to those of the Wittgensteinians. Gadamer's attack on the Enlightenment's transcendental definition of reason has much in common with Wittgenstein's point that logic is not a 'gift of God'. And Gadamer asserts, together with Winch, that the distinction between the natural and social sciences rests on the fact that the objects of these sciences are constituted in radically different ways (Gadamer, 1975:245–3; Winch, 1958:133).

A second major similarity between the position of Gadamer and that taken by the Wittgensteinian social scientists is their common refusal to discuss subjective intentionality. This refusal is, for both positions, rooted in the assumption that 'understanding' does not entail reference to mental events. Gadamer makes his position on this issue very clear in *Truth and Method*. His position that the meaning of a text is not dependent on the subjective intention of the author has, furthermore, become a hallmark of his hermeneutic theory (Palmer, 1969:185). It is likewise a hallmark of the Wittgensteinian position. One of the main theses of the works of both Winch and Louch is their insistence that subjective mental events cannot be discussed intelligibly and are therefore not a possible subject matter for the social sciences. The basic thesis of their approach to social analysis is that what Weber labelled 'subjective meaning' is publicly available data expressed in the ordinary language concepts of the social actors. Initially, this position was articulated in opposition to the *verstehen* tradition of Dilthey and Weber (Winch 1958:111–20). Today it is more likely to be cast in terms of opposition to Schutz's social phenomenology or ethnomethodology (Roche, 1973).[14] This position is, furthermore, one of the most distinctive and controversial aspects of the Wittgensteinian approach.

In the context of contemporary social theory the refusal to discuss subjective intentionality represents an important commonality between Gadamer and the Wittgensteinians. The significance of this commonality is best illustrated by reference to the on-going debate between Gadamer and Eric Hirsch on the role of authorial intention. Hirsch objects to Gadamer's position on the grounds that, by rejecting the author's intention as the basis for textual interpretation, Gadamer obviates the possibility of the objective interpretation of texts. He claims that Gadamer's theory, which he labels 'semantic autonomy', makes it impossible to judge one interpretation 'better' than another. Instead, in Gadamer's view, critics become paramount. Hirsch's counter to Gadamer centers on the distinction between meaning and significance. He defines the meaning of a text as what the author means to say, its significance as the relationship between that meaning and a person, conception, or situation. Thus, although Hirsch claims that the meaning of a text is fixed and 'objective' because it is determined by the author's intention, its significance may vary depending on specific conditions or questions of interpretation (Hirsch, 1967:4–10).

It should be clear from the preceding discussion of Gadamer's hermeneutics that he is not a proponent of 'semantic autonomy' as it is understood by Hirsch. Although Gadamer rejects the claim that subjective intentions fix the meaning of a text he does not espouse either of the major versions of semantic autonomy: the appeal to 'timeless truths' or the claim that interpreters alone determine textual meaning. The position of semantic autonomy denies the dialectical character of interpretation by claiming that the interpreter determines meaning; Hirsch also denies this dialectic by claiming that the author fixes meaning. Gadamer rejects both these positions by asserting that interpretation is the fusing of *both* horizons – that of the author and that of the interpreter. He thus transcends the limitations of both positions.

From the perspective of Gadamer's theory of understanding Hirsch's position is hardly a new one. Hirsch, like the historicists, fails to see that the determination of what he calls the 'meaning' of a text is a dialectical process. Rather, he assumes that interpreters can discover the author's intention from a position of objectivity free from the historical influences of their culture. The importance of Hirsch's criticism in this context, however, lies not in its novelty but in the fact that it highlights the commonality between Gadamer's approach and that of the Wittgensteinians. Although Hirsch's notion of intentionality is, as David Hoy points out, philosophically unclear, it can nevertheless be asserted that what Hirsch *seems* to be arguing is that the determination of authorial meaning entails recourse to subjectivity and consciousness (Hoy, 1978:29).[15] Appealing to Husserl's distinction between 'inner' and 'outer' horizons, Hirsch argues that 'objectivity in textual interpretation requires explicit reference to the speaker's subjectivity' (1967:224–37).

The fact that both Gadamer and the Wittgensteinians eschew reference to the speaker's subjectivity leads them to assume two common positions of considerable importance for the methodology of the social science. In the first place, it entails that both approaches avoid the error of assuming that the social actor's subjective intentions are the 'objective facts' of the social sciences that parallel those of the natural sciences. Thus they also avoid the error of mimicking the methods of the natural sciences by searching for those 'objective facts' that would make social science truly 'scientific'. Hirsch, on the contrary, makes this error in the most blatant way. Having argued that the author's subjective intention provides the social sciences with their objective data, he concludes:

> The identity of genre, pre-understanding, and hypothesis suggests that the much-advertized cleavage between thinking in the sciences and the humanities does not exist. The hypothetico-deductive process is fundamental in both of them, as it is in all thinking that aspires to knowledge. (1967:246)

The second common position dictated by the rejection of subjective intentionality is equally significant. By emphasizing the essentially intersubjective nature of understanding, both Gadamer and Wittgenstein place the human sciences squarely in the common world of human practices rather than in the shadowy private world of individual subjectivity. Gunnell has noted that Gadamer, along with Wittgenstein, is part of a movement in the human sciences away from seeing discourse as representing the ideas and thoughts of speakers. These thinkers, on the contrary, see the distinction between language and thought as untenable (Gunnell, 1979:116–17). The methodological convergence between Gadamer and the Wittgensteinians, furthermore, can be traced to their basic agreement on the definition of langauge: both define language as public discourse rather than the translation of inner discourse. It is this agreement between Gadamer and Wittgenstein on the public nature of language that, more than any other factor, accounts for the significant similarities exhibited by the approaches to the social sciences generated by their theories.[16]

It is therefore somewhat paradoxical to discover that it is their difference with regard to the issue of language that accounts for the most serious opposition between the two approaches. It was noted above that Gadamer's ontological approach to the study of language diverges from the Wittgensteinians' epistemological approach. This difference is significant for the social scientific methodology entailed by each position. The first point of difference concerns an issue that is fundamental to the basic argument that Gadamer presents in *Truth and Method*: the proper relationship between the natural and social sciences. One of Gadamer's foremost goals in *Truth and Method* is to remove what might be termed the 'inferiority complex' of the social sciences. Gadamer accomplishes this goal by arguing that because the subject matter of the human sciences, human understanding, is a precondition for all knowing, the human sciences are logically prior to the natural sciences.

On the face of it, it may seem that this view is not noticeably different from that espoused by the Wittgensteinians. Like Gadamer, the Wittgensteinians take great pains to distinguish the social from the natural sciences. But the Wittgensteinians' position differs from Gadamer's in a number of important ways. Although the Wittgensteinians clearly reject the view that the social sciences must mimic the model of the natural sciences, they, like Dilthey, implicitly accept the model of 'objective knowledge' employed by the natural sciences. Both Winch and Louch devote a significant portion of their analyses to proving that this model is not an appropriate one for the social sciences (Louch, 1966:163). But their analyses do not go beyond this negative point. Gadamer argues that the 'understanding' that is the subject matter of the human sciences precedes and makes possible the special form of knowledge characteristic of the natural sciences, effectively turning the tables on the natural sciences. Winch and Louch, in contrast, do not move beyond the narrow methodological point that the method of the natural sciences cannot be utilized in the social sciences. They fail, in other words, to provide a positive basis for the social sciences because they remain caught in the methodological disputes characteristic of nineteenth century hermeneutics, the diputes so sternly castigated in *Truth and Method*.

By rejecting the epistemological approach characteristic not only of Wittgensteinian social science but of Enlightenment thought in general, Gadamer provides the social sciences with a radically new self-understanding. Gadamer's linguistic-ontological approach to the definition of the human sciences moreover, offers a position that avoids some of the central criticisms that have been raised against the Wittgensteinian approach. A wide range of objections to Wittgensteinian social science has been advanced, but three basic lines of criticism stand out: first, the implicit relativism and nominalism of the Wittgensteinian approach; secondly, the monadic character of language game analysis; and, thirdly, the a-historical nature of Wittgensteinian analysis. Gadamer's linguistic-ontological definition of the human sciences offers a refutation of each of these criticisms not available to the Wittgensteinians.

The charge that the Wittgensteinian approach to the social sciences results in the 'total relativism' of social science has been most vehemently and eloquently stated by Ernst Gellner. Gellner declares that for most philosophers relativism is a problem, but for Wittgenstein and Winch it is a solution (1974:19–49). His argument is simply that the Wittgensteinian approach is unavoidably relativistic and thus an unacceptable basis for investigation in the social sciences. The nominalism of the Wittgensteinians also draws his fire. Analysis in the social sciences, Gellner claims, cannot be limited to the examination of 'mere words'. It must, on the contrary, be concerned with the 'reality' of social relations.

The Wittgensteinians' reply to these charges has been to argue the epistemological point that words form the boundary of what can be discussed, intelligibly and that to posit a realm of 'reality' beyond that which is linguistically constituted is to posit a reality about which we cannot speak. Although Gadamer would agree with this argument, his perspective supplies him with more substantive arguments against the charges of relativism and nominalism. First, and most importantly, Gadamer argues that relativism, or, in his words, prejudice, is not a 'problem' to be 'solved' but is the ontological condition of man in the world. By clearly revealing the error of identifying objective knowledge with freedom from prejudice, Gadamer reveals that Gellner's criticism is fundamentally misconceived. His approach also supplies a refutation of the charge of nominalism. For Gadamer language is central to understanding because being is revealed in language. The charge that the human sciences study 'mere words' thus becomes meaningless.[17]

The second criticism, the charge that Wittgenstein sees language games as monadic entities not subject to translation, is one that has figured prominently in Habermas's work and is best approached by referring to his comparative critique of Wittgenstein and Gadamer. Habermas argues that Gadamer's position is less relativistic than that of Wittgenstein because Gadamer emphasizes the 'porousness' of language games. While Gadamer's hermeneutic analysis focuses on the mediating function of language games, Wittgenstein, in contrast, defines language games as untranslatable (Gadamer, 1970:252 ff.; Apel, 1980b:23–33). Habermas uses this contrast between the two positions to argue for the superiority of Gadamer's view. But although Habermas has identified a valid difference between the positions of Gadamer and Wittgenstein, his argument must be carefully qualified. Although pointing to the monadic character of Wittgenstein's language games has become a stock criticism of his approach (Gellner, 1974:24; MacIntyre, 1974:71; Wellmer, 1971:30), this position has been attributed to Wittgenstein largely on the basis of his silence on this issue. Nowhere does Wittgenstein explicitly reject the possibility of translation between language games; the question simply never comes up. Although in some of his work Winch seems to deny the possibility of translation between language games, his position on this issue is less than clear.[18] Gadamer, in contrast, deals explicitly with the problem of translation throughout his work. The analysis of how translation or interpretation occurs is, in fact, the cornerstone of his theory of hermeneutics. But the reason for his interest in this issue should be clear. His approach to the human sciences emerges from the hermeneutic tradition of the translation of texts, a tradition that inevitably focuses on the problems raised by the process of translation. The opposition between Gadamer and Wittgenstein on this issue thus, represents less an explicit contrast between the two positions than a difference in emphasis rooted in the diverse traditions from which each position derives.

Much the same point can be made with regard to the third issue, also a frequently noted difference between Gadamer and Wittgenstein: the fact that Gadamer, unlike Wittgenstein, stresses the historicality of language, and, consequently, understanding. Habermas, makes much of this difference, praising Gadamer for his 'dialectical' account of tradition (1970:261 ff.). The difference between Gadamer and Wittgenstein on this issue has been exaggerated, however. Gadamer's emphasis on the historicality of understanding does, as Habermas claims, add an important dimension to language analysis. Although this dimension is, strictly speaking, lacking in many ordinary language discussions, it is not by any means in conflict with the basic assumptions of the approach. Winch and Louch have been frequently criticized for adopting an a-historical approach. But the work of others, whose perspective can broadly be defined as Wittgensteinian, suggests that a historical dimension is quite compatible with Wittgensteinian social science.[19] The difference between the two approaches, is again one of emphasis rather than incompatibility.

The significance of the dispute over the issues of translation and historicality is two-sided. Although the differences between the two positions on both issues have been overrated, Gadamer's emphasis on the issues of translation and the historicality of understanding still represent aspects of his approach that are particularly well suited to the necessities of social scientific analysis. They also represent, unfortunately, aspects that have been largely ignored by Wittgensteinian social scientists. The fact that the Wittgensteinian approach has been accused of ignoring the problems raised by the issues of translation and historicality has, furthermore, stood in the way of its acceptance as a viable methodology of the social sciences.

This comparison between the approaches to the social sciences dictated by the thought of Gadamer and Wittgenstein highlights a number of issues that are important in the present context. First, it reveals the liabilities of Wittgensteinian social science and why this approach has failed to provide a solution to the current 'crisis' of the social sciences. The radical critique of objectivism that Gadamer offers in *Truth and Method* reveals that the Wittgensteinians, despite their firm rejection of positivist social science, are rooted in the futile dichotomies of the positivist-humanist debate. Despite the strength of Wittgenstein's theory of language it is still caught up in the subject-object dichotomy that is characteristic of the Enlightenment theory of knowledge (Christopher Smith, 1979:306). Gadamer's rejection of this dichotomy, on the other hand, allows an entirely different approach to knowledge and understanding. It provides a means of transcending the epistemological assumption that knowledge is the product of the interaction between subject and object. It is this view of knowledge, as Gadamer shows in *Truth and Method*, that dooms the social sciences to subjectivity and exclusion from the realm of truth.

Secondly, the comparison reveals that the Wittgensteinians implicitly accept the definitions of 'science' and 'truth' that are characteristic of Enlightenment thought. Like other anti-positivist critics of the social sciences in recent decades, the Wittgensteinians do not challenge the Enlightenment's claim that truth is the exclusive product of the scientific method. They argue only that this method is inappropriate to the social sciences. It is one of Gadamer's greatest achievements in *Truth and Method* to show the futility of this argument and to offer a radical critique of Enlightenment thought that establishes the priority of the human sciences through an examination of the fundamental nature of human understanding.

Thirdly, this comparison shows that the Gadamerian approach to the social sciences contains elements that are particularly important for the kind of analyses that social scientists encounter in their work. Gadamer's emphasis on the historicality of understanding provides a necessary dimension to analysis in the social sciences. The Wittgensteinian's failure to emphasize historicality has proved to be a serious liability of their approach. Likewise, the Gadamerian emphasis on translation is especially relevant to problems that arise in social scientific analysis. Gadamer's assumption that translation is a necessary and integral part of all interpretation and, hence, all understanding, obviates the difficulty caused by Wittgenstein's position on the monadic character of language games. More importantly, it shows that communication between different cultures and different time periods is possible without presupposing an Archimedean point of objectivity.

In conclusion, it can be seen that the linguistic-ontological approach of Gadamer offers significant advantages to the social sciences even in comparison with the closely related anti-positivist approach of the Wittgensteinians. Because Wittgensteinian social science does not go far enough in rejecting the presuppositions of positivist social science it cannot offer a viable alternative to this approach. In contrast, Gadamer, because he challenges the Enlightenment–positivist conception of truth and knowledge at its very roots, can and does offer such an alternative.

III THE GADAMER–HABERMAS DEBATE

The debate between Gadamer and Habermas over the status of the social sciences has been a staple of German academic life for over a decade.[20] Many of the issues in this debate are central to the present discussion of Gadamer's relevance for the social sciences. Habermas directly attacks Gadamer's anti-foundational approach and counters it with one that, he claims, avoids the pitfalls of Enlightenment thought while retaining its advantages. Whether Habermas's claim can be substantiated thus is particularly germane to the argument for Gadamer's position.

The critique that Habermas advances against Gadamer is an exceedingly subtle one. Unlike many of Gadamer's other critics, Habermas does not simply dismiss Gadamer as a relativist.[21] He and Gadamer share a fundamental orientation that establishes a bond between them: the critique of instrumental reason (Habermas, 1983:196). Habermas makes it clear that he has much respect for the hermeneutic position and, furthermore, that he sees it as superior to both Wittgensteinian language analysis and phenomenology, the other 'interpretive' approaches that have gained popularity in recent years (Habermas, 1970). From the perspective of hermeneutics, he claims, phenomenology and linguistic analysis fall into the error of historicism (1977:344). Habermas sees hermeneutics as introducing a dimension of language analysis missing in the work of the later Wittgenstein: historicality. He observes that, in contrast to Wittgenstein, Gadamer re-introduced the unity of langauge that is established 'dialectically in the context of tradition' (1977:340).

Habermas also finds another aspect of Gadamer's approach particularly noteworthy: its 'self-reflexivity'. Unlike ordinary language analysis, Gadamer's approach makes use of the 'self-transcendence embedded in linguistic practice'. In a passage that echoes Gadamer's statement about the role of reason in language, Habermas states:

> Languages themselves possess the potential of a reason that, while expressing itself in the particularity of a specific grammer, simultaneously reflects on its limits and negates them as particular. Although always bound up in langauge, reason always transcends particular languages; it lives in language only by destroying the particularities of language through which alone it is incarnated. (1977:336)

Thus, as Habermas sees it, philosophical hermeneutics is 'useful' to the social sciences because the self-reflection fostered by hermeneutics reveals to the social sciences the errors of both objectivist social science and ordinary language analysis (1980:186–7).

Habermas asserts, however, that the hermeneutical perspective also has serious limitations for the social sciences. Although hermeneutic self-reflection allows for the transcendence of particular language games, it does not, as he sees it, take this transcendence far enough. Gadamer takes the position that we cannot, in his words, 'transcend the dialogue which we are'. Against this Habermas argues that 'Hermeneutic consciousness remains incomplete as long as it does not include a reflection upon the limits of hermeneutic understanding' (1980:190). This statement and many others like it that can be found scattered throughout Habermas' work represent the fundamental point of disagreement between Habermas and Gadamer. In the simplest terms this means that Habermas rejects Gadamer's claim of the universality of hermeneutic understanding, asserting that there is something beyond the 'dialoque that we are'. Gadamer, on the other hand, asserts that this dialogue constitutes the limit of our understanding.

This fundamental opposition between Gadamer and Habermas has been expressed in a number of different contexts as the extensive literature on the debate amply illustrates. One aspect of the debate is particularly relevant here: the opposition between prejudice and Enlightenment thought. Habermas's argument against Gadamer can be summarized in the claim that although hermeneutic understanding is a necessary first step in understanding, it cannot be the last. Hermeneutic understanding reveals what Habermas calls the 'pre-given' in thought. But, against Gadamer, he argues that once this pre-given is rendered transparent it need no longer be considered a 'prejudice'. This, he claims, Gadamer fails to see. Gadamer defines prejudice as a universal element of understanding and argues that even after hermeneutical reflection on the pre-judgements implicit in all thought, these pre-judgements remain 'prejudices'. Habermas challenges this conclusion by claiming that these prejudices can be dissolved by the power of a method he calls 'depth hermeneutics' (1977:358; 1980:201).

Habermas's objection to Gadamer's theory of prejudice, however, is not merely a methodological point; it involves more than a disagreement over prejudice and the power of reflection. Habermas is challenging what lies at the heart of Gadamer's approach: his assessment of Enlightenment thought. Underlying Habermas's position on prejudice is his claim that Gadamer was too hasty in rejecting the tradition of the Enlightenment. Although Habermas would be the first to admit that the objectivism fostered by Enlightenment thought has been detrimental to the social sciences, he nevertheless claims that Enlightenment thought also contained elements that are essential to a proper understanding of these disciplines. Quoting Wellmer, he argues:

> 'The Enlightenment knew what a philosophical hermeneutic forgets – that the "dialogue" which we, according to Gadamer, "are", is also a context of domination and as such precisely no dialogue. . . . The universal claim of the hermeneutic approach [can only] be maintained if it is realized at the outset that the context of tradition as a locus of possible truth and factual agreement is, at the same time, the locus of factual untruth and continual force.' (1980:204–5)

Gadamer's error, as Habermas sees it, is that he seeks to negate the tradition of modernity that began with the Enlightenment. The Enlightenment should be judged on more than what Habermas also concedes is its misunderstanding of knowledge. Against Gadamer he argues that 'one cannot simply strain the Enlightenment, the universalist eighteenth century, out of the humanist tradition' (1983:197). The Enlightenment, he claims, is an essential element of our tradition and Gadamer, despite all his emphasis on tradition, denies this fundamental fact (1977:358). Specifically, Gadamer denies that element of the Enlightenment that Habermas sees to be the most significant: the claim that reason can emancipate human beings from both prejudice and the forces of domination (1981c:11).

Habermas advances a corollary to this argument. He claims that Gadamer's opposition between truth and scientific method leads him to oppose 'methodic knowledge as a whole' (1977:356). Although I have argued that Gadamer does not in fact do this – he reveals, rather, that scientific method is a particular case of understanding – this objection nevertheless reveals an important aspect of Habermas's critique. Despite his sympathy for hermeneutic analysis Habermas is not willing to concede that methodic knowledge in either the social or natural sciences always presupposes a background of hermeneutic understanding.[22] Like the Enlightenment thinkers, Habermas posits a realm in which we can transcend prejudice and achieve objective knowledge. In the last analysis this is a reality that is not linguistically constituted and thus not subject to a 'linguistically articulated consciousness' (1977:361).

Habermas's search for a realm beyond prejudice, that is his search for a 'foundation' for social science, has aroused a great deal of controversy. The degree to which Habermas is a foundational or transcendental thinker has been hotly disputed by his critics.[23] In his early work, particularly *Knowledge and Human Interests* and *Zur Logik der Sozialwissenschaften*, this foundational impulse is quite evident. The knowledge-constitutive interests in *Knowledge and Human Interests* are widely acknowledged to be transcendental or quasi-transcendental and the search for an 'objective framework' in *Zur Logik* is very explicit. In his most recent work, however, Habermas's position on this issue is less clear. In *The Theory of Communicative Action* Habermas defines a position that, although retaining some elements of his earlier foundational tendencies, nevertheless appears to be moving closer to an anti-foundational stance. At the beginning of the work Habermas confronts the problem of foundations directly. In the introduction he states that:

> An investigation of this kind, which uses the concept of communicative reason without blushing, is today suspect of having fallen into the snares of foundationalism. (1984:xli)

But despite this caveat he also clearly defines his attempt to find something like these foundations by stating that:

> We would not be able to ascertain the rational internal structure of action oriented to reaching understanding if we did not already have before us – in fragmentary and distorted form, to be sure – the existing forms of a reason that has to rely on being symbolically embodied and historically situated. (1984:xli)

Throughout the book there is a constant vacillation between these two impulses: on the one hand the search for our 'existing reason' that allows us to transcend its particular historical manifestations, and, on the other hand, the recognition that all attempts at 'First Philosophy', that is, attempts to discover ultimate foundations, have broken down (1984:2).

The first impulse, that is the foundational strain in his work, is, at times, stated quite explicitly. His task, as he states it at the outset, is to define criteria of rational action. He specifies that these criteria must include a relation that is of the 'objective world (that is, a relation to the facts) and is open to objective judgment' (1984:9). He is seeking, in other words, to define reason in terms of a universal core that structures our ability to communicate. Arguing that society can be conceptualized either internally or externally, that is, either hermeneutically or structurally, he contends that defining it exclusively in terms of one or the other of these perspectives is limited; they must be integrated in social scientific analysis. In his clearest statement of the foundationalist perspective he is seeking, Habermas states that:

> the experiential basis of an interpretive [*sinnverstehenden*] sociology is compatible with its claim to objectivity only if hermeneutic procedures can be based at least intuitively on general and encompassing structures of rationality. From both points of view, the metatheoretical and the methodological, we cannot expect objectivity in social-theoretical knowledge if the corresponding concepts of communicative action and interpretation express a merely particular perspective on rationality, one interwoven with a particular cultural tradition. (1984:137)

Although he concedes that this is a 'difficult task' for him because he is 'no longer confident that a rigorous transcendental pragmatic program claiming to provide ultimate grounds can be carried out' (1984:137), he nevertheless proceeds with the attempt. This leads him to the development of a sociological approach to the theory of rationalization, a project that involves an extensive history of social theory beginning with the work of Max Weber.

Balancing this foundational tendency in Habermas' work, however, is his emphasis on hermeneutics. Habermas frequently reiterates the point made at the outset that reason is always historically situated. Thus he claims that we call someone rational who expresses desires and feelings in terms of culturally established values and can adopt a reflective attitude to these values (1984:20). In another context he defines rational action as a decision that issues from a consensus based on 'the interpretive processes of the participants themselves' (1984:339). Validity, furthermore, is always connected internally to reasons and grounds (1984:301). These theses, along with his reliance on the theories of Wittgenstein, Gadamer, Winch and Schutz, lend credence to a more anti-foundational reading of Habermas's work.

Ultimately, however, either a strict foundational or a strict anti-foundational interpretation of Habermas's latest work is misleading. A better conclusion is that he attempts to straddle the fence between the two positions and is, consequently, caught in a dilemma of his own making. On one hand he is convinced by the arguments against what Bernstein calls the 'Cartesian Anxiety' (1983), that is, the search for ultimate foundations. Yet, on the other hand, he is not, as Gadamer is, ready to eschew this tradition entirely and adopt an anti-foundational stance. What he opts for, finally, is a curious amalgam of the two: he seeks to define universal criteria by which historically situated reason operates. He establishes four criteria for what he calls a 'rationalized lifeworld' which he defines as one in which rational action is possible. In defining each of these four criteria he specifies conditions for the cultural tradition that would, he claims, provide the basis for rational action (1984:71–2). He summarizes this position in the following statement:

> We credit all subjects with rationality who are oriented to reaching understanding and thereby to universal validity claims, who base their interpretive accomplishments on an intersubjectively valid reference system of worlds, let us say, on a decentered understanding of the world. This underlying agreement, which unites us before the fact and in the light of which every actually attained agreement can be criticized, grounds the hermeneutic utopia of universal and unlimited dialogue in a commonly inhabited lifeworld. (1984:134)

Whatever ambiguity Habermas's position may exhibit, however, he is definite about one thing: his rejection of Gadamer's anti-foundational stance. The critique of Gadamer that he advanced in earlier works is reiterated in *The Theory of Communicative Action* (1984:134). Gadamer's reply to Habermas' critique, although formulated in response to earlier writings, is nevertheless relevant to this latest work. Like Habermas's own position, Gadamer's reply to Habermas' attack is a complex one. On one level, Gadamer's objection to Habermas appears to be a simple statement of opposition. Against Habermas's claim that we can, at least in some sense, transcend the prejudices that preform our consciousness, he asserts his thesis of the universality of hermeneutics. In his numerous writings on Habermas's challenge to his approach a common refrain appears: what can Habermas mean when he speaks of a position outside language and tradition (1971b:293 ff.)? For Gadamer the Archimedean point that Habermas posits for the social theorist is, at root, incomprehensible. He claims that he does not understand what it would mean to speak from a position outside what Habermas identifies as a linguistically constituted consciousness.

On a number of other levels, however, Gadamer's critique of Habermas seems to be based less on a simple opposition to his views than on the articulation of a position that constitutes only a difference of degree. Habermas' basic objection to Gadamer's position is that it precludes the possibility of critique. Gadamer vehemently denies that this follows from his position. His reference to 'critical reason' and a 'higher objectivity' are indications that he sees the possibility of critique as central to his conception of hermeneutics. Indeed, he defines the principal task of hermeneutics as the separation of true from false prejudice. The opposition between Gadamer and Habermas, does not therefore lie in whether or not critical reason can be said to exist, but rather in its definition and extent. As Gadamer sees it, Habermas, like the Enlightenment thinkers, overestimates the powers of reflection and reason. He implies that these faculties can be free from any ideology or prejudice in the exercise of analysis. Against this Gadamer takes the position that there can be no communication and no reflection without prior agreement (1975:315). While Habermas argues that the historicity of human beings narrows our understanding, Gadamer asserts that it widens that understanding, indeed makes it possible (Depew, 1981:427). Gadamer places our critical capacity firmly within history while Habermas attempts to remove what he calls our 'emancipatory interest' from history (Henning, 1982:94).

Gadamer reiterates this point in a number of contexts, but his basic objection to Habermas's position does not vary significantly in the different formulations. He defines hermeneutical critical reflection as the analysis of the 'bewitchment of ordinary language'. Habermas's claim that communication can exist outside ordinary langauge is thus incomprehensible to him (1971b:288–92). This point also informs his critique of Habermas's theory of the parallel between psychoanalysis and social theory. Gadamer makes the point that, unlike the psychoanalyst, the social theorist is a member of society and thus cannot step outside it and 'see through' it as psychoanalysts do with their patients (1971b:295; 1970:94–5). This criticism, as Gadamer sees it, negates this particular variant of Habermas's model of social theory. But it also leads to a conclusion that, significantly, has political implications. Because Habermas claims that emancipatory consciousness is free from tradition, authority and obedience, it follows that 'unconsciously, the ultimate guiding image of emancipatory reflection in the social sciences must be an anarchistic utopia' (1970:95).

The reason that Habermas misunderstands the role of hermeneutical understanding, Gadamer suggests, is that he approaches hermeneutics as a 'method' that might be 'useful' to the social sciences. But hermeneutics, as Gadamer has so often argued, cannot be conceived in terms of method:

> The hermeneutical experience is prior to all methodological alienation because it is the matrix out of which arise the questions that it then directs to science. (1976b:26)

In both his early and most recent work Habermas sees hermeneutics as an indispensable first step in the method of understanding characteristic of the social sciences. But there is a significant difference between arguing that hermeneutics is an examination of the fundamental nature of human understanding and arguing that hermeneutics is one of many useful methods for the social sciences. Gadamer asserts that this definition of the place of hermeneutics is fundamentally misguided. Habermas makes it clear that, ultimately, the purpose of sociological methodology is emancipation from tradition. But this puts it at odds with the traditional purpose and starting point of hermeneutics: the analysis of tradition (1970:84). Habermas' concept of the 'usefulness' of hermeneutics is thus from the very outset a misuse of the basic presupposition of hermeneutical analysis.

This analysis might seem to suggest that Gadamer's objection to Habermas is identical to that which would be advanced by Wittgenstein. Both Gadamer and Wittgenstein object to the positing of a non or supra-linguistic understanding of human social life. But the reasons for their objections are quite different. For Wittgenstein the objection is rooted in epistemology: what we know can only be apprehended through language. His point is that although there may be something 'out there' that precedes language, it is a realm about which we cannot speak because the limits of language are the limits of our world. For Gadamer, on the other hand, the objection is rooted in ontology. Gadamer's point that language is the 'house of being' throws an entirely different light on the statement that language is the limit of our world. While Wittgenstein's position comes dangerously close to nominalism, Gadamer's does not. Although, for Gadamer being must always be articulated through langauge this does not entail that it is any less 'real'. This perspective explains a rather curious passage in which Gadamer replies to Habermas's challenge:

> Fundamentally in our world the issue is always the same: the verbalisation of conventions and of social norms behind which there are always economic and dominating interests. But our human experience of the world, for which we rely on our faculty of judgment, consists precisely in the possibility of our taking a critical stance with regard to every convention. In reality, we owe this to the linguistic virtuality of our reason and language does not, therefore, present an obstacle to reason. (1975:495–6)

Gadamer, unlike Wittgenstein, has no difficulty in accepting the reality of 'economic dominating interests'. But, like Wittgenstein, he argues that they must be understood through language rather than, as Habermas suggests, in some hypothetical space beyond prejudice and tradition.[24]

In the now extensive commentary on the Gadamer–Habermas debate there is a growing body of literature that argues that the contrast between these two philosophers is less important than the disputants assume. What might be called the 'convergence' position has taken a number of forms. Ricoeur argues that critical theory and hermeneutics are complementary approaches, not contradictory; they merely operate on different levels of analysis (1973:163).[25] Bubner, on the other hand, argues that the debate between the two is 'bogus' in the sphere of methodology even though it is irreconcilable with regard to theory and practice. He asserts that the two disputants merely disagree over the relative importance of critical reflection (1975:338–41). In another analysis of the debate, Misgeld claims that Habermas's interest in Gadamer represents an important shift in critical theory that involves a major reorientation on the autonomy of reason. He implies that Habermas, by turning to Gadamer, is mediating the position on reason that has been the hallmark of critical theory (1976:165–6).[26]

Although these 'convergence' theories are to be commended for pointing out the frequently ignored point that Gadamer does not deny the possibility of critique, there is nevertheless a fundamental problem with this approach. Despite his recent questioning of 'First Philosophy' Habermas is, at root, a foundationalist; he has not definitively rejected the Enlightenment's search for a stable foundation for knowledge. Although he rejects many of the objectivist and scientistic elements of Enlightenment thought, he nevertheless wants to retain what he identifies as its 'emancipatory motive'. It is the virtue of Gadamer's critique to reveal that he cannot have it both ways. Gadamer shows that unless Enlightenment thought is rejected outright and the dichotomies on which it is founded transcended, the attempt to redefine the role of the social sciences is doomed to failure. Unless the social sciences reject both sides of the objective-subjective dichotomy posited by Enlightenment thought, they cannot surpass the self-understanding that this tradition of thought has imposed on them. Gadamer's radical critique of Enlightenment thought succeeds in doing so; ultimately, Habermas's does not.[27]

IV GADAMER AND THE METHODOLOGY OF THE SOCIAL SCIENCES

The arguments that have occupied the discussion to this point – that Gadamer provides a solid philosophical grounding for the social sciences and that his approach has certain advantages over two other post-positivist approaches to the social sciences – leave a number of questions unanswered. The first is the question of the relevance of Gadamer's position for some concrete issues in the methodology of the social sciences. Another is the question of the relationship between Gadamer's approach and Mannheim's sociology of knowledge. Both these questions are best addressed by looking in more detail at the implications of Gadamer's hermeneutics for the methodology of the social sciences.

Action as a text

In *Truth and Method* as well as in his more recent works, Gadamer states unambiguously that he has no intention of providing a methodology for the social sciences. In his argument against Habermas this claim takes the form of asserting that using his approach as a methodological 'tool' in the social sciences seriously distorts the meaning of the claim to universality that he posits for hermeneutical understanding. But arguing that hermeneutics is not a methodological tool for the social sciences on a par with, for example, statistical analysis, does not preclude arguing that hermeneutics has methodological relevance for the social sciences. Gadamer's hermeneutics provides an understanding not merely of the social sciences but of the phenomenon of human understanding itself. His approach dictates that although hermeneutics cannot be employed as a method in the social sciences, it can and should be employed as a means of understanding what the social sciences are about. An examination of Gadamer's position leads to the following question: if Gadamer's philosophical hermeneutics is correct, what kind of methodological approach to the social sciences is entailed by his position?

The first problem that arises in the attempt to answer this question is one that was mentioned briefly in connection with Mannheim's work: the relationship between the analysis of action and the analysis of texts. In his extensive exploration of the nature of hermeneutical understanding Gadamer is concerned almost exclusively with the analysis of written texts. Although he clearly means to establish universal principles of human understanding through this analysis, it is nevertheless the case that the actual descriptions he provides involve texts, and, in *Truth and Method*, works of art. This creates a particular problem for the social sciences. What social scientists normally deal with in their analyses are not written texts or artistic creations but *actions*. Although Gadamer's claim of the universality of hermeneutical understanding entails the claim that anything, and this includes actions as well as texts, must be understood and interpreted according to the principles he establishes, it is nevertheless important for social scientific analysis to specify precisely how the analysis of texts can be translated into the analysis of action.

Unfortunately, Gadamer offers the social scientist little help in answering this question; in *Truth and Method* as well as in his later works he never confronts the issue directly. He has a good reason, however, for avoiding this question: he is not concerned with an essentially methodological problem because he has no intention of formulating a methodology. The most that can be gleaned from his works is that he assumes that action, like any other human phenomenon, is to be understood hermeneutically and that the model of textual interpretation that he presents is also applicable to the analysis of action. The first indication of this assumption can be found in his discussion of Ranke, Droysen and Dilthey in *Truth and Method* (1975:174 ff.). Gadamer praises Dilthey for the innovation of interpreting historical reality as a text, a method that is repeated in the work of Ranke and Droysen. Gadamer quotes Dilthey with approval when he states that 'Life and history have meaning like the letters of a word' (1975:213). A second indication of this assumption is found in his discussion of style. In the course of making the point that style is a unity of expression he argues that actions can have a style that would be expressed in a series of events. His aim is to show that his analysis of style can also be applied to the study of political history (1975:452). Finally, Gadamer's clearest statement of the link between actions and texts can be found in a discussion with Paul Ricoeur. Gadamer states:

> Consequently, by text-interpretation is implied the totality of our orientation of ourselves in the world, together with the assumption that deciphering and understanding a text is very much like encountering reality. (Ricoeur and Gadamer, 1982:300)

But, as far as the social scientist is concerned, these brief comments are not sufficient, especially for a point so central to the social sciences. The connection between the analysis of texts and that of action must be made much more explicitly than Gadamer has done before a hermeneutically grounded methodology for the social sciences can be articulated. Although, as was argued above, Mannheim also makes this assumption, he fails to provide the necessary philosophical grounding for the connection. That philosophical grounding has, however, been provided by a contemporary social philosopher, Paul Ricoeur. In 'The model of the text' (1977a:316–34) Ricoeur supplies the link between actions and texts that is missing in Gadamer's work. Even though Ricoeur's effort is flawed by his reliance on the Enlightenment conception of 'objective knowledge' his effort is nevertheless a noteworthy and necessary step in the task of formulating a hermeneutically grounded social science.

Ricoeur makes it clear at the outset that his purpose in developing a model of textual analysis that is applicable to the social sciences is to provide 'objective data' for those sciences. He argues that texts have an 'objective meaning' and that this meaning is distinct from the author's intention because it is fixed in the process of writing. It is the objective meaning of texts that, as Ricoeur sees it, constitutes the objective data of the social sciences. Thus when Ricoeur claims that the social sciences are hermeneutical, he means that they employ a methodology based in the exegesis of the objective meaning of texts. In another context he clarifies this point:

> The kind of hermeneutics which I now favor starts from the recognition of the objective meaning of the text as distinct from the subjective intention of the author. This objective meaning is not something hidden behind the text. Rather it is a requirement addressed to the reader. The interpretation accordingly is a kind of obedience to this injunction starting from the text. (1977b:319)

After establishing this point, Ricoeur goes on to make the distinction between written and spoken discourse that informs the main thesis of his analysis.

> The subjective intention of the speaking subject and the meaning of the discourse overlap each other in such a way that it is the same thing to understand what the speaker means and what his discourse means. . . . With written discourse, the author's intention and the meaning of the text cease to coincide. . . . But the text's career escapes the finite horizon lived by the author. What the text says now matters more than what the author intended to say. . . (1977a:320)

Although neither speech nor writing is context-free, and thus there is a certain continuity between them, the distinction that Ricoeur wishes to emphasize here is that writing is fixed, that is, it becomes a text, while speech is an on-going event. Two aspects of this parallel between written discourse and accomplished actions on the one hand and spoken discourse and on-going events on the other are of central importance. First, the essence of the parallel between an action and a text that Ricoeur is advancing lies in the fact that both are detached from their author–actor and, hence, can be 'read' apart from the author or actor's subjective meaning. Furthermore, the meaning of an action as well as a text is established by appealing to common (ordinary language) understandings. The contention here is that actions, like words, have meanings that are constitutive of everyday understandings and these meanings are, in both cases, fixed.

Secondly, by positing a parallel between actions and texts, Ricoeur is not arguing for an equivalence or an identity between them. What he is arguing is that because of the 'fixed' nature of both phenomena they can be analyzed with a similar methodology. This becomes clear when Ricoeur attempts to sketch the methodological implications of the parallel between action and written discourse. To do so he returns to what he sees to be the central problematic of the human sciences: providing 'objective data' that would allow them to claim the status of a science. It now emerges that Ricoeur solves this problem by appealing to the objectification of action that, he asserts, parallels the objectification of meaning in texts. The objective data of the human sciences, he concludes, lies in the objective meaning of accomplished actions.

But for Ricoeur a further issue must be addressed before the human sciences can be securely established in the realm of the scientific: the problem of the logic of scientific analysis. Up to this point Ricoeur has shown in what sense the subject matter of the social sciences is objectified. He now asserts, along with the positivists, that if the social sciences are to be 'scientific' they must use the distinctive logic of scientific analysis. His argument differs from that of the positivists, however, in that he asserts that the model of objectivity which allows the human sciences to claim the status of 'science' can be derived not from the natural sciences but from one of the human sciences: linguistics (1977a:328). This point reveals the full relevance of Ricoeur's analysis of spoken discourse. He argues that recent advances in the sciences of linguistics provide, in a sense, a 'native' concept of objectivity and scientific method that offers a satisfactory answer to the question of the scientific status of the human sciences. As Ricoeur sees it, this solution, although it places the human sciences firmly in the scientific realm by providing them with a model of scientific method, does so by appealing not to a model of the natural sciences but to a model indigenous to the social sciences.

What Ricoeur has accomplished in the 'The model of the text' is, without doubt, a significant achievement. He shows in concrete terms how the hermeneutical method of textual analysis can be extended to the analysis of social action in the human sciences. But from the perspective of Gadamer's hermeneutics Ricoeur's analysis is seriously flawed. Ricoeur's concern is not merely to show the relevance of hermeneutics for the social sciences but also to establish the 'objectivity' of analysis in these disciplines. He argues that if the social sciences are to be classed as sciences then, first, the data of these sciences must be objectified and, secondly, the logic of analysis employed must conform to the standards of scientific method. In short Ricoeur implicitly accepts the model of knowledge embodied in the scientific method and attempts, in effect, to fit the social sciences into that model. Although Ricoeur argues that the model of objectivity sought in the social sciences differs from that of the natural sciences, there is no doubt that objectivity is his goal.[28]

Gadamer's analysis in *Truth and Method* reveals a central problem with Ricoeur's goal of objectivity: his failure definitively to dispel the ideal of objectivity embodied in the scientific method of the natural sciences. By continuing the search for a model of objectivity appropriate to the social sciences, he retains the notion that objectivity is the ideal toward which knowledge in both the natural and social sciences should strive. Gadamer's analysis, in contrast, reveals the error inplicit in this idealization of objectivity. But even more importantly, Gadamer, by definitively rejecting the Enlightenment's conception of knowledge, establishes the epistemological priority of the social sciences. Although Ricoeur moves away from the natural scientific model by positing a 'native' concept of objectivity for the social sciences, this move is surpassed by Gadamer's more radical step of transcending the model altogether.

If it can be assumed, however, that despite Ricoeur's errors with regard to objectivity his connection between actions and texts is sound, then his analysis is an important achievement. It means that all of the dimensions of Gadamer's understanding of how we interpret texts, including the fusion of horizons, effective historical consciousness, and the role of prejudice, apply to the analysis of action as well as texts. This has important implications for the social sciences. In terms of the most significant aspect of Gadamer's analysis of hermeneutic understanding, the fusing of horizons, what this conclusion entails for the analysis of action is that actors, like authors, are not the exclusive determinants of the meaning of actions. Rather, the meanings of actions, like texts, are a product of the fusing of the horizons of the actor and the interpreter; both the social actor and the social scientist participate in establishing the meaning of an action.

Interpreting action in terms of a fusing of the horizons of social actors and social scientific interpreters has significance for a controversy that has raged in the social sciences for several decades. This controversy, furthermore, forms a parallel to the controversy between Gadamer and Hirsch on the issue of semantic autonomy. In his dispute with Gadamer, Hirsch argued that the author's meaning fixes the meaning of the text while Gadamer claimed that meaning is established by the fusion of the horizons of author and interpreter. It is possible to identify a parallel to Hirsch's position in the social sciences in the position of what have been labelled 'interpretive' social scientists. It is a common characteristic of Wittgensteinian social science, Schutzian phenomenology and ethnomethodology to insist that the meaning of an action is determined by the meaning bestowed on it by the actor. Interpretive social scientists use this argument to combat the positivist position that the actor's 'subjective' meaning must be replaced by the social scientist's 'objective' meaning if the social sciences are to be scientific. They argue that the actors' understanding of their actions, that is, their subjective meaning, not only establishes the meaning of the action but must be the point of departure of all social scientific analysis. This is most clearly stated by the theorist who has been hailed as the founding father of the interpretive school, Max Weber. Weber states:

> We shall speak of 'action' insofar as the acting individual attaches a subjective meaning to his behavior. . . . Action is 'social' insofar as its subjective meaning takes account of the behavior of others and is thereby oriented in its course. (1968:4)

Although most interpretive social scientists now argue that 'subjective meaning' is not established by probing the internal mental events of the social actor but, rather, is established by the intersubjective meanings of the social context, they nevertheless assert that this meaning is the fundamental unit of social scientific analysis.

From the perspective provided by Gadamer's theory of the fusion of horizons, however, this assertion can be shown to be, at best, misleading. Gadamer's position entails that actors, like authors of texts, do not fix the meaning of their actions; rather, they are fixed by the fusion between the horizons of meaning of the interpreter and that of the actors. Interpretive social scientists would argue against this criticism that they do not ignore the role of the interpreter in the process of establishing meaning, but, rather, that they also examine the role played by the interpreter's values. What they fail to do, however, is to explain how the interpreter's values and the actor's subjective meaning are fused in the process of interpretation. Furthermore, because interpretive social scientists define their task as the interpretation of subjective meaning it follows that the actor's meaning is given epistemological primacy in the constitution of meaning. Gadamer, in contrast, emphasizes both sides of the dialectic of interpretation. His position does not grant epistemological primacy to either side of the dialectic but sees both as equal contributors.

Gadamer's theory of the fusion of horizons, however, does more than merely correct an oversight on the part of interpretive social science. It also obviates a particular problem that interpretive social science has faced in its effort to establish a methodology for the social sciences: the difficulty of justifying the movement beyond the actors' conceptions of their action. Although several of the interpretive approaches to the social sciences advance theories that provide a means of moving beyond the actors' concepts to an 'explanatory' framework, the assumption of the epistemological primacy of the social actors' constitution of the meaning of their actions calls into question the legitimacy of another interpretive framework. This problem has been extensively discussed in the cases of Peter Winch and Alfred Schutz. Both Winch and Schutz claim that the social scientist must begin with the actors' understanding of their actions, an understanding that both define in terms of the intersubjective understandings constituted by the social context rather than, with Dilthey, the subjective meanings of actors. Both also claim that the social scientist can then go on to a further level of explanation as long as it presupposes this basic understanding. Winch calls this level 'more reflective understanding' and gives the example of the economist's concept of 'liquidity preference' (1958:89). Schutz calls this level that of 'second order concepts' and insists that they meet the postulates of subjective interpretation, rationality, adequacy and logical consistency (1962:5; 1964:43–4, 86).

The problem in both cases, however, is similar. The analyses of Winch and Schutz as well as of those social scientists who have adopted their theoretical perspectives have, in actual practice, rarely moved to this 'second level' of explanation despite the attempts on the part of both Winch and Schutz to legitimize it. It is not difficult to show that the reason for this failure is implicit in the interpretive approach. Because both theorists insist on the epistemological primacy of the actors' constitution of meaning, it follows that any other construal of meaning is necessarily suspect. Thus it is little wonder that both they and their followers have rarely moved to this level of analysis; neither theorist offers any substantive justification for this second level of conceptualization on the part of the social scientist.

If the analysis of social action is approached from the perspective provided by Gadamer's hermeneutics, however, this problem of legitimizing a 'second level' of explanation imposed by the interpreter is removed. Gadamer's approach to the analysis of texts parallels the basic postulate of the interpretive school with regard to the analysis of social action. Gadamer argues that the author's concepts (defined in terms of the historical horizon of meaning) play a constitutive role in the meaning of a text, while the interpretive social scientist argues that the social actors' concepts (defined intersubjectively) play a constitutive role in the meaning of social action. But Gadamer denies that this constitutive role amounts to epistemological primacy. A Gadamerian perspective entails that understanding an action does not occur simply by appropriating the social actors' concepts. Rather, understanding is always from a certain perspective. The interpreter understands the action from a specific historical and cultural position and through the concepts and questions that are brought to the investigation. Thus the understanding of the action is neither an appropriation of the actors' concepts nor the imposition of the interpreter's categories, but a fusing of the two into a distinct entity: the interpretation. This position reveals that both the approach labelled 'semantic autonomy' and that of the interpretive social scientists emphasize only one half of the dialectic of interpretation.

It can thus be concluded that Gadamer avoids the interpretive social scientist's problem of legitimizing the interpreter's concepts because he defines the interpreter's conceptual scheme as a necessary, constitutive element of the act of interpretation. This conclusion combined with Ricoeur's examination of the analogy between texts and actions makes it possible to complete the task at hand: providing a concrete description of how a Gadamerian analysis of action might proceed. Ricoeur has revealed that an accomplished action, like a text, is autonomous. In the analysis of social action the first task of the interpreter is to understand the 'horizon' of action, that is, what the action meant to the participants. But for both Gadamer and Ricoeur understanding action in the actor's terms does not involve probing subjective intentions or 'getting inside the actor's mind'. As Ricoeur points out, accomplished action has a meaning that is detached from the actor's subjective intentions. What it 'means' thus becomes what it means in the social context in which it occurred. For Gadamer, however, understanding the action in the actor's terms is only the first movement in the dialectic of interpretation. To stop at this point is to deny the fundamental insight of historical understanding: that understanding always takes place within a context. What Hirsch forgot, and what interpretive social science fails to emphasize, is that the interpreter's understanding also derives from a particular context and this context is fused with the actor's context. In Gadamer's words, the action is always seen in terms of the horizon of the interpreter and, more particularly, the specific question posed in the interpretation.

Interpretive social scientists have undeniably shown considerable interest in what they define as the problems of the interpreter's values. Weber's famous discussion of 'value freedom' and Charles Taylor's examination of the 'value slope' of an investigation (1962) are notable examples of the importance of this issue for the interpretive approach. What I am arguing here, however, is not that interpretive social scientists deny the issue, but that by continuing to insist on the epistemological primacy of the actor's meaning they misunderstand what Gadamer defines as the dialectic of interpretation. For Gadamer the task of understanding is to explain how the horizon of interpreter and interpreted are fused; for the interpretive social scientist the question of fusion never comes up but, rather, the horizons of interpreter and interpreted are discussed as separate issues. It can further be argued that other elements of Gadamer's approach, his theory of prejudice and the workings of effective-historical consciousness are particularly useful to social scientists in their effort to understand action. Gadamer's approach forces interpreters to examine specifically the 'prejudices' informing their interpretive stance. It is this self-reflection that leads to the self-understanding that is such an integral part of the process of interpretation. What Gadamer identifies as the positive possibilities of prejudice is also of central importance. Ricoeur asserts that after an action has occurred it is removed from the immediate situation of its occurrence and becomes part of 'history'. If it is an action that attracts the attention of the social scientist it is most likely an action that has been identified as having an effect on history. Even more likely, it is an event that has been identified as central to the course of the history of the social scientist's society. The particular effect of the event, furthermore, could not have been completely foreseen by the actor or actors. It could not, in other words, have been part of the actor's conception of the action. But this effect necessarily becomes part of the interpretive schema of the social scientist; the interpreter is interested in the event to a large extent *because* of its effect. The effective-historical consciousness of the interpreter is thus a phenomenon that enhances rather than detracts from the act of interpretation.

How a Gadamerian social science would differ from the interpretive approach can best be illustrated by looking at an issue that has been problematic for interpretive social science in general but particularly for Winch and the Wittgensteinian school: the identification of false consciousness or unconscious motivation in the analysis of social action. In Winch's account attributing either false consciousness or unconscious motivation to a social actor is an illegitimate move for the social scientist because of the epistemological primacy of the actor's understanding. This position has been challenged by many social scientists because it seems an unacceptable restriction on the practice of social science. It is not difficult to show, however, that the inclusion of both these elements is compatible with the

Gadamerian framework. That this is the case is illustrated in an insightful article by Charles Reagan (1979:141–61). In the course of analyzing Ricoeur's treatment of Freud, Reagan shows how textual analysis alone cannot account for the uncovering of unconscious motives in the process of psychoanalytic interpretation. The 'text' of the psychoanalyst, that is, the patient's narrative, is, as a text, independent of the intention of its author. In the process of interpretation this text is fused with the interpreter's psychoanalytic horizon. What emerges is an interpretation that identifies motives not present to the patient, the author of the text. In fact, the whole point of the interpretation is precisely to identify these motives. But whereas neither Gadamer nor Ricoeur have any difficulty justifying the imposition of the psychoanalyst's conceptual scheme in this situation, in Winch's view such a move must be identified as illegitimate.[29]

This point can, furthermore, be extended to include the Marxist concept of false consciousness. A Marxist social scientist, imposing the Marxist framework of interpretation on a sequence of action might be led to the conclusion that a particular group of social actors in a particular situation exhibits false consciousness. Again, the Gadamerian would have no difficulty with such a conclusion. The 'text' of the action fused with the interpreter's Marxist horizon yields a particular, yet perfectly legitimate interpretation. It might even be argued that, given the influence of Marxist categories in the social sciences, it is difficult for contemporary interpreters to see past actions in anything *but* Marxist terms. That interpretive social science and especially the Wittgensteinian school has had a great deal of difficulty with the concept of false consciousness is, however, evident in the contemporary literature on this subject. This difficulty, furthermore, has been a major factor preventing the acceptance of this approach by social scientists.[30]

How, then, would a Gadamerian social scientist approach the analysis of a concrete event? First, the Gadamerian, like the interpretive social scientist, would seek to define the historical and cultural horizon of the actors involved in the event. This would entail understanding the action in terms of the social actors. Secondly, the Gadamerian would be aware that in the course of the interpretation a different horizon of meaning would necessarily be imposed on the actor's horizon, that of the interpreter. The horizon of the interpreter is defined jointly by the historical perspective of the interpreter and a specific ideological perspective such as the Freudian or Marxist perspectives discussed above. Awareness of this imposition of the 'prejudice' of the interpreter is the result, Gadamer claims, of the self-reflection that occurs in interpretation; in his words, I understand myself 'in front of the text'. Thirdly, the Gadamerian, unlike the interpretive social scientist would be aware of the effect of the analyzed event on subsequent history, the result of 'effective historical consciousness'. This consciousness enhances interpretation because the interpreter is aware that the effect of the event influences the interpretation. The awareness of prejudice, self-reflexivity, and effective historical consciousness together provide the Gadamerian with positive possibilities of interpretation not available to the interpretive social scientist.

Viewing action as a text through the interpretive schema of Gadamerian hermeneutics thus allows the social sciences to side-step one of the main problems of interpetive social science: restricting the explanation of action to the actors' concepts. Gadamer's position does not entail a rejection of the basic principle of interpretive social science, that is, that the analysis of social action must begin with an understanding of the actor's concepts. But Gadamer provides precisely what is missing in the interpretive approach: a legitimation of the integration of the actors' concepts with the conceptual scheme of the interpreter. Gadamer's approach thus removes one of the major impediments to the acceptance of interpretive social science without forsaking its basic precept or falling into the objectivism of the positivist approach to action explanation.

It can also be concluded, however, that such a Gadamerian approach to the methodology of the social sciences would not find ready acceptance among contemporary social scientists, interpretive, positivist, or Marxist. Two objections that would be advanced against a Gadamerian methodology are suggested by the preceding discussion. In the first place, the Marxist, positivist, or Freudian interpreter would object that Gadamer's approach excludes the possibility of declaring any one interpretation to be *the* correct interpretation. This position is also the basis of the objection advanced by Hirsch in the field of literary criticism. These objections, furthermore, are accurate in the sense that they correctly interpret Gadamer's position. Even though Gadamer's position does not entail an arbitrary stance in which any interpretation must be accepted, it nevertheless precludes the possibility that any one approach can be declared 'true'. Because interpretations necessarily change with interpreters and are the result of the fusing of horizons, one 'objectively correct' interpretation is not a possibility for Gadamer.

A second objection would be launched by the Wittgensteinians. It has been one of the principal arguments of interpretive social science and in particular the Wittgensteinian school, that the imposition of certain conceptual schemes by interpreters of social action is illegitimate. The Wittgensteinians, for example, assert that causal analysis, generalizations, and other tools of the scientific method are unacceptable in the social sciences because they violate the actors' understanding of their actions. On the face of it, a Gadamerian social science seems to oppose this view. Gadamer's understanding of the fusing of horizons seems to entail that any interpretive scheme, even one rooted in the 'objective method' of science is legitimate. In fact, he states explicitly that his position 'does not prevent the methods of modern natural science from having an application to the social world' (1975:xvii). It is not Gadamer's intent in *Truth and Method* to claim that the scientific method cannot produce truth but that other kinds of truth are more fundamental.

But this rendering of Gadamer's position on this issue must be carefully qualified. In discussing the relationship between the natural and the human sciences, Gadamer argues that the question is not one of method but, of the objectives of knowledge (1975:xvii). From this it follows that although the scientific method cannot be completely excluded from the human sciences the method that is employed in these sciences must be compatible with the object of knowledge in these disciplines. It also follows that, given that the object of knowledge in the human sciences is the *understanding* of human social life, the scientific method would not in most cases be compatible with this goal. Gadamer has much to say about the negative effects of the abstractness central to the scientific method. He claims that this abstraction excludes the historicity of the object constitutive of its being. Although he does not draw any specific conclusions for the human sciences from these remarks, his position entails that the object of knowledge in the human sciences would only rarely demand this method of scientific analysis.

These two objections involve issues that represent significant conflicts between Gadamer's position and those espoused by other contemporary approaches to the social sciences. Another set of objections, however, has been launched against Gadamer's approach from critics more sympathetic to his basic approach. In an insightful analysis of what he calls 'critical hermeneutics', John Thompson criticizes both Ricoeur's theory of action as a text and Gadamer's philosophical hermeneutics. Against Ricoeur Thompson argues that, like many other contemporary social theorists, he bases his theory on an illegitimate generalization from the linguistic sphere, a criticism that he would certainly also apply to Gadamer (1981:125). Thompson's argument against Ricoeur's position is a subtle one. He asserts on the one hand that 'lay actors may not have the first word in the interpretation of their action, but they do, in a fundamental epistemological sense, have the final word' (1981:127). In another passage, however, he deviates from what appears to be a strict Wittgensteinian line with the assertion that 'the interpretation of action is a relatively autonomous process in which the subject is not naively enthroned but rather systematically unveiled' (1981:143). This passage is an indication of Thompson's leaning toward Habermas's approach. Together with Habermas, Thompson claims that Ricoeur and Gadamer ignore the non-linguistic aspects of human life, aspects that are explored in Habermas's search for an 'objective framework'. Thus Thompson, like Habermas, is denying the universality of hermeneutic understanding that Gadamer asserts. He claims that the distantiation that is necessary for a critical social science is missing in the purely linguistic approach of Gadamer and Ricoeur.

In the light of Thompson's criticism of both Gadamer and Ricoeur on the issue of distantiation, it is interesting to note that Ricoeur himself criticizes Gadamer for failing to provide this critical distantiation while asserting that his own approach successfully employs it.[31] Ricoeur argues that Gadamer's hermeneutics cannot be critical because it rejects the 'alienating distantiation that makes critique possible' (1981:90). Against this Ricoeur argues that the text is already distantiated and, furthermore, that 'the emancipation of the text constitutes the most fundamental condition for the recognition of a critical instance at the heart of interpretation' (1981:91). But Ricoeur does not simply take the Habermasian line that such a 'critical instance' is possible. Rather, he attacks Gadamer for setting up an erroneous dichotomy in *Truth and Method* between alienating distantiation and belonging. As Ricoeur sees it, Gadamer claims that either we understand a text from the position of its belonging to a tradition that we share or we alienate it through the objectifying method of the sciences, thus distorting our understanding of it. Ricoeur wants to overcome this dichotomy by positing a 'positive distantiation' that is already present in textual interpretation. This positive distantiation, he claims, is not the product of methodology, but, rather, makes possible the critique of ideology that is missing in Gadamer's account (1981:131 ff.).

Ricoeur's critique of Gadamer thus falls short of Habermas's positing of an 'objective framework' while still rejecting what he sees to be Gadamer's exclusion of critique. In a sense, Ricoeur wants to have it both ways. By defining distantiation and belonging as 'dialectically opposed' he is seeking to retain both impulses in the human sciences. He argues that the critique of ideology can 'partially' free itself from its initial anchorage in preunderstanding and thus enter into the 'passage to theory' (1981:244–5). Like Habermas, he asserts that critique is legitimate because it is part of our tradition. It need not therefore be rejected outright as Gadamer claims (1981:99).

These criticisms are evidently more sympathetic to Gadamer's position. They suggest modifications of Gadamer's hermeneutics rather than, as in the case of the previous criticisms, rejection of its fundamental principles. But the nature of these criticisms reveals an important point. Both Thompson and Ricoeur question, although with reservations, the basic thesis of Gadamer's approach: the universality of hermeneutic understanding. And because they do so they are led, ultimately, to a position that exhibits aspects of foundational thought. Thus Thompson, like Habermas, appeals to an essentially non-linguistic realm by which action is constituted, denying Gadamer's claim to the universality and linguisticality of understanding. Ricoeur, on the other hand, denies Gadamer's point that objectifying method distorts the 'belongingness' of understanding. His thesis of the 'dialectical opposition' between the two fails to refute Gadamer's point that understanding is always an act of belonging to a tradition. It can thus be concluded, that, despite their proclaimed respect for Gadamer's position, both Thompson and Ricoeur reveal themselves as caught in the Enlightenment search for objectivity. Ultimately they cannot give up what Ricoeur identifies as the 'tradition of critique' that Gadamer rejects. Gadamer's point is that unless the tradition of critique as it was conceived by the Enlightenment is abandoned the human sciences cannot articulate the new self-understanding that both he and his critics are seeking. It does not follow from this, however, that critique itself must be abandoned. Rather, it follows that a new conception of critique that takes account of our 'belongingness' must be formulated.

Hermeneutics and the sociology of knowledge

The foregoing discussion of Gadamer's relevance for the methodology of the social sciences has attempted to show that Gadamer provides a radically new understanding of these disciplines by formulating a comprehensive conception of the phenomenon of human understanding. Several of the advantages of this new understanding have been discussed in terms of its relevance to some contemporary issues in social theory. The particular problem that is the concern of this work, however, must now be addressed: the relationship between Gadamer's approach and the sociology of knowledge. If, as I have argued, the sociology of knowledge is central to the enterprise of the social sciences and, furthermore, if Gadamer provides a new conception of the social sciences based on a radically different sociology of knowledge then the precise nature of this new relationship must be carefully defined.

Several sociologists of knowledge have commented on the relevance of Gadamer and the related approach of Heidegger to the social sciences. Janet Wolff argues that Gadamer solves several of the traditional problems of methodology in the sociology of knowledge by giving a detailed account of *verstehen* and resolving the problem of relativity in the social sciences (1975:117–18). In a similar vein Watson seeks to 'operationalize' Gadamer's hermeneutics into a kind of sociology or study of life history (1976:101–4) and Remmling, together with Mannheim, sees Heidegger's concept of '*das Man*' as relevant to the sociology of knowledge (1975:44). Finally, as was noted earlier, Simonds posits a close relationship between the approaches of Gadamer and Mannheim and asserts that Mannheim exemplifies a Gadamerian sociology of knowledge (1975; 1978).

Despite their admiration for Gadamer's approach, however, each of these commentators ultimately rejects Gadamer's 'relativistic' approach as unsuitable for the social sciences. Wolff, for example, questions whether Gadamer's approach is relevant to sociological methodology and states that Gadamer's rejection of the Enlightenment prevents him from providing a satisfactory conception of objectivity (1975:121). Simonds is even more explicit in his rejection of Gadamer's theory. He claims that because Gadamer rejects the whole idea of a uniquely correct interpretation, his position precludes the very possibility of the sociology of knowledge (1978:89). These critics misunderstand two important aspects of Gadamer's position. First, like Habermas, they fail to see that Gadamer is not attempting to offer a methodology for the social sciences and, thus, cannot be faulted for failing to do so. What he *is* offering is a new understanding for the social sciences that has methodological implications. That this is an entirely different project is crucial to a proper understanding of Gadamer's position. Secondly, and more importantly, they fail to see that Gadamer, by rejecting the Enlightenment conception of knowledge has made questions of the 'objectivity' of the social sciences and the notion of a 'uniquely correct interpretation' obsolete.

A defense of Gadamer's position must move beyond the narrow question of method that limits these criticisms. Gadamer provides an ontological explanation of human existence that reveals the universality and linguisticality of hermeneutic understanding. This theory demands an entirely new approach to the problems of the social sciences and the formulation of a method that is compatible with this ontological understanding. Such a method would reject the Enlightenment search for truth and objectivity, accept the role of prejudice in the universal phenomenon of human understanding, and define interpretation in terms of the fusion of horizons and effective-historical consciousness. A method that comes close to fulfilling these criteria is that of Karl Mannheim. Although Mannheim does not entirely eschew the search for objectivity, his approach goes a long way toward meeting the requirements of a Gadamerian approach to the social sciences in general and the sociology of knowledge in particular.

The compatibility between the two approaches can be summarized under four headings. First, both Mannheim and Gadamer reject the Enlightenment conception that knowledge is the appropriation of the object by the subject. Mannheim explicitly defines his approach as a corrective to the overemphasis on the subject in modern thought (1936:28). Secondly, both reject the exclusive identification of knowledge with science. Although Mannheim vacillates on this point and at times seems only to be saying that the social sciences embody a different type of knowledge rather than the universal form of all knowledge, at other times he espouses the more radical Gadamerian position. Thirdly, both Gadamer and Mannheim accept the participatory role of the interpreter in the process of understanding. Mannheim's sociology of knowledge comes very close to defining the fusion of horizons and effective-historical consciousness.[32] Finally, Mannheim echoes Gadamer's assumption of the universality of prejudice in his definition of the total conception of ideology.[33]

This is not to say that Gadamer and Mannheim are completely in harmony in their approaches to the social sciences. Mannheim's lapses into positivism conflict with Gadamer's complete rejection of Enlightenment thought. More importantly, the two theories operate on two different levels of analysis. While Gadamer deals with the ontological condition of human existence, Mannheim is concerned with the understanding of particular human phenomena. It is one thing to argue, as Gadamer does, that language preforms thought, and quite another to discuss, as does Mannheim, the way in which a particular ideology influences human thought and action.[34] But despite these differences the compatibility between the two approaches is striking. Furthermore, it is not difficult to show that the different levels on which the two approaches operate are complementary rather than contradictory. Gadamer supplies the basic understanding of what the social sciences are about while Mannheim provides a concrete method consistent with that understanding.

What a Gadamerian–Mannheimian methodology for the social

sciences would mean in specific terms is that social scientific problems would be approached with the assumption that understanding, not objectivity, is the goal of the social sciences. Although this dictum has been formulated many times before, what Gadamer means by it is significantly different. On the basis of his interpretation social scientists would accept not only the inevitability but the positive role of prejudice in the process of understanding while at the same time examining and critically assessing the tradition in which they find themselves.[35] Further, interpreters of social action would recognize that their understandings play an integral part in the interpretation that they produce, rejecting the notion that their interpretive position constitutes an Archimedean point of objectivity. Finally, they would see their position *vis-à-vis* the natural sciences in terms of the universality of hermeneutic understanding. Rather than defining the social scientific position as inferior to the natural sciences in their common search for 'objective knowledge', social scientists would see their discipline as prior to the natural sciences in a hermeneutical sense. Mannheim's investigations into particular belief systems and the way in which they influence thought and action illustrates the manner in which such a methodology would operate.

It does not follow from this that the kind of investigations that Mannheim pursues, that is, investigations into the social roots of particular belief systems, are the only kinds of investigations that would be allowed by a Gadamerian approach to the social sciences. What does follow from this is that a conception of the relationship between human thought and human existence is fundamental to a conception of what the social sciences themselves are about, not just a conception of the tasks of one field of social science, the sociology of knowledge. The Enlightenment's conception of the relationship between thought and existence embodied in its conception of the sociology of knowledge was and is definitive of the nature and extent of positivist social science. What I am arguing here is that Gadamer's understanding of this relationship, which I have described as an ontological sociology of knowledge, is also definitive of a distinctive approach to the social sciences in general, not just to the subfield of the social sciences labelled the sociology of knowledge. I am not suggesting that all investigations founded in Gadamer's approach would investigate the relationship between specific belief systems and particular human actions. But I am suggesting that the investigations of a Gadamerian, anti-foundational social science would rest on the presupposition that all human thought and action is preformed by language and tradition. What this would entail, most importantly, is that a Gadamerian social science would be concerned with language and the linguisticality of understanding in the interpretation of both action and texts. It entails a social science that provides an approach to understanding in the human social world that is rooted in the positive possibilities of prejudice as well as the critical evaluation of cultural tradition.

5

Beyond Objectivism and Nihilism

I INTRODUCTION

The argument for a social science understood in terms of a hermeneutic, anti-foundational sociology of knowledge has been developed along three lines: first, an argument for the necessity of an antifoundational approach based on an analysis of the historical evolution of the social sciences; secondly, an explication of the works of Mannheim and Gadamer and an argument for the intrinsic values of their approaches; and, thirdly, an argument for the advantages of a Gadamerian–Mannheimian approach relative to the positions espoused by the Wittgensteinians and Habermas. At this point it is necessary to complete the argument by examining a set of metatheoretical issues relating to the social sciences. What has been defined here as a hermeneutic sociology of knowledge is closely connected to certain current discussions in social theory and the philosophy of the social sciences. In order to conclude the argument for this hermeneutic approach the relationship between this position and the issues discussed in this debate must be made clear.

In the most comprehensive sense locating the argument for a social science rooted in a hermeneutic sociology of knowledge would necessitate presenting analyses of all the various approaches to social theory that are now current. Such a task is beyond the scope of this study, and would not, furthermore, add significantly to the thesis being advanced here. It should be clear from the foregoing that the anti-foundational approach is radically opposed to any social theory that seeks objective knowledge rooted in absolute truths. Thus there is little point in describing the relationship between hermeneutic sociology of knowledge and, for example, positivist social science, Husserlian phenomenology, or most varieties of Marxist social science. Detailing the opposition between Gadamer's thought and these approaches merely belabors the obvious.

What is both necessary and useful, however, is a discussion of the relationship between this approach and those of a number of writers whose works have contributed significantly to the anti-foundational movement. Although the anti-foundational approach is not the only position advanced in contemporary social theory it provides the appropriate context for a consideration of the work of Gadamer. Furthermore, the works of two writers within the anti-foundational context are particularly relevant to Gadamer's position and pose a challenge to the argument for a hermeneutic social science: Michel Foucault and Jacques Derrida. The relationship between Gadamer's approach and the work of these writers is a complex one. There is no doubt that there are strong similarities between both these writers' works and those of Gadamer and that, in this sense, Gadamer is connected to an important contemporary movement in the social sciences. But it is also the case that Gadamer's approach offers a better solution to the contemporary problems of the social sciences than can be found in the works of either of these writers. More precisely, although Gadamer's approach avoids the latent objectivism of much of contemporary social theory it does not incur what can be defined as the nihilism implicit in the works of Foucault and Derrida.

Before moving on to such a discussion, however, it is important to consider a number of general issues that will serve to locate the examination of these thinkers. In the past several decades theoretical discussions in both philosophy and the social sciences have revolved around issues that have also figured centrally in the preceding arguments: the errors of positivist social science; the public, rather than individual or subjective, constitution of meaning; the futility of looking for an absolute grounding for knowledge; the historicity of knowledge; the role of discourse in creating both knowledge and action; and the linguistic constitution of reality. Some of the works that fall into this category are Putnam (1981), Goodman (1978), Dallmayr (1981a,b; 1984), Shapiro (1981) and the collection of essays in Hollis and Lukes (1982).[1] Although this literature is by no means homogeneous it is possible to identify some broad themes that unite these discussions. In a general sense these works all question the foundational approach to knowledge that has been dominant since the Enlightenment. It is therefore tempting to subsume this literature under the rubric of the anti-foundational position advanced above. But to do so would be to ignore some significant divisions within this literature. A careful examination of these works reveals that two positions are advanced that conflict in important ways with the hermeneutic sociology of knowledge already outlined: the advocacy, albeit in a modified form, of a variety of forms of objectivism, and the espousal of a form of nihilism.

The argument that language and the social, historical and cultural influences that it embodies are constitutive of social reality has been a common refrain in social thought in the twentieth century. But all who have advocated this position have not come to the same conclusions. Some have argued, for example, that although language profoundly influences our perception of reality, we can still retain the notion that there is a 'reality' out there to which we can compare our (or another society's) perceptions. One of the best examples of this position can be found in the work of Benjamin Whorf. Although he does not offer an explicit argument to this effect, Whorf seems to adopt a view that retains a baseline in 'objective reality'. He attacks the notion of universal laws of logic or reason (1956:208) and talks about the 'background' character of language (1956:211) yet he also warns of the 'errors which unconscious acceptance of our language background otherwise engenders' (1956:222) and appeals to 'scientific, unbiased research into language' (1956:265).

Another example of a theorist who seems to accept the linguistic, even hermeneutic, viewpoint yet retains elements of objectivism is Karl-Otto Apel. In his espousal of a 'transcendental hermeneutics' Apel makes it very clear that he rejects positivist objectivism and scientism and advocates instead what he calls the 'a-priori of public language' that relieves the 'methodological solipsism' of Husserl and Descartes (1980a:122). He states that 'there is no other medium of definitively comprehending and expressing intersubjectively valid truth and meaning besides the public meaning of language' (1980a:136).

Yet when he seeks to define a proper methodology for the social sciences, elements of objectivism reappear. He argues that the methodology of the social sciences should be a 'dialectical mediation' between social scientific explanation and historical-hermeneutic understanding (1971b:43). He attacks the 'perspectival relativism' of modern social theorists by appealing to the positive heritage of the Enlightenment and the ideal of rational progress in knowledge (Holmes, 1975:221). The 'transcendental-logical presuppositions of a communicative community' (Apel, 1980b:287), a 'unitary-normative dimension' presupposed in our understanding (1980a:134), the 'anticipatory pre-conception of the ideal norm of possible true knowledge' (1980a:140), and a 'transcendental-pragmatic final grounding of ethics' (1981:28) all figure prominently in his discussion. Although each of these conceptions is informed by linguistic and historical elements, each finally rests on universal or absolute grounds. Ultimately Apel assumes that the conventional meanings of particular languages are the point of departure of analysis, not its terminus (1980a:134).[2]

Although Apel's position is, quite clearly, objectivist, his advocacy of a historically and culturally modified form of objectivism is not an isolated phenomenon among writers sympathetic to the anti-foundational position. That this is the case is illustrated by the analysis in Richard Bernstein's recent book, *Beyond Objectivism and Relativism* (1983). In this work Bernstein defines a position that is similar to the anti-foundational position outlined above. His discussion of four seminal thinkers, Rorty, Arendt, Gadamer and Habermas, is designed to show that the tendency of contemporary thought is to define a realm beyond the dichotomies of objectivism and relativism, objectivity and subjectivity, rationalism and irrationalism (1983:1). But, as Bernstein readily acknowledges, Habermas and Arendt, along with Apel, cling to a form of objectivism that, although historically and culturally sensitive, still seeks some metaphysical underpinnings for social knowledge. Even this modified objectivism, however, entails a position that, as Gadamer has so clearly illustrated, falls into the errors of Enlightenment thought. Gadamer has shown that unless objectivism is definitely rejected we cannot ascend to the realm 'beyond objectivism and relativism' that Bernstein seeks to define.

Bernstein's analysis also illustrates that a second position that is in opposition to Gadamer's anti-foundational approach is also present in this literature: a form of nihilism. Although explicit arguments for a nihilistic stance are rarely found in this literature, advocacy of what amounts to a modern form of nihilism has become fashionable in recent years.[3] Richard Rorty's important work, *Philosophy and the Mirror of Nature* (1979) is a good example of this trend. His principal concern in this work is to identify the error of attempting to define a philosophy that can mirror the reality of the world of nature, an error common to modern Western thought. In opposition to the history of Western philosophy originating with Plato, Rorty advocates what he labels a tradition of 'edifying philsophers' who, rather than seeking absolute foundations for knowledge seek rather to continue the 'conversation of mankind'. These philosophers, whom Rorty identifies as the American pragmatists (principally Dewey), Nietzsche, Wittgenstein, Heidegger, Gadamer and Derrida, reject the notion that the goal of philosophy is to mirror the world around us accurately and aim instead at 'continuing conversation rather than discovering truth' (1979:373).

On the face of it this sounds very similar to the kind of anti-foundational position argued for above. But in another context Rorty advances a criticism of Gadamer's work that reveals his nihilistic bent. In *Consequences of Pragmatism* Rorty makes the distinction between 'strong' and 'weak' textualists (1982:152). A weak textualist is one who argues that each work has its own vocabulary or secret code and seeks to discover it while strong textualists impose their own vocabulary on the work being interpreted. Identifying Nietzsche, James, Foucault and Bloom as strong textualists, Rorty argues that they realize that the idea of a method presupposes a privileged vocabulary and hence reject it. Weak textualists, on the other hand, are really just imitating the method of science because they seek to break the author's 'secret code'.[4]

Rorty identifies both Gadamer and Dilthey as weak textualists and criticizes their approaches accordingly. It is not difficult to show, however, that this categorization involves a misunderstanding of Gadamer. In *Truth and Method* Gadamer clearly distinguishes between his position and that of Dilthey and, furthermore, unambiguously rejects the idea that he is creating a method for the social sciences. He also emphasizes that interpretation does not involve the appropriation of the author's subjective intentions (Dilthey's position) but the fusion of the author's meaning, which is historically defined, with the interpreter's vocabulary. This is very different from seeking the 'secret code' of the author of a text.

There is, however, a deeper level on which Gadamer and Rorty clash here and on this level Rorty is at least partially correct in defining a distinction between Gadamer on the one hand and Nietzsche, Foucault and Derrida on the other. Rorty asserts, quite rightly, that a strong textualist argues that no vocabulary is privileged, neither that of the author nor that of the interpreter. Rorty puts this very succinctly in his summary of the pragmatists' viewpoint. He argues that the key to the pragmatists' position is

> the sense that there is nothing deep down inside us except what we have put there ourselves, no criterion that we have not created in the course of creating a practice, no standard of rationality that is not our appeal to such a criterion, no rigorous argumentation that is not obedience to our own conventions. (1982:xiii)

Gadamer would agree with this statement but would not agree with the conclusion that Rorty (together with Foucault and Derrida) draws from it. Rorty moves from the statement that all vocabularies and all standards are a result of conventions to the conclusion that no vocabulary is privileged. Gadamer's position, in contrast, is that at any given time a vocabulary, and this includes standards of rationality and definitions of truth, *is* privileged, not in any metaphysical or absolute sense, but in the sense that it is the shared vocabulary by which a group of people make sense of their common world. It is, in Wittgenstein's sense, the bedrock of their collective existence and the means of a common life. The implication is that if there were not a privileged vocabulary our collective life would degenerate into chaos and anarchy.

This is the sense in which Gadamer shows Rorty and, by extension, Foucault and Derrida to be in error. The position that no vocabulary is privileged, that interpreters impose any vocabulary they please on texts and, *ex nihilo*, create a unique interpretation, misunderstands the nature of collective life and the 'privileged' vocabulary on which it rests. On the basis of Gadamer's work it is possible to argue that, in the act of interpretation, two vocabularies are 'privileged' and together create the fusion of meaning that establishes the interpretation: the vocabulary defined by the tradition of the author and that defined by the tradition of the interpreter. This position is distinct from Dilthey's position that interpretation involves cracking the author's secret code. But it is also distinct from the nihilism that results from the rejection of any privileged vocabulary. Gadamer's work reveals that the traditions that make collective life coherent and even possible necessarily privilege a vocabulary in each historical period. As Gadamer puts it: 'the displacement of human reality never goes so far that no forms of solidarity exist any longer' (1983:264).[5]

Rorty's argument against Gadamer is closely related to a position that he takes in opposition to Charles Taylor and Hubert Dreyfus. In a debate published in the *Review of Methaphysics* Rorty argues against both Taylor and Dreyfus that there is no intrinsic method to the social sciences, but that both the natural and social sciences are hermeneutic in the same sense (Rorty:1980).[6] Taylor and Dreyfus maintain, against this, that there is a distinction between humans and things and hence a distinction between the natural and social sciences (C. Taylor, 1980; Dreyfus, 1980). Rorty's problem with this argument is that it appeals, he claims, to an a priori distinction between natural things and social things, a distinction that, as a good deconstructionist, he rejects. Taylor and Dreyfus have no reply to this argument other than to continue, somewhat dogmatically, to maintain this distinction.

Gadamer, however, has other options. Although he never explicitly puts forward the argument, his position, like Rorty's, entails that both the natural and the social sciences are hermeneutic (Bleicher, 1982:79). From the assertion of the universality of hermeneutic understanding it follows that all thought, including that of the natural sciences, is hermeneutic. In this Gadamer is in agreement with a growing number of philosophers of science who assert the hermeneutic character of the natural sciences (Heelan, 1983; Giddens, 1982:14; Toulmin, 1982; Lyotard, 1984). It also follows from Gadamer's position that the social sciences are prior to the natural sciences in that they study the fundamental nature of hermeneutic understanding. Gadamer's position on this issue also provides him with a reply to the argument between Rorty and Taylor/Dreyfus. Although Gadamer would not assert that there is an a priori reason why human beings must be treated differently from natural things, he would argue that there are two compelling practical reasons. One is that the vocabulary that we use about human beings and their actions is radically different from that which we use about natural things. This is not an a priori point, but a point about the tradition of discourse in which we live, a tradition that constitutes our collective life. The second reason is that, as a matter of practice, the kinds of questions that we ask in the social sciences result in the privileging of a certain vocabulary and, in most cases, the exclusion of the vocabulary employed in the natural sciences. Again, there is nothing a priori about this distinction but it has the result of establishing a certain vocabulary as appropriate to questions in the social sciences.[7]

The distinction between what I have labelled the nihilism of Rorty's position and the anti-foundational position espoused by Gadamer is central to a proper understanding of Gadamer's approach. Although Gadamer's thought is part of what can be identified as an anti-foundational movement in contemporary social thought, it is nevertheless important to distinguish his thought from both the objectivism and nihilism represented by some of the writers in this movement. Gadamer's rejection of any aspects of objectivism is not difficult to establish and should be obvious from the preceding discussion. The distinction between his thought and that of contemporary writers whose work has nihilistic tendencies is more difficult to show. Contrasting Gadamer's work with that of Foucault and Derrida reveals, however, that Gadamer's anti-foundationalism and the reliance on tradition and prejudice on which it rests is superior both practically and philosophically to the nihilistic approach of these writers.

II BEYOND HUMANISM: THE 'DEATH OF MAN'

In order to appreciate the full import of the anti-foundational movement in general and the work of Foucault and Derrida in particular it is necessary briefly to explore the history of a particular aspect of social theory in the twentieth century that has not been explicitly discussed above. It has frequently been noted that one of the main themes of social theory in this century is an on-going and ultimately sterile debate between positivism and humanism. Positivist thought in the social sciences, following the Enlightenment conception of scientific knowledge, has taken the position that the goal of the social sciences is to gather 'objective data' and subject it to scientific analysis. Humanism, in contrast, eschews the search for objective data and accepts the inherent 'subjectivity' of the social sciences. It would seem, then, that the humanists are offering a clear alternative to the positivist approach that rests on an entirely different epistemology. But closer examination shows this not to be the case. Both humanists and positivists share a fundamental epistemological assumption: the opposition of subject and object. The essence of the positivist approach has been to emphasize the object side of this opposition. Positivists claim that the goal of scientific investigation is the accumulation of 'objective knowledge' free from any taint of subjectivity. The humanists, on the other hand, have emphasized the subject side of the dichotomy. In the parlance of contemporary philosophy, what the humanists have effected is the 'deconstruction' of the object of knowledge in the social sciences. That is, they have attempted to show that the brute, 'objective' facts that provide the raw material for the positivist's production of knowledge simply do not exist in the social sciences. They argue, instead, that the subject matter of the social sciences is inherently 'subjective' because it deals with *meaningful* action.

This perspective suggests both why the humanist critique has failed and why the debate between positivism and humanism has persisted: positivism and humanism are, in essence, two sides of the same coin. This complementary relationship between positivism and humanism is increasingly coming to the attention of social and political theorists. Foucault, one of the pioneers in this line of thought, argues that rather than challenging the epistemological foundations of positivism the humanists have succeeded only in standing positivism on its head. Because they have failed to question the opposition of subject and object that lies at the heart of the positivist epistemology, the humanists have, in effect, chosen one side of this opposition as their exclusive domain. The subjectivism fostered by humanism is, in this sense, the counterpart of the objectivism of positivism.[8]

This assessment of the debate points to two conclusions. First, it suggests that the debate between positivism and humanism has not been resolved because the validity of the positivist epistemology has not been specifically challenged and the positivist definition of 'scientific knowledge' called into question. Secondly, it suggests that, as a first step, it is necessary to complete the critique of positivism begun by the humanists by 'deconstructing' the other side of the subject-object opposition: the knowing subject. It is necessary, in other words, to challenge the epistemological primacy of the knowing subject presupposed by the epistemology of both positivism and humanism. It has already been argued that Gadamer moves beyond the terms of the positivist-humanist debate by challenging the Enlightenment conception of knowledge and the dichotomies on which it rests and that he thus places the social sciences on a new footing. The way in which Gadamer challenges the epistemological primacy of the subject has also been explored. His rejection of subjective intentionality, his notion of the fusion of horizons, and his conception of language as 'I-less' are all central to his position on this issue.

Challenging the epistemological primacy of the subject through a deconstruction of the concept of 'man' has become a central theme of contemporary social theory. The rallying cry of those theorists who espouse this theory is the proclamation of the 'death of man'. The groups that claim principal responsibility for challenging the primacy of the knowing subject, particularly in humanist thought and thus 'killing' man, are the post-Second World War French structuralists and post-structuralists. Any number of books and articles can be cited as making the definitive proclamation of the death of man, but Foucault's *The Order of Things* (1971), Heidegger's 'Letter on humanism' (1977:189–242) and Derrida's 'The ends of man' (1969) stand out as particularly influential. Each proclaims in unambiguous terms that social and philosophical thought is moving away from the 'man' centered (homocentric) foundations that have characterized it since the last quarter of the eighteenth century (Lemert 1979:14).

The homocentrism that the proponents of the 'death of man'

are attacking is by no means a minor aspect of social theory. Rather, a man-centered approach is the epistemological foundation for most nineteenth and twentieth century social and political theory. It follows that the long-standing and pervasive impact of homocentrism that has been definitive of contemporary social and political thought has not been completely exorcized by the proclamation of the 'death of man'.[9] The continuing strength of phenomenology which, with Husserl's work, is the culmination of homocentric thought, testifies to the tenacity of the homocentric perspective. But since mid-century the reaction against homocentrism has begun to have a significant impact. Coincident with and, some have argued, the cause of the 'death of man' is the linguistic turn of twentieth century social and political thought. The emphasis on language results in the decentering of 'man' because the speaking subject is not the primary focus in the study of language. Human beings as individuals are participants in language; they are acted on by language and its rules and are only in a very tangential sense creators of language (Lemert, 1979:184). Wittgenstein's later philosophy has been particularly influential in promoting this attitude toward individuals and language. Wittgenstein rejects the notion that meaning is a mental event that in some way accompanies speech and carefully avoids any reference to the constituting human subject that is so central to phenomenology and other homocentric approaches (Giddens, 1979:33).

Neither Wittgenstein nor Gadamer actively proclaims the death of 'man' in their writings. Both Foucault and Derrida, in contrast, are explicit defenders of the 'death of man' thesis. On the basis of the foregoing analysis, however, it can be argued that Gadamer, like Wittgenstein, contributes to the 'death of man' even though he does not specifically proclaim it. Several commentators have noticed the similarity between Gadamer's hermeneutics and post-structuralists in this respect (Giddens, 1979:40; Jay, 1982:96; Apel, 1981:246). Although it is clear that Gadamer has not gone as far as the structuralists and post-structuralists in rejecting the subject, he is nevertheless clearly moving away from a homocentric emphasis. As Apel puts it:

> Modern hermeneutics, following Heidegger and Gadamer and drawing on certain affinities with French Structuralism has almost dismissed (dropped) the problematic of understanding *subjective*

> *intentions*, e.g., of the authors of texts, in favor of explicating the language of texts as an autonomous medium and even origin of meaning. (1981:246)

It is Gadamer's tendency to decenter 'man' and his rejection of the epistemological dichotomies of Enlightenment thought that form the bridge between Gadamer and post-structuralist thinkers.[10]

It would be premature to conclude, however, that Gadamer and the post-structuralists are completely in agreement on this issue. Like the post-structuralists Gadamer encourages us to be suspicious of 'subjects' as well as 'objects' and thus transcend the sterile dichotomies of the positivist-humanist debate. But Gadamer stops short of the extremes of the position espoused by the 'death of man' theorists. Many critics have suggested that the 'death of man' advocates have gone too far in their rejection of the concept and, consequently, have incurred a number of serious problems. Dallmayr, for example, argues that those who argue for the end of man are endangering both self-reflection and moral responsibility (1981b:30). In the same vein Giddens argues against the 'death of man' theorists that we must be able to retain a role for the subject without falling into subjectivism (1979:47). It can be argued that Gadamer's perspective does precisely this. Gadamer offers a sort of midway position on the 'death of man' issue that offers the advantages of avoiding the subjectivism that is the counterpart of objectivism without incurring the problems encountered by the 'death of man' theorists. Gadamer retains reference to agents and their moral responsibility without abandoning the collective perspective dictated by the thesis of the linguisticality of understanding.[11]

III FOUCAULT: MORAL NIHILISM

No account of contemporary anti-foundational thought could be considered complete without an examination of the work of Michel Foucault. In the context of the particular concerns of this study, however, an exploration of his work is especially compelling. Foucault, along with Derrida, illustrates most clearly the nihilistic dangers of some aspects of the anti-foundational position. It is especially important, therefore, to establish that Gadamerian hermeneutics can be clearly distinguished from Foucault's position, that Gadamer's position has distinct advantages, and, consequently, that the anti-foundational approach need not entail nihilism. This is significant in light of the fact that Foucault's work has many striking parallels with Gadamer's hermeneutics. Foucault's arguments, particularly in *The Order of Things*, are very similar to Gadamer's critique of the Enlightenment in *Truth and Method*. Establishing precisely the differences and similarities between these two works is thus central to the thesis being advanced here.

In a recent book, *Beyond Structuralism and Hermeneutics* (1982), Hubert Dreyfus and Paul Rabinow argue for a parallel between the hermeneutics of Heidegger and the work of Foucault. A consideration of this work is a good place to start a discussion of Foucault because it is directly relevant to the present thesis. Dreyfus and Rabinow argue, first, that Heidegger's 'background' and the 'unthought' that Foucault seeks to define are essentially the same thing and thus that the theories of the two thinkers are parallel in this important sense.[12] Secondly, they argue that Foucault moves beyond both structuralism and hermeneutics in his analysis. This thesis hinges on their particular definition of these two terms: they define structuralism as the subjectless search for objective laws and hermeneutics as the search for meaning in social practices (1982:xvii). This second thesis, however, is misleading. The authors define hermeneutics in terms of the search for 'deeper' meaning that probes the subjective intentions of authors of texts (1982:181). Their claim is that because Foucault does not probe this deeper meaning but merely attempts to describe and interpret the discursive practices he analyzes he is not engaged in 'hermeneutic' analysis (1982:124). It should be clear from the foregoing, however, that by this definition Gadamer is not a hermeneuticist. Significantly, this is precisely the claim that Dreyfus and Rabinow make for Heidegger's methodology.

Two arguments can be advanced against this interpretation of Foucault's work. First, although Dreyfus and Rabinow have made a valuable contribution in emphasizing the connection between Heidegger's background and Foucault's discursive analysis, they have failed to make a clear distinction between the tasks of the two programs of analysis or the liabilities of Foucault's approach. The philosopher's effort to understand the 'background' of human life and the fundamental nature of human understanding is related to, yet distinct from, the social scientist's effort to understand the presuppositions and implications of a particular belief system, what Foucault calls a 'discursive formation'. Although these two tasks are related in that Foucault's discursive analysis must presuppose Heidegger's 'background' it does not follow that they are identical. A similar argument was made above with regard to Mannheim and Gadamer: Mannheim's analysis of particular belief systems must presuppose Gadamer's prejudice. Secondly, it can be argued against Dreyfus and Rabinow that Heidegger, like Gadamer, is acutely conscious of the role of the questioner who searches for the meaning of Being in a particular epoch while Foucault, as Dreyfus and Rabinow themselves point out, is unconscious of the place of the investigator (archaeologist) in the investigation. This difference between the two approaches is, however, much more important than the authors concede. Foucault's failure to account for the role of the investigator causes him to misinterpret the phenomenon of human understanding that he seeks to explicate.

Foucault's work is one of the central influences in the movement discussed in the previous section – the attack on humanism and the proclamation of the 'death of man'. Foucault rejects both positivism and the interpretative or humanistic alternatives and seeks to present a theory without any center at all. If there is a center to Foucault's work it is that of texts and language. But, as one of his critics has noted, in the context of Western thought centering a theory on language is the closest thing to absolute decentering (Brown, 1975;158). An understanding of Foucault's work must therefore begin with an examination of his theory of discourse. Foucault's thesis that discourse creates subjects as well as objects is arguably his greatest contribution to social theory. Although critics of positivism came to the conclusion that scientific discourse in both the natural and the social sciences creates the objects of its analysis, Foucault's contribution was to explain how it also created subjects and particularly the subject 'man'. Foucault's discursive analysis begins with the presupposition that the examination of meaning is not centered in an author. Like Gadamer, Foucault is interested in the text itself, not who wrote it or the subjective intentions that guided its composition. He is interested in revealing the presuppositions informing the categories the text employs. Foucault is at his best when he is analyzing specific instances of discourse and the way in which they create unique subjects, subjects that did not exist before the discourse was deployed. In a methodological sense Foucault can be most accurately classified not as someone who is attempting to formulate a new social theory in opposition to the other post-positivist alternatives but, rather, someone who is interested in the concrete problems of social practice.

Foucault's theory of discourse has a second unique element: his contention that knowledge is a form of power. Discourse, he claims, is a regulated social practice and hence partakes of power as well as knowledge; power and knowledge are fused in the practices that comprise history (Lemert and Gillan, 1982:60). His view of power/knowledge separates his theory of discourse from other language-oriented theories (including Gadamer's) because it introduces a specifically political element. It is Foucault's thesis that the categories embodied in a particular discursive framework create not only knowledge but power as well. In his studies of prisons and mental institutions in particular he shows how categories of knowledge determine relationships of power and how the two interact to form a cohesive unit. His argument for this power/knowledge nexus, more than any other aspect of this theory, sets him apart from other theorists of discourse. It also sets him apart from other theorists of power. Foucault offers a radically different concept of power that avoids both agency and structure (Hoy, 1981:47). Against the Marxists he rejects the notion that the state is the focus of power relations (Poulantzas, 1978:44) and against the humanists he divorces power from human action and responsibility (Philip, 1983:48).

Since the focus of this work is an exploration of the method of the social sciences it would seem appropriate to center the discussion of Foucault around a close examination of his one explicitly methodological work, *The Archaeology of Knowledge* (1972). But there are a number of reasons why looking to *The Archaeology* for the key to his approach is ill-advised. It is widely acknowledged to be his worst book and presents a position that he later repudiates (Dreyfus and Rabinow, 1982:100). This may be due to the fact that *The Archaeology* attempts to define a method for a practice that is profoundly anti-theoretical (Sheridan, 1980:215). *The Archaeology* can, however, offer insights into the nature of Foucault's approach. It provides a clear idea of what Foucault does *not* see his method as doing. At the end of the book he presents a list of philosophical errors that his method seeks to avoid: transcendental reflection, anthropological themes, a search for origins, and a return to humanist ideologies, particularly that of the subject (1972:204). Further, in the course of the work he rejects both structuralism and hermeneutics as well as traditional intellectual history as definitons of his method (1972:15, 135–41). His description of what his method *is* doing, however, is not as clear. At the outset he declares that he is attempting to analyze discursive events without reference to anthropological categories (that is, whether those events are embodied in a book, work of art, etc.) and describe the relations between statements (1972:21–30). Later he claims that his aim is to analyze the 'positivity' of discourse without reference to subjective intention. This positivity plays the role of a 'historical *a priori*' or a condition of reality for statements. What this comes to is that he is seeking to discover the conditions under which it is possible for statements to emerge (1972:127). He defines these laws of what can be said as an 'archive', and claims that the uncovering of the archive forms a 'general horizon' to which discursive formations belong (1972:129–30).

The general conclusion that can be drawn from this list of repudiations and definitions is that Foucault, like Dilthey, is looking for a set of objective relations in the social world that he can analyze scientifically. Although he defines the data of his analysis as discursive relations, not, as Dilthey did, subjective intentions, his goal is much the same. He is looking for a method for the social sciences that is native to these disciplines yet will yield scientific results. Dreyfus and Rabinow refer to this method as 'phenomenological positivism' (1982:52). What sets his approach apart from both Marxist historical materialism and intellectual history is that he sees discourse-practice not as separate entities but as a unity that structures social life and defines power relations (Poster, 1982:149).

The method that Foucault outlines in *The Archaeology* is, without question, profoundly innovative. His replacement of both materialism and idealism, his discovery that discourse and practice form a unity that structures both knowledge and power relationships is a significant accomplishment. Yet there are also serious problems with his method. In the first place, Foucault, following Dilthey, is looking for a 'scientific' method to study social practices 'objectively'. Although he is, as an archaeologist, critical of the nature of the discursive practice of Enlightenment science and the presuppositions underlying it, he does not, like Gadamer, attack the notion of scientificity at its root. This problem is closely connected to a second deficiency in his method: his lack of awareness of the role of the archaeologist. Although Foucault takes great pains to define the 'horizon' of the discursive practice he is investigating, he fails to define or take account of his own horizon. Although he does not, like Dilthey, assume his position to be an Archimedean point of objectivity because he eschews the possibility of eternal truth, his lack of awareness of his own role as archaeologist in the task of interpretation seriously distorts his analysis.[13]

Foucault's other works form a sharp contrast to the abstract theorizing of *The Archaeology*. In *Madness and Civilization* (1973b), *The Birth of the Clinic* (1973a), *The Order of Things* (1971), *Discipline and Punish* (1977), and *The History of Sexuality* (1978) Foucault analyzes specific discursive formations of power/knowledge. The only methodological point he discusses after *The Archaeology* concerns his move away from the archaeological method. Beginning with *Discipline and Punish* he employs the word 'geneology' to describe his methodological approach. Following Nietzsche he defines geneology as

> a form of history which gives an account of the constitution of different kinds of knowledge, of discourse, and of the domains of the object, etc., without having to refer to a subject that would be transcendent to the field of events or that, in its contentless identity, would transverse the entire length of history. (1981:299)

He makes certain that his definition of geneology is clearly distinquished from ideology, arguing that 'ideology' is an unsuitable description of the goal of his analysis because it is always opposed to truth. Ideological statements, further, always refer to a subject and are in a secondary position to an infrastructure. In contrast to subject-oriented analyses Foucault defines geneological analysis as revealing the 'articulation of knowledge on power and power on knowledge' (1980:51). With regard to madness, medicine, the human sciences, punishment and sexuality he reveals how particular discursive formations define complexes of power and knowledge, how they have shaped practices in Western history and how their internal structure is constituted. In each case he shows the central role that language plays in this process. With regard to madness he asserts:

> Language is the first and last structure of madness, its constituent form; on language are based all the cycles in which madness articulates its nature. (1973b:100)

One of the leading themes that Foucault develops in these works is how these discursive practices are articulated onto bodies. Foucault defines his task not as probing the 'deeper' meaning of these discursive practices, if exploring deeper meaning entails uncovering the subjective intentions of individual authors. In this Foucault is making an explicit distinction between geneology and the kind of hermeneutics espoused by Dilthey. He defines his aim as revealing the relations of power, knowledge and the body in modern society and, most importantly, destroying the assumption of the primacy of origins and the existence of eternal, unchanging truth (Dreyfus and Rabinow, 1982:105–9). He is not attempting to oppose the 'unreality' of the discursive formation he analyzes to a 'true reality' that he has claimed to discover. He states this intention very clearly with regard to the concepts of 'sex' and 'sexuality'.

> We must not place sex on the side of reality and sexuality on that of confused ideas and illusions; sexuality is a very real historical formation; it is what gave rise to the notion of sex, as a speculative element necessary to its operation. (1978:157)

In *The Order of Things* Foucault presents a series of arguments that are the most relevant to a consideration of the state of the social sciences in the twentieth century and, specifically, to the thesis presented here. This work is similar to Gadamer's *Truth and Method* because in it Foucault offers a critique of Enlightenment thought and an explanation of why the sciences of man have necessarily failed. The two analyses are also linked in that they are both concerned with language and the way in which it structures thought. For Gadamer this means defining the horizon of meaning in a given era, for Foucault, defining the 'a priori' of thought. But there are important differences as well. The most essential difference concerns Foucault's attempt to uncover the 'positive unconscious of knowledge'. He defines this as that level of knowledge that eludes the consciousness of the scientific investigator yet is an integral part of scientific discourse. He states:

> Thus in every culture, between the use of what one might call the ordering codes and reflections upon order itself, there is the pure experience of order and of its modes of being. (1971:xxi)

This level, he claims, is the most clearly visible, yet something that must be sought out because it is the most hidden (1971:29). Later he defines this realm as the 'a priori of knowledge':

> This a priori is what, in a given period, delimits in the totality of experience a field of knowledge, defines the mode of being of the objects that appear in that field, provides man's everyday perception with theoretical powers, and defines the conditions in which he can sustain a discourse about things that is recognized to be true. (1971:158)

The explicit goal of Foucault's analysis in *The Order of Things* is to analyze the transition from classical to modern thought. In a complex and detailed discussion he identifies the 'a priori' of classical thought–representation and the reflection on order – and explores the contrast between these concepts and the 'a priori' of modern thought. In an argument reminiscent of Kuhn he asserts that the break between the two modes of thought came not through a 'rational' process of scientific analysis, but through a shift in 'what it makes sense to say' in the three areas of scientific thought that he analyzes. But his analysis is more complex than Kuhn's because he argues, further, that

> Philology, biology, and political economy were established, not in the places formerly occupied by *general grammar, natural history,* and *the analysis of wealth*, but in an area where those forms of knowledge did not exist, in the space they left blank, in the deep gaps that separated their broad theoretical segments and that were filled with the murmur of the ontological continuum. The object of knowledge in the nineteenth century is formed in the very place where the Classical plenitude of being has fallen silent. (1971:207)

Much of Foucault's work is devoted to defining the particular a priori of knowledge at the root of modern thought. He asserts that at the end of the eighteenth century a new opening of thought appeared: the transcendental. It is this concept that he defines as providing the basis for the modern episteme: 'Labor, life and language appear as so many "transcendentals" which make possible the objective knowledge of living beings, of the laws of production, and of the forms of language' (1971:244).

The most intriguing part of Foucault's analysis, however, is his treatment of the human sciences and the concept 'man'. In his exploration of the modern episteme he makes the observation that the human sciences are excluded from this epistemological domain (1971:347). Their anomalous position explains the problematic status of the human sciences in modern thought. Foucault claims that they are not false sciences but simply not sciences at all (1971:366). And central to the difficulty of the human sciences is the concept of 'man':

> Western culture has constituted, under the name of man, a being who, by one and the same interplay of reasons, must be a positive domain of *knowledge* and cannot be an object of *science*. (1971:366)

What Foucault defines as three 'doublets' have defined man's mode of being since the nineteenth century: the empirical-transcendental, the cogito and the unthought, and the retreat and the return of the origin (1971:320–35). Each of these 'doublets' has an object pole and a subject pole and the concept of 'man' consists of the impossible attempt to integrate the two poles. Each pole tries to exclude the other, yet because each requires the other, the attempt must fail. It is the existence of these doublets that has made it impossible to integrate 'man' into the modern episteme. As a kind of solution to this dilemma, however, Foucault takes the controversial position that ethnology, psychoanalysis and linguistics, because they 'dissolve' the concept of 'man', presage a new era in which 'man' is coming to an end. He ends the book with a rhetorical question that leaves no doubt as to how he stands on this issue:

> Since man was constituted at a time when language was doomed to dispersion, will he not be dispersed when language regains its unity? (1971:386)

Even this brief outline of Foucault's argument in *The Order of Things* reveals the similarity between his account and some aspects of Gadamer's argument in *Truth and Method*. Both accounts define language as the determinant of thought, that is, the 'horizon' or 'a priori' by which certain kinds of thought are made possible. Furthermore, both define the structure of the modern episteme as problematic for the human sciences. Gadamer approaches this problem in explicitly philosophical terms, arguing that the identification of truth with scientific method leaves no space for the human sciences. Foucault deals with the issue more historically, arguing that the epistemological domain of thought created in the nineteenth century excludes the human sciences. But the net result is much the same. Both deplore the status of the human sciences in the twentieth century and seek in their work to move it to a new plane of thought by changing the terms of the argument.

But on a deeper level there are significant differences not only in the form but also in the substance of the two works. Dreyfus and Rabinow claim that Foucault is examining the same thing as what Heidegger calls the 'background'. They claim that Foucault analyzes this 'background' through his examination of the unconscious, unformed level of thought preceding explicit belief systems. But a careful reading of *The Order of Things* shows that Foucault's analysis operates on a different level than Heidegger's anlaysis of 'background' or Gadamer's examination of 'prejudice'. Although Foucault is undoubtedly probing deeper than traditional intellectual history in seeking to define what it is possible to say in certain periods, he is not, as are Gadamer and Heidegger, probing the nature of human understanding itself. What Gadamer explores in his notion of prejudice is how human beings understand each other. What Foucault explores, in contrast, is the underlying epistemological basis of scientific thought in a particular age. And this is quite a different phenomenon.

Despite this difference, however, the approaches of Gadamer and Foucault are, at root, compatible. The difference between the two approaches is the same difference that divided Gadamer and Mannheim: their sociologies of knowledge operate on different but compatible levels. While Gadamer explores the philosophical point that all human thought is socially structured, Foucault and Mannheim explore how particular human thought systems are structured in specific historical instances. But Foucault, like Mannheim, presents a position that diverges from traditional sociology of knowledge. There are three respects in which Foucault's work moves beyond the traditional approach. First, he firmly rejects any absolute grounding of knowledge. The only a priori of knowledge is, Foucault makes clear, historically constituted. Secondly, unlike Mannheim, Foucault probes beyond the obvious levels of belief systems normally explored by intellectual historians to the underlying epistemological level. He discovers what it makes sense to say, not just what is said. Thirdly, unlike both intellectual historians and Marxist philosophers he shows the unity of discourse and practice, the interplay between social practice and social discourse.

In these respects Foucault exemplifies in *The Order of Things* the kind of anti-foundational sociology of knowledge for which I am arguing here. Eschewing any absolute grounding for knowledge he explores, at a level that has eluded previous analysis, the basis for knowledge in particular eras. He illustrates through his theory of the constitutive power of discourse what Gadamer calls the linguisticality of understanding. He moves beyond Mannheim in that he probes a deeper level in his analysis and beyond Gadamer in the clarity of this demonstration of the unity of thought and social existence. Foucault's work can thus be seen as an important addition to the anti-foundational position because it adds the dimension of social practice to the analysis of discourse. He fleshes out what is only implicit in Gadamer – the social and political implications of the linguisticality of understanding. Even though Foucault rejects hermeneutics because it is rooted in an appeal to subjective intentions, this rejection does not apply to Gadamer's particular definition of hermeneutics. The explicit anti-foundationalism of both, furthermore, forms a significant bond between them.

Despite these important similarities, however, there are at least three respects in which Gadamer's approach diverges from that of Foucault. The first concerns the issue of the 'death of man'. Many commentators have criticized Foucault's attitude toward the subject in his work, arguing that his analysis necessitates reference to it although he rejects it as a methodological concept (Lemert and Gillan, 1982:104–5). Foucault's attitude toward the subject has caused him to be labelled an 'anti-humanist' by many of his critics. Although it has been argued above that Gadamer also rejects the concept of the constituting subject and that this forms an important parallel between the two, Gadamer's position avoids the extremes of Foucault's anti-humanism. Gadamer claims that texts are to be interpreted through reference to the horizon of meaning definitive of the author's era, not through reference to subjective intentions. Yet Gadamer does not exclude reference to authors and subjects altogether. Unlike Foucault he does not abandon the subject as a methodological category, he merely places the subject where it belongs – in the context of meaning supplied by the historical, cultural setting.

The second difference between Foucault and Gadamer involves an issue central to Gadamer's approach, the fusion of horizons. Correcting the historicist's one-sided notion that the interpreter appropriates the meaning of the text from an Archimedean point of objectivity, Gadamer argues that understanding is a dialectical process in which both interpreter and interpreted participate. For Gadamer, the notion that the meaning of both participants fuse to create the interpretation is essential to an understanding of the phenomenon of human understanding. Foucault, in contrast, fails to account for the role of the interpreter adequately in his analysis. Although a brief passage in *The Archaeology* refers to the impossibility of describing our own archive because 'it is from within these rules that we speak' (1972:130), the theme of reflexivity is not prominent in Foucault as it is in Gadamer. Rather, like the historicists, he does not describe the role of the interpreter as integral to the interpretation but, as one commentator has put it, renders the role of the investigator in the passive mode (Shapiro, 1981:163). This deficiency has been noted by several critics of Foucault's work (Shapiro, 1981:167; Dreyfus and Rabinow, 1982:87; Hoy, 1979:87).[14] Given his sensitivity to the historical determination of thinking this is a somewhat surprising although unmistakable error on his part.

The third respect in which the perspectives of Gadamer and Foucault diverge is, however, the most important and overshadows the other two issues. It was asserted at the outset that Foucault's anti-foundationalism leads to a kind of nihilism, particularly in the area of morality, that is not entailed by Gadamer's position. This claim involves a number of complex issues. Whether or not Foucault's work entails nihilism is not at all easy to determine, a fact indicated by the disagreement of his critics on this issue. Although many admit that Foucault comes close to the nihilism of Nietzsche, many others claim that he stops short of a nihilistic position or that, at the very least, he claims to avoid this extreme. Still others simply concede that Foucault's position on nihilism is ambiguous. This ambiguity is freqently excused with the argument that Foucault is better at criticizing specific patterns of authority than at offering an alternative.

Support for a nihilistic interpretation of Foucault's work is not difficult to find. The main thrust of his books is to attack the 'will to truth' that has dominated Western thought since Plato. His stated aim is to replace this impulse with the analysis of a particular regime of truth (Sheridan, 1980:222). Truth, Foucault claims, is a consequence of multiple constraints within this world; it is not beyond power in another world. He asserts that the intellectual does not battle on behalf of truth, but, rather, about its status. He defines truth as 'the totality of rules according to which the true is distinguished from the false and the concrete effects of power are attached to what is true' (1981:306). It follows that no regime of truth can be declared superior to any other; they are all products of particular conceptual schemes.

There is some evidence, however, that Foucault offers hope beyond this nihilistic conclusion. At various points in his work he seems to indicate that nihilism is not our only option in the present situation. In *The Order of Things* he begins to discuss the possibility of a new vocabulary (and, hence, set of practices) for the human sciences that is not 'man' centered. To those who still wish to talk about man, he states, we can only answer 'with a philosophical laugh – which means, to a certain extent, a silent one' (1971:343). This enigmatic statement may be intended to hold out the possibility of a less repressive social system in the future. Although Foucault defines truth as lodged in particular social systems, he seems to indicate here and elsewhere that the truth–power relationship under which we live is especially destructive. He states that in our society 'the relationship between power, right and truth is organized in a highly specific fashion' (1980:93). Although he is very clear that our task is not to free truth from power because, of course, truth *is* power, he insists that we should detach the power of truth from the 'forms of hegemony' (social, economic and cultural) within which it now functions (1981:307). He further argues that the specific task of the intellectual in this process is to determine whether it is possible to constitute 'a new politics of truth' (1981:306). He even seems to indicate that although the will to truth has been the 'tyrant' that ruled Western thought, the problem posed by this fact is not that the quest for truth is in itself futile but that it has been perverted in practice to a point where we can no longer recognize it (1972:216).

What Foucault seems to be indicating in these passages is that it is possible to construct a new truth–power relationship that is less repressive than the ones we have seen so far. It may be possible, that is, to create a regime in which the will to truth is not perverted. His references to this possibility, however, are very sketchy. In the *History of Sexuality* he refers to a 'different economy of bodies and pleasures' (1978:137) and in 'The subject and power' to a 'new economy of power relations' (1982b:210). What is entailed by these statements, however, is never specified. On the basis of passages such as these several of Foucault's defenders have argued that he offers a kind of implicit moral alternative. Lemert and Gillan claim that Foucault's solution is the 'forging of a revolutionary link between power and knowledge', a link that would create a 'nomadic joy' (1982:91). Lemert further claims that the decentering of man does not necessarily entail a dehumanizing of moral life (1979:230–1). Shapiro, who praises Foucault's 'radical partisanship model of political interpretation' (1984:391), argues that although Foucault does not answer our questions of 'what now?' he does offer criteria by which we might select a less repressive interpretive scheme (1980:24). Finally, in a particularly provocative essay, Fraser suggests that Foucault's work is compatible with the modern humanist values of autonomy, reciprocity, mutual recognition and human dignity (1981a:4). She claims that 'Foucault's deconstruction of metaphysical humanism does not entail the delegitimation of the normative ideals of moral humanism' (1981a:36) and that 'we can and should combine post-modern antifoundationalism and anti-transcendentalism with substantive modern normative humanism' (1981a:38).

What can be made of these claims for Foucault's rejection of nihilism? Although it is quite clear that Foucault does not offer the goal of emancipation held out by the critical theorists, it might be argued that he does motivate his readers to social and political action and holds out the possibility of a better relationship of truth and power in the future. It might be argued, for instance, that his approach is compatible with the method of 'sociological intervention' proposed by Touraine (1981). But, as even his defenders will admit, the evidence for an anti-nihilistic reading of Foucault is quite thin. The principal difficulty is that Foucault's method dictates that there is no reason to accept one conceptual scheme rather than another. And although, as Fraser argues, there is nothing in Foucault that obliges us to reject the humanist values (1981a:24), it can also be argued that there is nothing that obliges us to accept them either. Foucault leaves us with little more than the faint hope that a 'new economy of bodies and pleasures' will emerge but with no sense of what that state might be.

It follows from this that Foucault's position is, at root, inconsistent. Those who argue against a nihilistic reading of Foucault are, on one level, correct. Foucault's work has a clearly moral thrust. His intent is to unmask repressive power relationships and even to argue for resistance to regimes of power. He claims that his position with regard to the contemporary situation is one of 'optimism' based on the possibility of change (1982a:35). What is wrong with this interpretation is that it ignores that his method denies that any conceptual scheme is true and, thus, can be used as a basis for such a critique. As Charles Taylor puts it in his criticism of Foucault, the notions of mask and falsehood make no sense without a corresponding notion of truth (1984:174). The paradox in Foucault's work is that he seems to be revealing a good repressed in history, yet his method precludes the possibility of offering any particular definition of good because all definitions are equally products of conceptual schemes and we have no way of choosing among them. Several other critics have pointed to this inconsistency in Foucault's work (Fraser, 1981b:282; Philip, 1983:42; Major-Poetzl, 1983:42). Although this interpretation of Foucault rescues him from nihilism it does so only at the expense of incoherence. In the end Foucault can most accurately be portrayed as a theorist who argues for resistance to power without being able to justify such resistance because he can offer no positive basis for political action.

The implicit nihilism of Foucault's position, however, can be corrected by turning to the perspective offered by Gadamer and Heidegger. Unlike Foucault, Gadamer offers a reason to accept a particular set of norms, the normative values of our tradition, and thus avoids the nihilistic implications of Foucault's work. Gadamer argues, following Heidegger, that we are ontologically bound to our tradition and to our prejudices; we cannot express ourselves, in either a normative or epistemological sense, outside the reference point of that tradition. Heidegger argues that the historical setting is the 'clearing' in which Being is revealed for us:

> In analysing the historicality of Dasein we shall try to show that this entity is not 'temporal' because it 'stands in history' but that, on the contrary, it exists historically and can so exist only because it is temporal in the very basis of its Being. (1962:428)

The most significant aspect of this position is that, for both Heidegger and Gadamer, the reliance on tradition does not entail a negative resignation to its arbitrary power. This is the case, first, because tradition is not arbitrary. By destroying the Enlightenment dichotomy between reason and authority/tradition, Gadamer has shown that the two are not incompatible, but actually complementary. Secondly, the power of tradition and prejudice is a positive possibility of understanding, not a negative restriction on it. What this comes to is that tradition provides us with the context that allows us to make moral judgements.[15] It is precisely this context that is lacking in the work of Foucault.

This reference point provided by tradition, furthermore, does not preclude the possibility of critique. As Gadamer makes so clear in *Truth and Method* the critical assessment of tradition is the main task of hermeneutics. It not only leaves open the possibility of the internal critique of social norms, it defines such critique as the basic requirement of hermeneutic thought. This can be illustrated by using one of Foucault's own examples. From a Gadamerian perspective it can be argued that what Foucault identifies as the carceral society violates some of the basic norms of Western civilization: autonomy and human dignity. An internal critique of these practices dictates that the social practices associated with carceral institutions must be resisted. Foucault's position, in contrast, precludes the possibility of such a critique. Instead he holds out the hope of a new discourse that would dictate less repressive social practices. The difference between the two positions is this: Foucault agrees with Gadamer that each society generates its own truth and its own moral code but, for him, this fact has only nihilistic significance. For Gadamer, in contrast, it has ontological significance. His position entails that as human beings we express our morality through the moral codes of our society, codes that allow for self-reflection and internal critique. This possibility is a positive expression of our presence in the world, not the basis for a negative, arbitrary judgement of the subjectivity of moral judgements. It provides us with what Giddens calls 'ontological security' (1981:194). Foucault's error is that although he sees the social world, along with Gadamer, as linguistically constitued, his view is not tempered by the ontological perspective that allows for the possibility of critique.

IV DECONSTRUCTION: CONCEPTUAL NIHILISM

There is a second approach within the anti-foundational camp which, in addition to the work of Foucault, is gaining attention in contemporary social theory: deconstruction, and particularly the deconstructive theories of Jacques Derrida. Although this approach is, unlike that of Foucault, not specifically concerned with social and political issues, it has captured the attention of social and political theorists and is, perhaps to the surprise of its proponents, being seriously discussed outside the philosophical and literary circles where it originated. This approach is important to the present thesis for a number of reasons. In the first place, Derrida, the foremost spokesman of the approach, relies heavily on the work of Heidegger and thus his perspective is relevant to an analysis of Gadamer's work. Secondly, and more importantly, the issue of deconstruction has come to define anti-foundational thought in the minds of many contemporary thinkers. It is thus important to show that although there are similarities between the two approaches of Derrida and Gadamer the nihilistic implications of Derrida's definition of deconstruction can be distinguished from Gadamer's anti-foundational position.

Derrida's work presents a formidable challenge to his interpreters. Unlike Foucault he has written no methodological work that, however flawed, can serve as a guide to his work. Furthermore, approaching Derrida's work by looking for his 'method' is false to the underlying theme of that work because Derrida eschews the whole notion of a method. Even more vexing is the fact that Derrida offers unique definitions of a number of words that he uses to identify his approach. These definitions are complex and easily misunderstood yet central to an understanding of his perspective. Because of the idiosyncratic meanings he attaches to terms such as deconstruction, *différance*, trace and presence, precisely what he means to convey by them is not easily discovered.

Derrida has been one of the leading proponents of the movement discussed at the beginning of this chapter: the advocacy of the 'death of man'. In his seminal article, 'The ends of man' (1969) he traces the demise of French humanism after the Second World War and the rise of what is today identified as post-structuralism. But the real thrust of his work is not the proclamation of the 'death of man' but rather an attack on what he regards as a more fundamental issue: the 'metaphysics of presence'. His most explicit statement of this theme can be found in *Of Grammatology* which focuses on the metaphysical opposition of speech to writing in Rousseau's account of the origin of languages. Derrida identifies Rousseau's work as a kind of paradigm of the tradition of Western metaphysics, a tradition he defines as fundamentally in error:

> If the history of metaphysics is the history of a determination of being as presence, if its adventure merges with that of logocentrism, and if it is produced wholly as the reduction of the trace, Rousseau's work seems to me to occupy, between Plato's *Phaedrus* and Hegel's *Encyclopedia*, a singular position. (1976:97)

In the context of his condemnation of what he identifies as Rousseau's 'privileging' of speech over writing a number of key elements of Derrida's approach emerge. First, he condemns what has been at the heart of Western metaphysics since its inception: the binary opposition of positive and negative terms. Derrida identifies the relationship of speech to writing as one instance of this opposition that is central to the metaphysical enterprise.

Secondly, he condemns the identification of being with presence that has also characterized this tradition. Rousseau is, once again, an excellent example of this tradition. He defines writing as the destruction of presence and the disease of speech (1976:142).

In opposition to Rousseau's understanding of the origin of language Derrida claims that writing, not speech, is primary. Writing, he claims, opens the field of history and of historical becoming. He asserts that the origin of language and the origin of writing are inseparable (1976:27–8). Further, he argues:

> I would wish rather to suggest that the alleged derivativeness of writing, however real and massive, was possible only on one condition: that the 'original', 'natural', etc. language had never existed, never been intact and untouched by writing, that it had itself always been a writing. (1976:56)

By the end of the work Derrida completely reverses Rousseau's formulation. Overturning the presupposition that speech is prior to writing, he argues instead that 'writing precedes and follows speech, it comprehends it' and that 'writing is the eve of speech' (1976:238).

But there is much more involved in *Of Grammatology* than merely questioning Rousseau's understanding of speech and writing. Following Nietzsche and Heidegger, Derrida is launching an attack on Western metaphysics itself. By attacking the privileging of speech, Derrida is attacking an opposition – between speech and writing – that has been fundamental to Western philosophy since the work of Plato. In an examination of Plato's *Phaedrus* Derrida argues that Plato presents writing as an occult power (1981b:97). Writing has no intrinsic essence; it is a tool that can be used positively or negatively and thus is linked with sophism (1981b:105). Derrida's attack on the opposition between speech and writing is part of two broader arguments: first, that the metaphysics of presence rests on a series of binary oppositions that can be traced to Plato (1981b:92) and, secondly, that this tradition is a tradition of violence (1978:102). In the writings that follow *Of Grammatology* Derrida develops each of these themes. The binary oppositions that have defined Western philosophy since Plato constitute the essence of the metaphysics of presence that Derrida is attacking in *Of Grammatology*. He claims that this tradition, in its attempt to comprehend the whole of being, is essentially a totalitarian tradition that, rather than revealing being, does violence to it.

Attempting to identify Derrida's condemnation of Western metaphysics and his reversal of its central position is not simple, but at least fairly straightforward. What is much more difficult, is to identify what he opposes to that tradition. This difficulty is largely a product of the fact that Derrida is fundamentally anti-methodological. He forcefully insists that he is not proposing a new method to replace the traditional one that he rejects. Although many of his critics identify grammatology as a 'science' Derrida claims that it is 'less another science, a new discipline charged with a new content or domain, than the vigilant practice of this textual division' (1981b:36). He argues:

> Grammatology must deconstruct everything that ties the concept and norms of scientificity to ontological, logocentrism, phonologism. This is an immense and interminable work that must ceaselessly avoid letting the transgression of the classical project of science fall back into a prescientific empiricism. This presupposes a kind of *double register* in grammatological practice: it must simultaneously go beyond metaphysical positivism and scientism, and accentuate whatever in the effective work of science contributes to freeing it of the metaphysical bonds that have borne on its definition and its movement since its beginnings. Grammatology must pursue and consolidate whatever, in scientific practice, has always already begun to exceed the logocentric closure. (1981b:35–6)

What Derrida is opposing to the metaphysics of presence can best be summarized in his conceptions of '*différance*' and 'trace'. The concept of *différance* combines the sense of the English verbs 'to differ' and 'to defer'. In the simplest sense Derrida uses this word to convey his claim that everything exists only as it differs from or defers to something else. But there is more involved in this concept than the mere combination of these two words. He contrasts *différance* as a ground of being, truth, or knowledge. Derrida claims that *différance* cannot be conceived on the basis of the opposition between presence and absence, the opposition that is central to the metaphysics of presence (1981a). Rather, *différance* is an attempt to define existence without grounds or binary oppositions between positives and negatives. *Différance* always connotes a difference in both space and time: while 'difference' indicates spatial distinction, 'defer' connotes temporal distinction. One commentator even claims that *différance* is not a concept at all, but rather a strategy of writing or a process of textual work (Johnson, 1981:xvi). Much the same idea governs Derrida's use of the concept of 'trace'. 'Trace' is the word Derrida uses to describe the radically other within the structure of *différance*. Again, he does not see this concept as providing a ground or a presence, but uses it to convey otherness without relying on the opposition of positive or negative. The notion of 'trace' rejects the concept of origins altogether.

His use of these concepts reveals that, for Derrida, the metaphysics of presence errs, first, because it privileges one set of terms over another (the positive over the negative) and, secondly, because it attempts to define the origin and ground of knowledge and truth. Against this he argues that no vocabulary is privileged and that no origins or grounds exist. The structure of presence, he claims, is defined not by origins or oppositions but by *différance*. And at the center of these conceptions, defining their structure and employment, is Derrida's primary concern: language. Derrida's basic assumptions derive from his attitude toward language: *différance* is always expressed in language; writing is prior to speech. Language, for Derrida is infinite play. It does not reflect a reality outside itself because we have no access to a reality outside langauge (Callinicos, 1982:88). Further, deconstruction, the concept with which Derrida is most closely associated, is commonly defined as Derrida's 'method' of language analysis. But to call deconstruction a 'method' is misleading. Deconstruction is rather the rejection of method, of grounding, of the search for origins and of the privileging of vocabularies. It is the kind of interpretation (not 'method') that is opposed to the metaphysics of presence. Derrida puts it this way:

> Thus there are two interpretations of interpretation, of structure, of sign, of freeplay. The one seeks to decipher, dreams of deciphering, a truth or an origin which is free from freeplay and from the order of the sign, and lives like an exile the necessity of interpretation. The other, which is no longer turned toward the origin, affirms freeplay and tries to pass beyond man and humanism, the name man being the name of that being, who, throughout the history of metaphysics or of ontology – in other

> words, through the history of all of his history – has dreamed of full presence, the reassuring foundation, the origin and the end of the game. The second interpretation of interpretation, to which Nietzsche showed us the way, does not seek in ethnography, as Levi-Strauss wished, the 'inspiration of a new humanism'. (1970:264–5)

This second kind of interpretation, the kind of interpretation that Derrida himself employs, he defines as deconstruction.

Deconstruction as it is conceptualized by Derrida has, on some accounts, caused a 'revolution' that challenges the fundamental premises of much of Western philosophy. It has been argued that deconstruction calls into question the possibility of defining a ground for absolute knowledge, the correspondence theory of truth, the primacy of consciousness, and the self-evidentness of binary opposition (Ryan, 1982:33). As Derrida sees it, however, deconstruction is positive, not negative. It involves 'being alert to the implications of the historical sedimentation of language which we use – and that is not destruction' (1970:271). It is not skepticism but a teasing out of significations within a text (Johnson, 1981:xiv). It is at the same time a critique of history and historical understanding and an argument that meaning is historically determined (Culler, 1982:129). The decentering that led to deconstruction began, Derrida claims, with the Nietzschean critique of metaphysics, the Freudian critique of self-presence and the Heideggerean destruction of metaphysics (1970:250). Derrida sees his project of deconstruction as continuing this tradition and extending beyond the limits observed by these writers.

In his comprehensive analysis of the deconstruction movement Jonathan Culler argues that deconstruction has been the leading source of energy and innovation in recent literary theory (1982:12). It is undeniable that the deconstruction movement fostered by Derrida's theories has become an important force in contemporary intellectual life. One could argue that it has caused, if not a revolution, at least significant interest in social theory.[16] For social theorists as well as literary critics deconstruction always involves a 'taking apart' of concepts and, specifically, taking apart concepts that serve as central axioms or principles for a whole period of thought (Allison, 1973:xxxii). The analyst deconstructs these central concepts by identifying in the text the operations that produce the supposed ground of the argument (Culler, 1982:86). But, as the deconstructionist sees it, the task of deconstruction is not merely to discard the concepts thus revealed, but, rather, to re-inscribe them in another way, to situate them differently. This re-inscribing of concepts defines a distinctive aspect of the program of deconstruction. It is one of the principal arguments of the deconstructionists that interpretation is a species of production. The deconstructionist does not attempt to find the 'true' meaning of the text or even to identify the author's intention, but, rather, defines interpretation as creating a product that is a literary production in its own right. Thus, for the deconstructionist, different readings are not illegitimate distortions of the text, but merely different species of production (Culler, 1982:38). Deconstructionists have called this the 'birth of the reader', a birth that necessarily caused the death of the author. This position entails that since all readings of a text are productions, there can never be an exhaustive science of deconstruction. Another, equally legitimate, reading can always be produced by another interpretation. For Derrida, the meaning of the text is the creative experience of the reader and is produced through the process he calls 'grafting'. The meaning bestowed by the reader is 'grafted' onto the text, producing a creation unique to that particular reading.

It should be clear from even this brief sketch of the deconstructive program that there are some significant parallels between this approach and Gadamer's anti-foundational thought. These similarities stem from the fact that deconstruction as defined by Derrida represents a powerful critique of foundational thought. First, like Gadamer, Derrida attacks the foundations of Western metaphysics and, also like Gadamer, eschews the notion of ultimate foundations altogether. Secondly, Derrida echoes Gadamer's insistence in *Truth and Method* that it is not his intention to offer an alternative 'method' for philosophy or the social sciences. Rather, like Gadamer, Derrida rejects the concept of method and the grounding that it entails. Thirdly, both Gadamer and Derrida reject an appeal to the author's intention as the basis for the meaning of the text. And, finally, both see language as a kind of play and define interpretation as participation in that play. Although there are differences as well –

Gadamer's decentering of the subject is not as extreme as that of Derrida's and his work does not emphasize ruptures and discontinuities as do the deconstructionists – the similarities are significant enough to warrant serious attention (Jay, 1982:96).

To uncover the root of both the similarities and differences between the two approaches, however, it is necessary to probe more deeply into the nature of the deconstructive enterprise. In a scathing attack on Derrida's work, John Searle has argued that Derrida's problem is that he is a kind of closet foundationalist. Searle argues that Derrida implicitly accepts that foundations are necessary, and that it therefore matters that they are shown to be false. Against Derrida he argues:

> The real mistake of the classical metaphysicians was not the belief that there were metaphysical foundations, but rather the belief that somehow or other such foundations were neccessary, the belief that unless there were foundations something is lost or threatened or undermined or put in question. (1983:78)

Another critic, Altieri, echoes a similar sentiment in his claim that Derrida assumes that if determinant meanings mirror the world then it follows that indeterminate meanings do not (1978:83). These critics have identified a weak point in Derrida's position. It is possible, however, to launch another, even stronger, line of criticism against Derrida. It can be argued that, in his compulsive effort to deconstruct all founding concepts Derrida has simply gone too far, that is, that he has replaced the metaphysics of presence with arbitrariness, capriciousness and, implicitly, nihilism. Some critics have argued that there are a few slight indications in Derrida's work that he does not see deconstruction as a completely arbitrary enterprise. Culler claims that Derridian deconstruction is not free association, that it does not denigrate literature, eliminate meaning and referentiality or reject history (1982:128, 280). He further claims that the phrase 'all readings are misreadings' does not deny truth (1982:178). But even the most positive reading of Derrida must conclude that, in his rejection of all foundations, Derrida supplies no basis for judging the legitimacy of interpretations. Unlike Gadamer, it makes no sense for Derrida to talk about legitimate or illegitimate prejudices. He attacks the positive unity of the metaphysics of presence, but opposes it with only a negative unity (Seung, 1982:277).

The inability to distinguish between legitimate and illegitimate prejudice defines the basic error of Derridean deconstruction. A two-pronged argument against the deconstructive program can be launched from the perspective of Gadamer's anti-foundational approach: a methodological argument and a philosophical-anthropological argument. Methodologically Gadamer differs from Derrida principally in his insistence that interpretation is defined by horizons of meaning. For Gadamer interpretations must take place within two horizons – that of the text and that of the interpreter. The horizons place limits on the interpretation and form the basis for the judgement of correct and incorrect interpretations. Deconstructionists, who deny any limits on interpretation, must accept the conclusion that 'anything goes'. Although Gadamer does not espouse foundations in any metaphysical or ultimate sense, he does argue that the historical horizons of both the interpreter and the text necessarily impose limits on the interpretation and provide criteria by which the interpretation can be evaluated. Gadamer's notion of the fusing of horizons, furthermore, offers another corrective to Derrida's understanding of the nature of interpretation. It is interesting that Derrida, who is so insistent in his argument against the historicists that the author's intention does not establish the meaning of the text, falls prey to their error: the assumption that interpretation is one-sided. But while the historicists focused exclusively on the author's side of the dialectic of interpretation, Derrida focuses exclusively on the other side, that of the interpreter. Derrida sees interpretation as the function of the reader alone, the historicists saw it as a function of the author alone. Gadamer corrects both positions by revealing interpretation to be a function of the interaction of both participants.[17] In her commentary on the deconstructive program, Kristeva makes the point that the contemporary interpreter rejects the classical meaning of the concept of interpretation: to be mutually indebted (1983:86). Nothing could summarize the contrast between Gadamer and Derrida more aptly. For Gadamer interpretation is an act of mutual indebtedness because both interpreter and interpreted participate in the meaning of the interpretation. For Derrida, in contrast, interpretation is not mutual and does not involve indebtedness. Rather, interpretation is a literary production that is independent rather than dependent.

The philosophical-anthropological argument against Derrida derives from these methdological criticisms. Derrida rejects the notion that convention, tradition, authority or historical norms serve as 'grounds' for interpreting texts. Gadamer, on the other hand, embraces this notion, arguing that prejudice is both a necessary and a positive element in interpretation. In defense of Gadamer's position on this issue it can be argued that tradition supplies the means by which understanding is possible in human social life. Prejudice is not simply another concept to be deconstructed but, rather, creates the possibility of human understanding itself. Gadamer's ontological perspective reveals that human beings live inside tradition and prejudice. They cannot transcend it or, as Derrida suggests, completely deconstruct it. The claim to do so denies not only the possibility of human communication but what Gadamer and Heidegger have revealed to be the ontological condition of human beings.

What this entails is that Derrida, like Foucault, strays toward nihilism because he denies the 'background' of human life. But Derrida's nihilism, unlike Foucault's, is primarily conceptual. He argues that no vocabulary is privileged, that is, that no conceptual scheme can .serve as a ground for interpretation. Although Foucault's nihilism is primarily moral, much the same argument can be used against both authors.[18] Derrida and Foucault both claim that what we call 'truth' is the result of superior power. Against this Gadamer claims that 'truth' is the result of tradition, prejudice, authority and, significantly, reason. In rejecting this Derrida and Foucault have thrown the baby out with the bath water. In their obsessive desire to reject foundations they have forgotten that historical, social and cultural grounds are necessary to human life because they make human understanding possible. Derrida and Foucault lead us toward a kind of nihilistic Tower of Babel in their rejection of historically grounded foundations for human understanding. Gadamer, in contrast, shows us that although absolute grounds are impossible, we are grounded ontologically in our historical existence.

Notes

SOCIAL SCIENCE AND THE SOCIOLOGY OF KNOWLEDGE

1. Goff argues that the sociology of knowledge represents a contradiction to positivist social science because it challenges the objective truth of positivism (1980:19). Against this I am arguing that the two kinds of knowledge are interdependent, not incompatible.
2. The notable exceptions to this characterization, Berger and Luckmann's phenomenological sociology and the 'strong program' of Bloor and Barnes, will be discussed in the next chapter. The distinction between objective and subjective knowledge employed here is equivalent to the distinction between impure (socially determined) and pure (universal, absolute) knowledge. This distinction will also be more fully discussed in the next chapter.
3. This argument has certain similarities to Paul Ricoeur's thesis in *The Conflict of Interpretations* (1974).

A BRIEF HISTORY OF THE SOCIOLOGY OF KNOWLEDGE

1. See Burger (1976) and Janoska-Bendl (1965) for a description of the *Methodenstreit* and particularly Weber's role in it.
2. For a discussion of Weber's epistemology see Hekman (1983b).
3. Scheler published *Schriften zur Soziologie und Weltanschauungslehre* in 1923–4 and *Die Wissensformen und die Gesellschaft* in 1926.
4. See Schutz (1967; 1964; 1962).
5. Schutz inherits this problem from Husserl who, many commentators have claimed, fails to establish a basis for the intersubjective constitution of meaning (Peritore, 1974).
6. The one exception to this is the work of Lucien Goldman. Goldman's work is an excellent example of a contemporary neo-Marxist sociology of knowledge that retains the Enlightenment's quest for objective knowledge. In describing the 'battle of dialectical sociology' Goldman states that it is a 'struggle against

particular ideologies for a free, objective and human knowledge' (1969:84).

7. Habermas's emphasis. The translation here is Dallmayr and McCarthy (1977:361).
8. Giddens also shares Habermas' quest for objective knowledge. He states: 'The approach to ideology I shall suggest certainly implies accepting that social science can deliver objectively valid knowledge' (1979:186).
9. See especially Kortian (1980) and Weiner (1981).
10. The principal works in the Gadamer–Habermas debate are Gadamer (1975), Habermas (1970) and the collection of essays in Karl-Otto Apel (1971a).
11. It should be noted, however, that Barnes rejects the 'realist' label as a description of his work. Instead, he labels his position 'naturalism', a position that is in many ways similar to the realists' account. Like the realist the naturalist argues that the 'post-empiricist' philosophy of science is applicable to both the social and natural sciences. Using the post-empiricist definition of scientific method the naturalist argues that there can be a natural scientific study of society (Thomas, 1980).
12. See Laudan (1981) for a critique of the strong program and its approach to science.

MANNHEIM'S HERMENEUTIC SOCIOLOGY OF KNOWLEDGE

1. Alexander makes this point in his commentary on Mannheim (1982:123–4).
2. Simonds makes a similar observation in his discussion of this issue (1978:130–1).
3. Remmling (1975:57) and Rempel (1965:19) both offer interpretations of Mannheim's concept along these lines but, unlike the present account, do not explore the anti-foundational implications of it. Many commentators, however, attribute to Mannheim the traditional definition of ideology as a distortion of thought (Mullins, 1979:141; S.Taylor, 1956:21).
4. Simonds argues that Mannheim's position on expressive meaning does not involve recourse to the mind or psyche (1975:97). He is referring rather to shared social meaning in the manner of Wittgenstein. It should also be noted that although Mannheim's early works are strongly influenced by phenomenology, by 1924 he attacks phenomenology in a way that presages Gadamer's later criticism (1982:169).
5. It is interesting to note in this context that Garfinkel refers to Mannheim's documentary method as a means for studying common-sense knowledge (1967:78).

6. Simonds argues that in his theory of knowledge Mannheim treats both subject and object as problematic (1975:100).
7. Kettler makes a similar argument in his commentary on Mannheim's theory (1967:421–3). In his book, *Karl Mannheim's Sociology of Knowledge*, Simonds presents a persuasive argument that Mannheim's sociology of knowledge consists of a hermeneutic method of interpretation. He argues that the ultimate aim of Mannheim's sociology of knowledge is the self-understanding of the human community as a whole (1978:187). This argument will be discussed in more detail at a later point in the chapter.
8. Callinicos argues that Mannheim derived his 'perspectivism' from Nietzsche who also rejected relativism (1982:106).
9. The complexity of Mannheim's position on the genetic fallacy has led his critics to disagree on his standing on the issue. While most critics (e.g., Carlsnaes, 1981:207; Mandelbaum, 1938:76) conclude that he rejects the genetic fallacy, others (Simonds, 1978:120; Simon, 1982:156) deny that he falls prey to it. Simon points out, quite correctly, that Mannheim holds out the possibility that a purely physical description or a statement such as $2 \times 2 = 4$ is not dependent on social context. But if we keep in mind that Mannheim's claim is that *meaning* is always dependent on social context and that the analysis of ideas is concerned with meanings, not factual description, this qualifier becomes insignificant.
10. During this phase of his career Mannheim the remote academic, contemplating the abstract philosophical and epistemological questions of the sociology of knowledge, becomes Mannheim the politically involved, activist social planner. Some critics have claimed that this phase represents Mannheim's break with his former 'relativism and detached fatalism' (Eros and Stewart, 1957:xxi) as well as his holistic approach (Kecskemeti, 1953:4). Such an assertion is hard to justify. Although Mannheim's interest clearly changed in these years, his basic presuppositions remained the same. His attention moved from the underpinning of the social sciences to its concrete workings in a particular locale. Although this renders his work methodologically uninteresting, it does not represent a contradiction to his previous work.
11. In addition to those authors mentioned in the text and previous notes the commentaries on Mannheim consulted were: Gardiner, 1981; Thomas, 1980; Lichtheim, 1967; Laudan, 1977; Abercrombie, 1980; Abercrombie and Longhurst, 1983; Lavine, 1950–1; Lavine, 1964–5; Giddens, 1979; Maquet, 1951; Seliger, 1976; Neiser, 1965; Wagner, 1952; Bauman, 1978; Charles Smith, 1982; Merton, 1968; K. Wolff, 1984; Connolly, 1967; Hesse, 1980; Meja, 1975; Kettler, 1975; Adorno, 1967; Ashcraft, 1981; Jay, 1974; Shmueli, 1977; Bloor, 1973.

12. It should be noted that Simonds does not see Mannheim siding completely with Hirsch in the Gadamer–Hirsch debate. He points out that Mannheim, like Gadamer, claims that the interpreter's perspective cannot be entirely eliminated from the interpretation (1975:83).
13. Simonds also makes this point (1978:138 ff).

GADAMER'S HERMENEUTICS AND THE METHODOLOGY OF THE SOCIAL SCIENCES

1. For information on this controversy see Palmer (1969).
2. Gadamer takes this thesis directly from Heidegger who argues that art is *the* experience of truth (Heidegger, 1977:179 ff.).
3. It is interesting to note that Bauman's conception of hermeneutics as well as, to some extent, that of Ricoeur, is an attempt, like Dilthey's, to mimic the objectivism of the natural sciences (Bauman, 1978).
4. For a discussion of the transcendental elements of Heidegger's ontology see Seung (1982:173 ff.).
5. Derrida challenges this priority of speech over writing. His thesis on this matter will be discussed in chapter 5.
6. Heidegger simply states 'Language is the House of Being' (1977:193).
7. The challenges to this thesis will be discussed more later in the chapter.
8. J. Wolff along with many other critics of Gadamer claims that his position on objectivity is ambiguous (1975:108).
9. The most famous of these critiques of Gadamer is that of Eric Hirsch in *Validity in Interpretation* (1967). A refutation of Hirsch's attack on Gadamer will be presented in the next section of the chapter.
10. In a curious passage Gadamer claims that 'behind' the verbalization of social norms there are always 'economic and dominating interests' (1975:495–6).
11. See Hinman for an extended critique of Gadamer's concept of truth (1980).
12. In his assessment of Gadamer's philosophical hermeneutics Bernstein also argues that Gadamer goes beyond both objectivism and relativism (1983:166).
13. The understanding of the 'ordinary language methodology' for the social sciences used in this discussion is taken primarily from Ludwig Wittgenstein, *Philosophical Investigations* (1953), Peter Winch, *The Idea of a Social Science* (1958), A. R. Louch, *Explanation and Human Action* (1966), Hanna Pitkin, *Wittgenstein*

and Justice (1972) and Richard Bernstein, *The Restructuring of Social and Political Theory* (1976).

14. It should be noted that although those in the Wittgensteinian tradition frequently engage in discussions of intentionality, they define this concept in a fundamentally different way than do the Husserlians. For the Wittgensteinians, intentions are publicly available data that do not entail recourse to subjective mental events.
15. Hirsch's confusion on this point is indicated by the fact that at one point he explicitly states that the author's intention is *not* to be defined as a 'mental process' (1967:32). But he freely refers to the subjective intention of the author and insists that the verbal meaning of a text is a 'willed type' that an author expresses by linguistic symbols and can be understood by another through those symbols (1967:49). I think that it can be concluded that Hirsch fails to see the importance of the distinction between viewing the author's intention as a subjective mental event that is translated into language and viewing language and thought as indistinguishable.
16. On this point see Hacking (1975).
17. In this respect Gadamer sees his view in conflict with that of Wittgenstein. He explicitly states that the relationship between language and being obviates the nominalism implicit in Wittgenstein's approach (1976b:75).
18. In his discussion of this issue Hacking makes the point that Winch does not derive his position from that of Wittgenstein (1975:153).
19. I am thinking here particularly of J. G. A. Pocock (1971).
20. For the principal works in the Gadamer–Habermas dispute see chapter 2, note 10.
21. In a much less sophisticated critique, for example, Wellmer dismisses hermeneutics because it cannot deal with questions concerning the 'fundamental norms of a society – their truth and justice' (1976:255).
22. Keat makes the point that Habermas posits two ontologically distinct realms: that of the social sciences and that of the natural sciences. Although he is willing to concede that the social sciences are hermeneutic, he denies that the natural sciences are. Thus not only does he implicitly accept the Enlightenment dichotomy between these two branches of science, he also precludes the possibility of a scientific social science or a hermeneutic aspect to natural science (1981:87–91). There is some question, however, as to whether this criticism applies to Habermas's most recent work.
23. For a discussion of Habermas's transcendentalism see Hesse (1982:114), McCarthy (1982:58 ff.), Geuss (1981:65), Lemert (1979:215), Rorty (1979) and Bernstein (1983:194).

24. In Bernstein's assessment of the Gadamer–Habermas debate he makes much of the fact that both Gadamer and Habermas see social science as an activity in which application plays a key role (1983:182). Although this is not central to my argument, it is an important similarity between the two theories (see Gadamer, 1975:281 ff.). It should also be noted that, while both Habermas and Gadamer appeal to Aristotle to establish the notion of the social sciences as a science of application, Gadamer notes that, for Aristotle, practical philosophy presupposes that we are already shaped by the normative ideas and images of our society (1981b:135).
25. Ricoeur argues at another point, however, that the difference between Gadamer and Habermas on the assessment of tradition is irreconcilable (1981:63–70).
26. Misgeld also notes that it is Gadamer's 'transcendental' position that appeals to Habermas, an interpretation that I have attempted to refute above (1976:168).
27. In *The Theory of Communicative Action* Habermas argues that Gadamer's approach is dated because it does not take into account the hermeneutic character of natural science (1984:108). It is not difficult to argue, however, that Gadamer's point about the priority of the human sciences remains intact. As Giddens has pointed out, the social sciences operate according to a 'double hermeneutic' (1976:158).
28. In another article Ricoeur elaborates on the differences between the objectivity of the natural and the social sciences (1976:683–95).
29. In this regard see also R. S. Peters, *The Concept of Motivation* (1958).
30. In his *Radical Reflection* Calvin Schrag advocates extending the concept of 'text' to the 'texture of lived through world experience' (1980:98). Although his approach is compatible with the one suggested here, I do not find it to be developed to the point that it is as methodologically fruitful as that of Ricoeur.
31. Thompson criticizes Ricoeur's theory of distantiation, arguing that he violates the primordial bond between subject and object presupposed by Heidegger and Gadamer (1981:163).
32. Simmel also comes very close to defining the concept of effective history in his statement that it is impossible to identify an act independent of its consequences (1980).
33. Ricoeur also praises Mannheim for his total conception of ideology (1981:240).
34. Gadamer specifically rejects the notion that language is an 'ideology' in the narrow sense of the word (1975:493).
35. It is significant that Gadamer praises Francis Bacon, who can be

identified as the father of the sociology of knowledge, for examining 'the prejudices that hold the human mind captive and lead it away from the true knowledge of things' (1975:313).

BEYOND OBJECTIVISM AND NIHILISM

1. Also included are Schrag's *Radical Reflection and the Origin of the Human Sciences* (1980) and Bourdieu's *Outline of a Theory of Practice* (1977).
2. In a similar vein, Putnam states that arguing about the nature of rationality presupposes a notion of rationality wider than the positivist notion and wider than institutionalized criterial rationality (1981:113). It is interesting to note, furthermore, that all the contributiors to the Hollis and Lukes volume (1982) with the exception of the article by Bloor and Barnes and that by Hacking advocate some form of universalism.
3. Several authors have identified this trend in contemporary discussions and linked it to Nietzsche (Giddens, 1982:221; DeMan, 1979:105).
4. Bernstein argues that Rorty is *not* a nihilist because he does not take the position that, in knowledge or morals, anything is just as good as anything else (1980:762). The following argument seeks to disprove this.
5. This position is also related to Heidegger's point that Being is revealed in a particular way in each historical epoch, and thus cannot be arbitrarily interpreted.
6. For an insightful critique of this controversy see Okrent (1984).
7. Curiously, Rorty seems to make much the same point when he claims that the actor's account is not epistemologically privileged, but is morally privileged (1982:202).
8. See Fred Dallmayr's excellent analysis of this theme in his recent *Twilight of Subjectivity* (1981b). Michael Shapiro pursues a similar argument in *Language and Political Understanding* (1981).
9. Toulmin claims that we are still vulnerable to the claims of the belief in the epistemological primacy of the subject even though we may be convinced that it is fallacious (1982:68).
10. Gadamer's work also has an affinity to some aspects of the work of another post-structuralist, Louis Althusser. For a comparison of the work of Gadamer and Althusser see Hekman (1983a).
11. In a similar vein Dallmayr argues that Heidegger presents a midway position on the 'death of man' thesis (1981b:31).
12. Foucault, following Nietzsche, even employs the concept of effective history (1977:154–5).
13. In an innovative study of Foucault's method Major-Poetzl claims

that Foucault's method is unclassifiable – it operates simultaneously as philosophy, history, science and literature yet can be classified as none of these (1983:195).

14. Dreyfus and Rabinow claim, however, that Foucault only incurs this error in his role as archaeologist. They insist that when he switches to geneology he becomes aware of his role as interpreter (1982:103).
15. Charles Taylor comes to a similar conclusion in his critique of Foucault (1984:178).
16. Ryan argues forcefully for the relevance of deconstruction for Marxist social theory. He concludes, however, that Derrida's position leads to 'epistemological nihilism' (1982:40).
17. Culler's comparison between Derrida and pragmatism offers much the same contrast (1982:153).
18. See Henning for a comparison of the positions of Derrida and Foucault (1982:166 ff.).
19. Gunnell argues that it is precisely the lack of methodological guidance on the part of Gadamer that disqualifies his approach (1982:327).
20. For the attempt to justify relativism see the essays in *Relativism, Cognitive and Moral* edited by Meiland and Krausz (1982).
21. Bourdieu's concept of 'doxa' (1977:164 ff.), Bubner's concept of 'concrete knowledge' (1981:46) and Wittgenstein's famous statement that 'If a lion could talk we could not understand him' are also relevant in this context.

References

Abercrombie, Nicholas 1980: *Class Structure and Knowledge*. Oxford: Basil Blackwell.

Abercrombie, Nicholas and Longhurst, Brian 1983: Interpreting Mannheim. *Theory, Culture and Society*, 2, 5–15.

Adorno, T. W. 1967: The sociology of knowledge and its consciousness. In *Prisms*, London: Spearman, 35–49.

Alexander, Jeff 1982: *Theoretical Logic in Sociology. Volume I: Positivism, Presuppositions and Current Controversies*. Berkeley: University of California Press.

Allison, David 1973. Translator's introduction. In Derrida, *Speech and Phenomena*, Evanston: Northwestern University Press, xxxi–xlii.

Altieri, Charles 1978: The hermeneutics of literary indeterminacy: a dissent from the new orthodoxy. *New Literary History*, 10, 71–99.

Apel, Karl-Otto (ed.) 1971a: *Hermeneutik und Ideologiekritik*. Frankfurt: Suhrkamp.

1971b: Szientistik, Hermeneutik, Ideologiekritik. In *Hermeneutik und Ideologiekritik*. Frankfurt: Suhrkamp, 7–44.

1980a: Three dimensions of understanding meaning in analytic philosophy. *Philosophy and Social Criticism*, 7, 115–42.

1980b: *Toward a Transformation of Philosophy*. London: Routledge and Kegan Paul.

1981: Social action and the concept of rationality. *Phenomenology and the Human Sciences*. Supplement to *Philosophical Topics*, 12, 9–35.

Ashcraft, Richard 1981: Political theory and political action in Karl Mannheim's thought. *Comparative Studies in Society and History*, 23, 23–50.

Bacon, Francis 1970: On the interpretation of nature and the empire of man. In Curtis and Petras (eds), *The Sociology of Knowledge*, London: Duckworth.

Barnes, Barry 1974: *Scientific Knowledge and Sociological Theory*. London: Routledge and Kegan Paul.

1976: *Interests and the Growth of Knowledge*. London: Routledge and Kegan Paul.

1981: On the conventional character of knowledge and cognition. *Philosophy of the Social Sciences*, 11, 303–33.

1982: *T. S. Kuhn and Social Science*. New York: Columbia University Press.

Barth, Hans 1976: *Truth and Ideology*, trans. Frederic Lilge. Berkeley: University of California Press.

Bauman, Zygmunt 1978: *Hermeneutics and Social Science*. New York: Columbia University Press.

Berger, Peter 1970: Identity as a problem in the sociology of knowledge. In Curtis and Petras (eds), *The Sociology of Knowledge*, London: Duckworth, 373–84.

Berger, Peter and Luckmann, Thomas 1966: *The Social Construction of Reality*. New York: Anchor Books.

Bergner, Jeffrey 1981: *The Origin of Formalism in Social Science*. Chicago: University of Chicago Press.

Bernstein, Richard 1976: *The Restructuring of Social and Political Theory*. New York: Harcourt Brace Jovanovich.

1980: Philosophy in the conversation of mankind. *Review of Metaphysics*, 33, 745–75.

1983: *Beyond Objectivism and Relativism*. Philadelphia: University of Pennsylvania Press.

Betti, Enrico 1955: *Teoria Generale della Interpretatione* (2 vols), Dott. A. Giuffre (ed.). Milan: Istituto di Teoria della Interpretazione.

Bhaskar, Roy 1979: *The Possibility of Naturalism*. Atlantic Highlands, New Jersey: Humanities Press.

Bleicher, Josef (ed.) 1980: *Contemporary Hermeneutics*. London: Routledge and Kegan Paul.

1982: *Hermeneutic Imagination: outline of a positive critique of scientism and sociology*. London: Routledge and Kegan Paul.

Bloor, David 1973: Wittgenstein and Mannheim on the sociology of mathematics. *Studies in the History and Philosophy of Science*, 4, 173–91.

1976: *Knowledge and Social Imagery*. London: Routledge and Kegan Paul.
1983: *Wittgenstein: a social theory of knowledge*. New York: Columbia University Press.
Bourdieu, Pierre 1977: *An Outline of a Theory of Practice*. Cambridge: Cambridge University Press.
Brown, P. L. 1975: Epistemology and Method: Althusser, Foucault, Derrida. *Cultural Hermeneutics*, 3, 147–63.
Bubner, Rudiger 1975: Theory and practice in the light of the hermeneutic-criticist controversy. *Cultural Hermeneutics*, 2, 337–52.
1981: Hermeneutics: understanding or edification. *Phenomenology and the Human Sciences*. Supplement to *Philosophical Topics*, 12, 37–48.
Burger, Thomas 1976: *Max Weber's Theory of Concept Formation*. Durham: Duke University Press.
Callinicos, Alex 1982: *Is There a Future for Marxism?* Atlantic Highlands, New Jersey: Humanities Press.
Carlsnaes, Walter 1981: *The Concept of Ideology in Political Analysis: a critical examination of its usage by Marx, Lenin, and Mannheim*. Westport, Conn.: Greenwood Press.
Child, Arthur 1941a: The problem of imputation in the sociology of knowledge. *Ethics*, 51, 200–19.
1941b: The theoretical possibility of the sociology of knowledge. *Ethics*, 51, 392–418.
1942: The existential determination of thought. *Ethics*, 52, 153–85.
Congdon, Lee 1977: Karl Mannheim as philosopher. *Journal of European Studies*, 7, 1–18.
Connolly, W. E. 1967: *Political Science and Ideology*. New York: Atherton.
Cox, Richard 1979: Karl Mannheim's concept of ideology. *Cahiers Vilfredo Pareto*, 17, 209–22.
Culler, Jonathan 1982: *On Deconstruction: theory and criticism after structuralism*. Ithaca: Cornell University Press.
Curtis, J. E. and Petras, J. W. (eds) 1970: *The Sociology of Knowledge*. London: Duckworth.
Dallmayr, Fred 1981a: *Beyond Dogma and Despair*. Notre Dame, Indiana: University of Notre Dame Press.
1981b: *The Twilight of Subjectivity*. Amherst: The University of Massachusetts Press.

1984: *Language and Politics: why does language matter to political philosophy?* Notre Dame, Indiana: University of Notre Dame Press.

Dallmayr, Fred and McCarthy, Thomas 1977: Introduction. In Dallmayr and McCarthy (eds), *Understanding and Social Inquiry* Notre Dame, Indiana: University of Notre Dame Press, 285–91

DeGre, Gerard 1955: *Science as a Social Institution: an introduction to the sociology of knowledge*. Garden City, New York: Doubleday.

DeMan, Paul 1979: *Allegories of Reading*. New Haven: Yale University Press.

Depew, David 1981: The Habermas-Gadamer debate in Hegelian perspective. *Philosophy and Social Criticism*, 8, 425–46.

Derrida, Jacques 1969: The ends of man. *Philosophy and Phenomenological Research*, 30, 31–57.

1970: Structure, sign and play in the discourse of the human sciences. In Richard Macksey and Eugenio Donato (eds), *The Structuralist Controversy*, Baltimore: Johns Hopkins University Press, 246–72.

1976: *Of Grammatology*, trans. Gayatri Spivak. Baltimore: John Hopkins University Press.

1978: *Writing and Difference*. Chicago: University of Chicago Press.

1981a: *Dissemination*, trans. Barbara Johnson. Chicago: University of Chicago Press.

1981b: *Positions*, trans. Alan Bass. Chicago: University of Chicago Press.

Dixon, Keith 1980: *The Sociology of Belief*. London: Routledge and Kegan Paul.

Dreyfus, Hubert 1980: Holism and hermeneutics. *Review of Metaphysics*, 34, 3–23.

Dreyfus, Hubert and Rabinow, Paul 1982: *Michel Foucault: beyond structuralism and hermeneutics*. Chicago: University of Chicago Press.

Eros, J. S. and Stewart, W. A. C. 1957: Introduction. In Mannheim, *Systematic Sociology*, New York: Grove Press.

Foucault, Michel 1971: *The Order of Things: An Archaeology of the Human Sciences*. New York: Random House.

1972: *The Archaeology of Knowledge*, trans. A. M. Sheridan Smith. New York: Random House

1973a: *The Birth of the Clinic*. New York: Pantheon.
1973b: *Madness and Civilization*. New York: Vintage.
1977: *Discipline and Punish*, trans. Alan Sheridan. New York: Random House.
1978: *The History of Sexuality*, volume 1, trans. Robert Hurley. New York: Random House.
1980: *Power/Knowledge*. New York: Pantheon Books.
1981: Truth and power. In Charles Lemert (ed.), *French Sociology: Rupture and Renewal*, New York: Columbia University Press, 293–307.
1982a: Is it really important to think? *Philosophy and Social Criticism*, 9, 29–40.
1982b: The subject and power. In Dreyfus and Rabinow, *Michel Foucault: beyond structuralism and hermeneutics*, Chicago: University of Chicago Press, 208–26.
Fraser, Nancy 1981a: Foucault and the problem of the normative foundations of post-modern social critique. Unpublished manuscript.
1981b: Foucault on modern power: empirical insights and normative confusions. *Praxis International*, 1, 272–87.
Gadamer, Hans-Georg 1970: On the scope and function of hermeneutical reflection. *Continuum*, 8, 77–95.
1971a: Replik. In Apel (ed.), *Hermeneutik und Ideologiekritik*, Frankfurt: Suhrkamp, 283–317.
1971b: Rhetorik, Hermeneutik und Ideologiekritik. In Apel (ed.), *Hermeneutik und Ideologiekritik*, Frankfurt: Suhrkamp, 57–82.
1975: *Truth and Method*. New York: Continuum.
1976a: *Hegel's Dialectic: Five Hermeneutic Studies*, trans. P. Christopher Smith. New Haven: Yale University Press.
1976b: *Philosophical Hermeneutics*, trans. David E. Linge. Berkeley: University of California Press.
1979: The problem of historical consciousness. In Paul Rabinow and William Sullivan (eds), *Interpretive Social Science*, Berkeley: University of California Press, 103–60.
1981a: Heidegger and the history of philosophy. *Monist*, 64, 434–44.
1981b: *Reason in the Age of Science*, trans. Frederick G. Lawrence. Cambridge, Mass.: MIT Press.
1981c: The religious dimension in Heidegger. In Alan M.

Olson (ed.), *Transcendence and the Sacred*, Notre Dame, Indiana: University of Notre Dame Press, 193–207.

1983: A letter by Professor Hans-Georg Gadamer. In Bernstein, *Beyond Objectivism and Relativism*, Philadelphia: University of Pennsylvania Press, 261–5.

Gardiner, Patrick 1981: German philosophy and the rise of relativism. *Monist*, 64, 138–54.

Garfinkel, Harold 1967: *Studies in Ethnomethodology*. Englewood Cliffs, New Jersey: Prentice Hall.

Gay, Peter 1966: *The Enlightenment: An Interpretation*. New York: Random House.

Gellner, Ernst 1974: Concepts and society. In B. Wilson (ed.), *Rationality*, Oxford: Basil Blackwell, 18–49.

Geuss, Raymond 1981: The Idea of a Critical Theory: Habermas and the Frankfurt School. Cambridge, Mass.: Cambridge University Press.

Giddens, Anthony 1976: *New Rules of Sociological Method*. New York: Basic Books.

1979: *Central Problems in Social Theory*. Berkeley: University of California Press.

1981: *A Contemporary Critique of Historical Materialism*. Berkeley: University of California Press.

1982: *Profiles and Critiques in Social Theory*. Berkeley: University of California Press.

Goff, Tom 1980: *Marx and Mead: Contributions to a Sociology of Knowledge*. London: Routledge and Kegan Paul.

Goldman, Lucien 1969: *The Human Sciences and Philosophy*. London: Jonathan Cape.

Goodman, Nelson 1978: *Ways of Worldmaking*. Indianapolis: Hackett.

Gunnell, John 1979: *Political Theory: tradition and interpretation*. Cambridge, Mass.: Winthrop Publishers, Inc.

1982: Interpretation and the history of political theory. *American Political Science Review*, 76, 317–27.

Habermas, Jurgen 1970: *Zur Logik der Sozialwissenschaften*. Frankfurt: Suhrkamp.

1971: *Knowledge and Human Interests*, trans. Jeremy J. Shapiro. Boston: Beacon Press.

1977: A review of Gadamer's *Truth and Method*. In Dallmayr and McCarthy (eds), *Understanding and Social Inquiry*, Notre

Dame, Indiana: University of Notre Dame Press, 335–63.
1979: *Communication and the Evolution of Society*, trans. Thomas McCarthy. Boston: Beacon Press.
1980: The hermeneutic claim to universality. In Bleicher (ed.), *Contemporary Hermeneutics*, London: Routledge and Kegan Paul, 181–211.
1981: Modernity versus post-modernity, trans. Seyla Gen-Haabib. *New German Critique*, 22, 3–14.
1983: *Philosophical-Political Profiles*, trans. Frederick G. Lawrence. Cambridge, Mass.: MIT Press.
1984: *The Theory of Communicative Action*, volume 1, trans. Thomas McCarthy. Boston: Beacon Press.

Hacking, Ian 1975: *Why Does Language Matter to Philosophy?* New York: Cambridge University Press.

Hamilton, P. 1974: *Knowledge and Social Structure*. London: Routledge and Kegan Paul.

Hartung, Frank 1970: Problems of the sociology of knowledge. In Curtis and Petras, (eds), *The Sociology of Knowledge*, London: Duckworth, 686–705.

Heelan, Patrick 1983: Natural science as a hermeneutic of instrumentation. *Philosophy of Science*, 50, 181–204.

Heidegger, Martin 1962: *Being and Time*. New York: Harper and Row.
1977: Letter on humanism. In *Basic Writings*, New York: Harper and Row, 189–242.

Hekman, Susan 1983a: Beyond humanism: Althusser and the methodology of the social sciences. *Western Political Quarterly*, 36, 98–115.
1983b: *Weber, the Ideal Type and Contemporary Social Theory*. Notre Dame, Indiana: University of Notre Dame Press.

Henning, E. M. 1982: Archaeology, deconstruction, and intellectual history. In Dominick LaCapra and Steven L. Kaplan (eds), *Modern European Intellectual History*, Ithaca: Cornell University Press, 153–96.

Hesse, Mary 1980: *Revolutions and Reconstructions in the Philosophy of Science*. Bloomington, Indiana: Indiana University Press.
1982: Science and objectivity. In John Thompson and David Held (eds), *Habermas: Critical Debates*, London: Macmillan, 97–115.

Hinman, Lawrence 1980: *Quid facti or quid juris*: the fundamental ambiguity of Gadamer's understanding of hermeneutics. *Philosophy and Phenomenological Research*, 40, 512–35.

Hinshaw, Virgil 1943: The epistemological relevance of Mannheim's sociology of knowledge. *Journal of Philosophy*, 40, 57–72.

Hirsch, Eric 1967: *Validity in Interpretation*. New Haven: Yale University Press.

Hollis, Martin 1978: Action and context. *Aristotelian Society*, supplementary volume 52, 43–50.

Hollis, Martin and Lukes, Steven (ed.) 1982: *Rationality and Relativism*. Cambridge, Mass.: MIT Press.

Holmes, Stephen 1975: Review of Apel's *Transformation der Philosophie*. *International Philosophical Quarterly*, 15, 215–26.

Holzner, Burkart 1972: *Reality Construction in Society*. Cambridge, Mass.: Schenkmann.

Horowitz, Irving Louis 1961: *Philosophy, Science, and the Sociology of Knowledge*. Springfield, Illinois: Charles C. Thomas.

Horton, Robin 1979: Material-object language and theoretical language: towards a Strawsonian sociology of thought. In S. C. Brown (ed.), *Disputes in the Social Sciences*, Atlantic Highlands, New Jersey: Humanities Press, 197–224.

House, J. Douglas 1977: In defence of Karl Mannheim: the sociology of knowledge, epistemology, and methodology. *Sociological Analysis and Theory*, 7, 207–25.

Howard, Roy 1982: *Three Faces of Hermeneutics*. Berkeley: University of California Press.

Hoy, David Couzens 1978: *The Critical Circle: literature and history in contemporary hermeneutics*. Berkeley: University of California Press.

1979: Taking history seriously: Foucault, Gadamer, and Habermas. *Union Seminary Quarterly Review*, 34, 85–95.

1981: Power, repression, progress: Foucault, Lukes and the Frankfurt school. *Triquarterly*, 52, 43–63.

Janoska-Bendl, Judith 1965: *Methodologische Aspekte des Idealtypus*. Berlin: Dunker und Humblot.

Jay, Martin 1974: The Frankfurt School's critique of Karl Mannheim and the sociology of knowledge. *Telos*, 20, 72–89.

1982: Should intellectual history take a linguistic turn:

reflections on the Habermas–Gadamer debate. In Dominick LaCapra and Steven L. Kaplan (ed.), *Modern European Intellectual History*, Ithaca: Cornell University Press, 86–110.

Johnson, Barbara 1981: Translator's Introduction. In Jacques Derrida, *Dissemination*, Chicago: University of Chicago Press, vii–xxxiii.

Jung, Hwa Yol 1979: *The Crisis of Political Understanding: a phenomenological perspective in the conduct of political inquiry*. Pittsburg: Duquesne University Press.

Keat, Russell 1981: *The Politics of Social Theory: Habermas, Freud and the critique of positivism*. Chicago: University of Chicago Press.

Kecskemeti, Paul 1953: Introduction. In Mannheim, *Essays on Sociology and Social Psychology*, New York: Oxford, 1–11.

Kettler, David 1967: Sociology of knowledge and moral philosophy. *Political Science Quarterly*, 82, 399–426.

1975: Political theory, ideology, sociology: the question of Karl Mannheim. *Cultural Hermeneutics*, 3, 69–80.

Kortian, Garbis 1980: *Metacritique: the philosophical argument of Jürgen Habermas*. Cambridge: Cambridge University Press.

Kristeva, Julia 1983: Psychoanalysis and the polis. In W. J. T. Mitchell (ed.), *The Politics of Interpretation*, Chicago: University of Chicago Press, 83–98.

Laudan, Laurens 1977: *Progress and its Problems*. Berkeley: University of California Press.

1981: The pseudo-science of science. *Philosophy of the Social Sciences*, 11, 173–98.

Lavine, Thelma 1950–1: Knowledge as interpretation: an historical survey, part II. *Philosophical and Phenomenological Research*, 11, 88–103.

1964–5: Karl Mannheim and contemporary functionalism. *Philosophical and Phenomenological Research*, 25, 560–71.

Lemert, Charles 1979: *Sociology and the Twilight of Man: homocentrism and discourse in sociological theory*. Carbondale: Southern Illinois University Press.

Lemert, Charles and Gillan, Garth 1982: *Michel Foucault: social theory and transgression*. New York: Columbia University Press.

Lichtheim, George 1967: *The Concept of Ideology and Other Essays*. New York: Vantage.

Louch, A. 1966: *Explanation and Human Action*. Berkeley: University of California Press.

Lyotard, Jean Francois 1984: *The Post-Modern Condition: a report on knowledge*, trans. Geoff Bennington and Brian Massumi. Minneapolis: University of Minnesota Press.

MacIntyre, Alasdair 1974: Is understanding religion compatible with believing? In B. Wilson (ed.), *Rationality*, Oxford: Basil Blackwell, 62–77.

1976: Contexts of interpretation. *Boston University Journal*, 24, 41–46.

1980: Epistemological crises, dramatic narrative, and the philosophy of science. In Gary Gutting (ed.), *Paradigms and Revolutions*, Notre Dame, Indiana: University of Notre Dame Press, 54–74.

Major-Poetzl, Pamela 1983: *Michel Foucault's Archaeology of Western Culture*. Chapel Hill: University of North Carolina Press.

Mandelbaum, Maurice 1938: *The Problem of Historical Knowledge: an answer to relativism*. New York: Liveright Publishing Corp.

Mannheim, Karl 1936: *Ideology and Utopia: an introduction to the sociology of knowledge*, trans. Louis Wirth and Edward Shils. New York: Harvest Books.

1952: *Essays on the Sociology of Knowledge*, ed. by Paul Kecskemeti. London: Routledge and Kegan Paul.

1953: *Essays on Sociology and Social Psychology*, ed. by Paul Kecskemeti. London: Routledge and Kegan Paul.

1956: *Essays on the Sociology of Culture*, ed. by Ernest Mannheim. London: Routledge and Kegan Paul.

1957: *Systematic Sociology*. New York: Grove Press.

1971: *From Karl Mannheim*, ed. by Kurt Wolff. New York: Oxford University Press.

1982: *Structures of Thinking*, ed. by David Kettler, Volker Meja and Nico Stehr. London: Routledge and Kegan Paul.

Maquet, J. 1951: *The Sociology of Knowledge*. Boston: Beacon Press.

Marx, Karl and Friederick Engels 1947: *The German Ideology, Parts I and II*. New York: International Publishers.

McCarthy, Thomas 1982: Rationality and relativism: Habermas' 'overcoming' of hermeneutics. In John Thompson and David Held (eds), *Habermas: critical debates*, London: Macmillan, 57–78.

Meiland, Jack and Krausz, Michael (eds) 1982: *Relativism: cognitive and moral*. Notre Dame, Indiana: University of Notre Dame Press.

Meja, Volker 1975: The sociology of knowledge and the critique of ideology. *Cultural Hermeneutics*, 3, 57–68.

Merton, Robert 1968: The sociology of knowledge. In *Social Theory and Social Structure*, New York: Free Press, 493–582.
1970: Social conflict over styles of sociological work. In Curtis and Petras (eds), *The Sociology of Knowledge*, London: Duckworth, 507–30.

Misgeld, Dieter 1976: Critical theory and hermeneutics: the debate between Habermas and Gadamer. In John O'Neill, *Critical Theory*, New York: Seabury Press, 164–83.

Mulkay, Michael 1979: *Science and the Sociology of Knowledge*. London: George Allen and Unwin.

Mullins, Willard 1979: Truth and ideology: reflections on Mannheim's paradox. *History and Theory*, 18, 141–54.

Nagel, Ernest 1961: *The Structure of Science*. New York: Harcourt Brace and World.

Neiser, Hans 1965: *On the Sociology of Knowledge*. New York: Heinemann.

Newton-Smith, W. H. 1981: *The Rationality of Science*. Boston: Routledge and Kegan Paul.

Okrent, Mark 1984: Hermeneutics, transcendental philosophy, and social science. *Inquiry*, 27, 23–49.

Oliver, Ivan 1983: The 'old' and the 'new' hermeneutic in sociological theory. *British Journal of Sociology*, 34, 519-53.

Palmer, Richard 1969: *Hermeneutics: interpretation theory in Schleiermacher, Dilthey, Heidegger, and Gadamer*. Evanston, Illinois: Northwestern University Press.

Peritore, N. Patrick 1974: Some problems in Schutz's phenomenological methodology. *American Political Science Review*, 69, 132–40.

Peters, R. S. 1958: *The Concept of Motivation*. London: Routledge and Kegan Paul.

Philip, Mark 1983: Foucault on power: a problem in radical translation? *Political Theory*, 11, 29–52.

Pitkin, Hanna 1972: *Wittgenstein and Justice*. Berkeley: University of California Press.

Pocock, John 1971: *Politics, Language, and Time*. New York: Atheneum.

Poster, Mark 1982: The future according to Foucault. In Dominick La Capra and Steven L. Kaplan (ed.), *Modern European History*, Ithaca: Cornell University Press, 137–52.

Poulantzas, Nicos 1978: *State, Power, Socialism*. London: New Left Books.

Putnam, Hilary 1981: *Truth and History*. Cambridge: Cambridge University Press.

Reagan, Charles 1979: Psychoanalysis as hermeneutics. In Charles Reagan (ed.), *Studies in the Philosophy of Paul Ricoeur*, Athens: Ohio University Press, 141–61.

Remmling, Gunter 1971: Philosophical parameters of Karl Mannheim's sociology of knowledge. *Sociological Quarterly*, 12, 531–47.

1975: *The Sociology of Karl Mannheim*. London: Routledge and Kegan Paul.

Rempel, F. W. 1965: *The Role of Value in Karl Mannheim's Sociology of Knowledge*. The Hague: Mouton.

Ricoeur, Paul 1973: Ethics and culture: Habermas and Gadamer in dialogue. *Philosophy Today*, 17, 153–65.

1974: *The Conflict of Interpretations*, ed. by Don Ihde. Evanston: Northwestern University Press.

1976: History and hermeneutics. *Journal of Philosophy*, 73, 683–95.

1977a: The model of the text: meaningful action considered as a text. In Dallmayr and McCarthy (eds), *Understanding and Social Inquiry*, Notre Dame, Indiana: University of Notre Dame Press, 316–34.

1977b: *The Rule of Metaphor: multi-disciplinary studies of the creation of meaning in language*. Toronto: University of Toronto Press.

1978: The task of hermeneutics. In Michael Murray (ed.), *Heidegger and Modern Philosophy*, New Haven: Yale University Press, 141–60.

1981: *Hermeneutics and the Human Sciences*. Cambridge: Cambridge University Press.

Ricoeur, Paul and Gadamer, Hans-Georg 1982: The conflict of interpretations. In Ronald Bruzina and Bruce Wilshire (eds), *Phenomenology: dialogues and bridges*, Albany: SUNY Press, 299–320.

Roche, Maurice 1973: *Phenomenology, Language, and the Social Sciences*. London: Routledge and Kegan Paul.

Rorty, Richard 1979: *Philosophy and the Mirror of Nature*. Princeton: Princeton University Press.
1980: A reply to Dreyfus and Taylor. *Review of Metaphysics*, 34, 39–46.
1982: *Consequences of Pragmatism*. Minneapolis: University of Minnesota Press.
Rubinstein, David 1981: *Marx and Wittgenstein: social praxis and social explanation*. London: Routledge and Kegan Paul.
Ryan, Michael 1982: *Marxism and Deconstruction*. Baltimore: Johns Hopkins University Press.
Sayer, D. 1979: *Marx's Method: Ideology, Science and Critique in Capital*. Atlantic Highlands, New Jersey: Humanities Press.
Scheler, Max 1980: *Problems of a Sociology of Knowledge*. London: Routledge and Kegan Paul.
Schrag, Calvin 1980: *Radical Reflection and the Origin of the Human Sciences*. Lafeyette, Ind.: Purdue University Press.
Schutz, Alfred 1962: *Collected Papers*, volume 1, ed. Maurice Natanson. The Hague: Martinus Nijhoff.
1964: *Collected Papers*, volume 2, ed. Avrid Brodersen. The Hague: Martinus Nijhoff.
1967: *The Phenomenology of the Social World*, trans. George Walsch and Frederick Lehnert. Evanston, Ill.: Northwestern University Press.
Searle, John 1983: The world turned upside down. *New York Review of Books*, 30, 74–79.
Seliger, Martin 1976: *Ideology and Politics*. New York: The Free Press.
Seung, T. K. 1982: *Structuralism and Hermeneutics*. New York: Columbia University Press.
Shapiro, Michael 1980: Interpretation and political understanding. Paper presented at the annual meeting of the American Political Science Association.
1981: *Language and Political Understanding*. New Haven: Yale University Press.
1984: Literary production as politicizing practice. *Political Theory*, 12, 387–422.
Sheridan, Alan 1980: *Michel Foucault: The Will to Truth*. London: Tavistock.
Shils, Edward 1974: Review of *Ideology and Utopia*. *Daedelus*, 103, 83–9.

Shmueli, Efraim 1977: Objectivity and presuppositions: a re-evaluation of Karl Mannheim's sociology of knowledge. *Sociology and Social Research*, 62, 99–112.

Simmel, Georg 1980: *Essays on Interpretation in Social Science*, trans. Guy Oakes. Totowa, N. J.: Rowman and Littlefield.

Simon, Michael 1982: *Understanding and Human Action*. Albany: SUNY Press.

Simonds, A. P. 1975: Mannheim's sociology of knowledge as a hermeneutic method. *Cultural Hermeneutics*, 3, 81–105.

1978: *Karl Mannheim's Sociology of Knowledge*. Oxford: Clarendon Press.

Smith, Charles 1982: The sociology of mind. In Paul Secord (ed.), *Explaining Human Behavior*, Beverly Hills: Sage, 211–28.

Smith, Christopher 1979: Gadamer's hermeneutics and ordinary language philosophy. *The Thomist*, 43, 296–321.

Sorokin, Pitirim 1947: *Society, Culture, and Personality*. New York: Harper and Brothers.

Stark, W. 1958: *The Sociology of Knowledge*. London: Routledge and Kegan Paul.

Stehr, Nico 1981: The magic triangle: in defense of a general sociology of knowledge. *Philosophy of the Social Sciences*, 11, 225–9.

Taylor, Charles 1962: Neutrality in political science. In Peter Laslett and W. B. Runciman (eds), *Philosophy, Politics and Society*, series 3, Oxford: Basil Blackwell, 25–57.

1977: Interpretation and the sciences of man. In Dallmayr and McCarthy (eds), *Understanding and Social Inquiry*, Notre Dame, Indiana: Notre Dame University Press, 101–31.

1980: Understanding in human science. *Review of Metaphysics*, 34, 25–38.

1984: Foucault on Freedom and Truth. *Political Theory*, 12, 152–83.

Taylor, Stanley 1956: *Conceptions of Institutions and the Theory of Knowledge*. New York: Bookman Associates.

Thomas, David 1980: *Naturalism and Social Science*. New York: Cambridge University Press.

Thompson, John 1981: *Critical Hermeneutics: a study in the thought of Paul Ricoeur and Jurgen Habermas*. New York: Cambridge University Press.

Toulmin, Stephen 1982: The construal of inquiry: criticism in modern and post-modern science. *Critical Inquiry*, 9, 93–111.

Touraine, Alain 1981: *The Voice and the Eye*, trans. Alan Duff. Cambridge: Cambridge University Press.

Vallas, Steven 1979: The lesson of Mannheim's historicism. *Sociology*, 13, 459–74.

Von Schelting, Alex 1936: Review of *Ideology and Utopia*. *American Sociological Review*, 1, 664–74.

Wagner, Helmut 1952: Mannheim's historicism. *Social Research*, 19, 300–21.

Watson, Lawrence 1976: Understanding a life history as a subjective document. *Ethos*, 4, 95–131.

Weber, Max 1968: *Economy and Society*, ed. Guenther Roth and Claus Wittich. New York: Bedminster Press. 3 vols.

Weiner, Richard 1981: *Cultural Marxism and Political Sociology*. Beverly Hills: Sage.

Wellmer, A. 1971: *Critical Theory of Society*. New York: Seabury.

1976: Communications and emancipation: reflections on the linguistic turn in critical theory. In John O'Neill (ed.), *Critical Theory*, New York: Seabury Press, 231–63.

Whorf, Benjamin 1956: *Language, Thought, and Society*. Cambridge, Mass.: MIT Press.

Winch, Peter 1958: *The Idea of a Social Science and Its Relationship to Philosophy*. London: Routledge and Kegan Paul.

Wittgenstein, Ludwig 1953: *Philosophical Investigations*. New York: Macmillan.

Wittgenstein, Ludwig 1980: *Culture and Value*. Oxford: Basil Blackwell.

Wolff, Janet 1975: *Hermeneutic Philosophy and the Sociology of Art*. London: Routledge and Kegan Paul.

Wolff, Kurt 1959: The sociology of knowledge and social theory. In Llewellyn Gross (ed.), *Symposium on Sociological Theory*, Evanston: Row Petersen and Co., 567–602.

1984: Karl Mannheim: an intellectual itinerary. *Society*, 21, 71–4.

Index

Althusser 17, 203
antifoundationalism 8–12, 14–16, 23, 39, 44, 46, 49, 160–4, 167, 171–2, 181–2, 184, 187, 193, 195, 198
  Gadamer 91, 98, 129, 133–5, 159
  Mannheim 51, 64, 66, 73, 78–90
antipositivist social science 78, 128
Apel, Karl-Otto 162–3, 170, 198

Bacon, Francis 4, 17–18, 35, 37–8, 65–6, 202
Barnes, Barry 40–4, 46–7, 197, 198, 203
Berger, Peter and Thomas Luckmann, *The Social Construction of Reality* 27, 197
Bergner, Jeff 2–4
Bernstein, Richard 163–4, 200–3
Betti, Enrico 92
Bhaskar, Roy 40, 43–4, 46–7
Bloor, David 40, 42–4, 46–7, 197, 203

Chicago School 23, 26
Child, Arthur 31
Comte, Auguste 2, 13
critical theorists 7, 35, 117, 138
Culler, Jonathan 9, 192, 194, 204

Deconstruction 9, 166, 168–9, 187–8, 191–6, 204
DeGree, Gerard 31–3
Derrida, Jacques 9, 161, 164–5, 167, 169, 170–1, 187–96, 200, 204
DeTracy, Destutt 17
Dilthey, Wilhelm 13, 15, 24, 94, 98–9, 122, 125, 141, 164–6, 175–7, 200
Dreyfus, Hubert 166–7, 172–3, 204
Durkheim, Emile 2, 13, 23, 78

Enlightenment 4–11, 14–18, 20–22, 29–31, 35, 37–8, 45, 47–9, 162–3, 168–9, 171–2, 176–7, 186, 197, 201
  Gadamer 97, 100, 102–3, 105, 107, 112, 114–16, 120–1, 125, 128–9, 132, 139, 141, 144, 155–8
  Mannheim 50, 53–6, 60, 62, 64, 66, 72, 75, 78, 89
epistemology 2, 31, 52, 61–2, 66, 78–9, 111, 114, 116, 137, 168–9, 197

false consciousness 18, 20, 149–50
Foucault, Michel 161, 164–5, 167–88, 196, 203, 204
foundationalism 8, 132–4, 139, 154, 162, 193–4
Freud, Sigmund 9, 37, 151

Gadamer, Hans-Georg 10–12, 14–16, 24, 29, 38, 46, 47, 49–51, 54, 62, 67, 71, 79–86, 88–9
  hermeneutic method 91–117
  social scientific method 117–159, 160–1, 163–7, 169–73, 176–7, 179–82, 186–7, 193–6, 198, 200–4
Gellner, Ernst 125–6
Giddens, Anthony 171, 187, 198, 202

Habermas, Jürgen 35–8, 42, 116–17, 120–1, 126–39, 153–4, 156, 160, 163, 198, 201–2
Heidegger, Martin 8–10, 29, 51–2, 62, 81–2, 86–8, 99–101, 110–112, 119, 155–6, 164, 169–70, 172–3, 180, 186–7, 189, 196, 200, 202–3
hermeneutic method 33, 69, 85–6, 121, 125–6, 199
  Gadamer 91–117
hermeneutics 3, 24, 31, 36, 43–4, 46, 50–1, 80, 89, 120, 122, 127, 130–1, 134–40, 142, 144, 150, 153–5, 160, 162–3, 166, 170–2, 175, 177, 181, 186, 200–1
  Gadamer 91–117
Hesse, Mary 37, 44–5
Hirsch, Eric 83, 85, 122–3, 145, 148, 150, 200–1
historicism 51–2, 55, 57, 60, 66, 73, 111, 130
humanism 168–9, 173, 184, 188, 191–2
humanists 22, 171, 174
Husserl, Edmund 27, 29, 87, 99–100, 104, 123, 162, 170, 197

ideology 17–21, 24, 58, 64–66, 87, 136, 157, 176, 198, 202

Kant, Immanuel 4, 55, 58

language 94–5, 100, 109–13, 115–17, 121, 124, 126–7, 129–30, 135, 138, 157, 159, 162–3, 169–70, 173, 177, 179, 188–9, 191–3, 201–2
Louch, A. R. 121, 125, 200
Lukács, Georg 17, 52

Mannheim, Karl 6, 11, 24, 26, 27, 30–1, 34, 39, 41–2, 45–6, 48–9, 140–1, 155–8, 160, 173, 180–1, 198–9, 200, 202
  sociology of knowledge 50–90
Maquet, J. 31–2
Marx, Karl 2, 13, 15–22, 24–5, 35, 48, 59, 61, 88–9
Marxist sociology of knowledge 30, 35–8, 197
Mead, George Herbert 28–9
Methodenstreit 15, 22–4, 50, 197
Montesquieu 6, 15, 17

natural sciences
  Gadamer 92–3, 95, 97–8, 105–7, 112
  history 5–8, 14–16, 22, 34–5, 37, 39, 41–2, 44–7
  Mannheim 51, 56, 58, 67–76, 78–80
  methodology of the social sciences 121, 123–5, 132,

143–4, 153, 158, 166, 173, 198, 200–2
Nietzsche 9, 104, 164–5, 176, 183, 199, 203
nihilism 161–2, 164, 167, 171–2, 182–7, 189, 194, 196, 203–4

objective knowledge 6–10, 14–16, 20–1, 30, 34–5, 46–9, 53–7, 121, 126, 141, 160, 168, 179, 197, 198
objectivity 8, 29, 32, 35, 37–8, 40, 163, 176, 182, 200, 202
  Gadamer 98, 104, 107, 112–13, 156–8
  Mannheim 60, 62, 66, 70, 74–6, 78
ontology 90, 95, 99–101, 111–12, 115, 119, 120, 124–5, 128, 138, 191, 200
ordinary language 35, 36, 127, 136, 200

phenomenologists 7, 16, 30, 41, 55, 70–1
phenomenology 27–9, 36, 52, 55, 70, 98, 122, 130, 161, 170
positivist social science 1, 7, 8, 10, 22, 25, 30–2, 34–5, 38–9, 43–5, 49, 51–2, 55, 65, 68–72, 76, 143, 145, 150, 158, 161, 168–9, 171, 173, 197
pragmatism 8, 76, 204
prejudice 6, 11–12, 51, 84–5, 88, 101–3, 105, 107, 113–17, 126, 131–2, 135–6, 138, 149, 156–9, 173, 180, 186, 194–6

Rabinow, Paul 172–3, 204
realists 39–48, 198
reason 4, 17–21, 53–5, 58, 60, 102, 113, 121, 130, 132–3, 136, 138, 162, 186
relativism 24–5, 34, 36, 38, 42–5, 47, 53–4, 57–60, 71–2, 79, 103, 116, 125–6, 163, 199, 200, 204
relational knowledge 56–8, 60, 71–4
Ricoeur, Paul 138, 141–5, 148–50, 153–5, 197, 200, 202
Rorty, Richard 8, 163, 164–7, 203
Rousseau 188–9

Scheler, Max 2, 15, 24, 27, 30, 48, 55, 57, 197
Schutz, Alfred 27–30, 82, 122, 134, 146–7, 197
self-reflexivity 80–1, 85, 88, 114–15, 130, 151
semantic autonomy 82–5, 122, 145, 147–8
Simmel 13, 24, 79, 82, 202
Simonds, A. P. 3, 4, 82–5, 156, 198–200
social sciences
  antifoundational 160–1, 163, 165–9, 173–5, 177, 193, 198, 200–2
  crisis of 1–7, 9–11
  Gadamer 91–2, 95–6, 98, 100, 105–6, 112
  history 12–17, 22–3, 26–8, 31, 34, 36–8, 43–9
  Mannheim 67, 70–4, 76, 78, 80
  method 117–159
sociology of knowledge 1–4, 6–11
  antifoundational 155–60, 162, 180–1, 197–9, 203
  history 13–49
  Mannheim 50–90
Sorokin, Pitirim 31–3
Stark, Werner 31–3
subjective knowledge 6, 8–10, 14–16, 20–1, 47–9, 53–4, 197
subjectivity 29, 163, 168, 187

Taylor, Charles 82, 148, 166–7, 185, 204

Thompson, John 153–4, 202
truth 3–6, 8–9, 12, 16, 19, 20–1, 31–2, 34, 40–1, 45–6, 162, 164–6, 176–7, 180, 183–5, 187, 190–2, 194, 196–7, 200–1
  Gadamer 93–4, 100, 102–3, 105–7, 109, 115–17, 128, 132, 156
  Mannheim 50–1, 55, 57, 67, 74–6, 79, 82

Vico 6, 15–17, 94

Weber, Max 1–2, 13, 15, 23, 50, 76, 78–9, 82, 122, 134, 145, 148, 197
Whorf, Benjamin 162
Winch, Peter 82, 121, 125, 134, 146–7, 149, 200–1
Wittgenstein, Ludwig 8, 10, 29, 87, 88, 118–20, 124–30, 134, 137–8, 164, 170, 198, 200–1, 204
Wittgensteinian social science 116–30, 145, 149, 150, 152, 160, 201